Contents

Visit **www.suexch.com** for access to companion tutorial videos and other resources related to the book.

THE
SKETCHUP
WORKFLOW
FOR ARCHITECTURE

PART I

Starting the Flow

Get ready to elevate your SketchUp skills and design workflow to the highest radical extremes of efficiency. *The SketchUp Workflow for Architecture* contains tips, tricks, and strategies for modeling in SketchUp, as well as methods to leverage SketchUp and LayOut during every step of the design process. Let's start with a few tips on how to get the most out of this book, how BIM plays a part in the SketchUp workflow, and how to effectively manage a PROJECT folder.

Chapter 1

Introduction

This book is the missing set of standards for SketchUp and LayOut. *The SketchUp Workflow for Architecture* provides a flexible, clear set of rules for organizing any type of building project in SketchUp: renovation, new construction, residential, commercial, high-rise, low-rise, industrial. It is up to the user to process these techniques and strategies, and then apply them to projects. In this chapter you will pick up a few tips on how to best absorb the information and get the most out of this book.

This book covers advanced concepts performed with advanced operations. These are not workarounds; rather they are clever ways to use SketchUp to expedite the design process. With *The SketchUp Workflow for Architecture* and some practice, you will be able to:

- ☑ Speak knowledgeably about Building Information Modeling (BIM).
- ☑ Organize and manage PROJECT folders in an efficient manner.
- ☑ Effectively use the Modeling tools and organization containers in SketchUp.
- ☑ Create and customize a timesaving SketchUp template.
- ☑ Tailor the SketchUp modeling environment to fit your professional needs.
- ☑ Create and organize collections for materials, components, styles, and templates.
- ☑ Find, install, and utilize valuable ruby scripts.
- ☑ Fully understand the value of LayOut and its dynamic links to SketchUp and other insertable content.

- ☑ Tailor the LayOut drafting environment to fit your professional needs.
- ☑ Create and organize collections for scrapbooks and title blocks.
- ☑ Create site plans and topographic surveys using Google Earth terrain and aerial imagery.
- ☑ Find or create building context models around a specific site.
- ☑ Efficiently document existing buildings and create extremely accurate as-built drawings using SketchUp Pro and LayOut.
- ☑ Transition a design model into an accurate 3D model.
- ☑ Create inspiring LayOut presentations that accurately represent your designs.
- ☑ Accurately model and organize various types of buildings in SketchUp Pro.
- ☑ Prepare, render, and post-process convincing photorealistic images.
- ☑ Extract information from SketchUp and LayOut in useful formats for use in other CAD programs.
- ☑ Compile and draft construction documents using SketchUp Pro and LayOut.

THE WORKFLOW

The term "workflow" loosely describes the collection of tools designers use and the order in which they use those tools to produce a final design. Designers use many different tools and software to produce their final products, which are typically new, built environments; some of many initial products are construction documents.

Many different workflows can be used to design and create construction documents; however, the best workflows minimize the use of several different softwares because something is always lost during translation between programs.

The workflow explained in this book uses SketchUp and LayOut for every phase of the design process. You can use other programs to supplement SketchUp, but SketchUp Pro and LayOut are at the core of this process. For example, you could use an image editor to post-process exports and modify textures, but you will simply be using the image editor to complement SketchUp. As another example, you could use a spreadsheet program for schedules, but keep all of your drafting in SketchUp and LayOut.

This workflow is not a regimented design process; you can adapt all or part of it and use the organizational and design tips. The process of moving from sketches to construction documents is expedited by *The SketchUp Workflow for Architecture* (Figure 1.1).

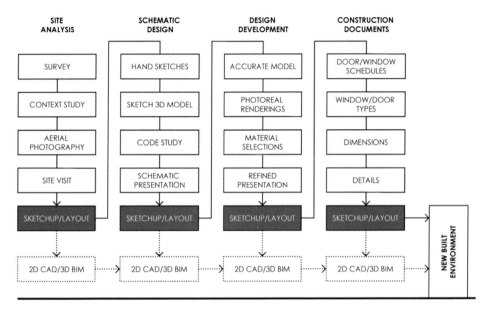

Figure 1.1 The SketchUp Workflow for Architecture

The evolution of a client's vision to an actual building involves many small steps and phases. There is no right or wrong way to produce a design, but there are critics out there who will judge your designs. The most important audiences, however, are your clients. The more time you spend on the design, the better. *The SketchUp Workflow for Architecture* is focused on design and will ultimately provide more time for you to explore real designs in three dimensions.

WHO SHOULD READ THIS BOOK?

Anyone interested in mastering SketchUp will benefit greatly from this book— architects, landscape architects, designers, interior designers, contractors. Large firms, one-man-shows, and every office size in between can benefit from this book. If you are using SketchUp to design built space, you should practice *The SketchUp Workflow for Architecture*. Most sizable firms already have a design workflow with 3D Building Information Modeling (BIM) software and standards in place. BIM is excellent for huge projects with extensive scheduling and square footage, but does it really help on the smaller projects? For large firms, *The SketchUp Workflow for Architecture* will fit in where a bloated, over-featured software suite is not necessary. The techniques in this book give you the freedom to simplify your model by including only the building information you need to get the project done on time.

On the other end of the spectrum is the one-man-show looking to cut overhead. When compared to other popular design and documentation programs available on the market, this workflow is very inexpensive. By adding a few plugins to SketchUp Pro, you'll have full capability to efficiently design, draft, render, analyze, and document any project.

Anyone who reads this book will take away excellent organization and problem-solving strategies for SketchUp. The techniques presented will help any designer create more engaging and accurate 3D models that are easily shared across several platforms.

WHAT'S IN THIS BOOK?

The advanced concepts and operations covered in this book are organized into four separate and distinct parts.

Part I: Start the Flow

Part I takes care of some administrative tasks and disclaimers common in an instructional software book. In Part I, you will learn the benefits of using SketchUp Pro and LayOut, and you will be introduced to the power of this system. Also, you will be exposed to a new way of thinking about BIM. Part I wraps up by explaining folder and file organization techniques that will help keep your projects running smoothly.

Part II: SketchUp

In Part II you will learn the basic, intermediate, and advanced SketchUp skills necessary to complete the exercises in this book. You will also tune your SketchUp environment for professional use. You will learn to create utility styles and scenes, custom layers, and ultimately your own custom default template. Even if you are an experienced SketchUp user, you will benefit from the refresher and most likely will develop a new understanding of the old features.

Part III: LayOut

Part III is an "everything you need to know" guide for LayOut. At times, this section may read more like a manual than a tutorial because it explains every menu, dialog, and setting you will come across in LayOut. It also contains tutorials for creating custom scrapbooks and templates. Study this part closely even if you have used LayOut previously. The skills you learn in Part III will make you a fast and effective LayOut draftsman.

Part IV: The Architectural Design Process

The traditional architectural design process consists of five major phases: schematic design, design development, construction documents, bidding and negotiations, and construction administration. The design process presented in Part IV has been whittled down to four main phases: site analysis (SA), schematic design (SD), design development (DD), and construction documents (CD).

Although they are very important steps in the design process, this book will not directly address construction administration (CA), or bidding and negotiation (BN). SketchUp can be used for cost estimating, but does not typically play a major role in negotiating numbers with a contractor. SketchUp can also play a role in CA, but the skills you will learn in the other four phases can be easily applied to the construction administration phase.

WHAT ARE THE PREREQUISITES?

This is an extremely advanced book. It assumes that you are already familiar with many of the tools and basic functions in SketchUp, including groups, components, edges, surfaces, dividing surfaces, styles, layers, and scenes. You also need to know and understand basic computer terms and concepts such as right-click, left-click, windows, files, folders, drop-down menus, zipped, unzip, extract, etc.

To make the most of this book, you should have some experience with SketchUp, but even if you don't you can still benefit. You don't have to have any experience with LayOut. Parts II and III cover the essential skills you'll need to complete the advanced exercises in Part IV.

The following resources will help you make the most of this book.

- ☑ SketchUp 101 is an excellent class to help you get over the initial SketchUp learning curve; it is offered for free at **www.suexch.com**. The topics covered in SketchUp 101 include creating geometry, modifying geometry, and inference locking. It includes two building exercises that pull everything together.

- ☑ SketchUp 201 is a commercially available class that covers the next level of intermediate concepts; it is available at **www.suexch.com**. The topics covered include: groups, components, layers, scenes, styles, layout, geomodeling, and general model organization.

These classes are helpful, but they are not required to utilize *The SketchUp Workflow for Architecture*. Everything you need is included in this book.

FREE SKETCHUP OR SKETCHUP PRO?

The free version of SketchUp is for hobbyists; it is intended for the weekend warrior designing a deck or a student working on a school project. The free version has been stripped of many capabilities that are needed to create professional presentations; it lacks exporters for 3D models and can't create high-resolution images or animations, features that professionals need.

SketchUp Pro contains everything a professional needs to create engaging and precise presentations that accurately represent their designs. Using the Pro version, you can present and explain 3D designs in LayOut (2D page-creation software included with SketchUp Pro), use several export options to share work (including **.dwg** format), and create HD animations and high-resolution renderings. Figure 1.6 compares the features of SketchUp and SketchUp Pro.

SketchUp

Intuitive and fun to use

- Re-imagine your living space
- Model buildings for Google Earth
- Use SketchUp for free

SketchUp Pro

with LayOut

Powerful, fast, and accurate

- Build precise 3D models on the fly
- Exchange files with other software
- Create compelling 2D design documents
- Generate reports, PDFs, and more

Figure 1.6 Features of SketchUp and SketchUp Pro

ONLINE CONTENT

Many of the exercises in this book require digital files to illustrate certain points in the tutorials. You can download all of the class files for the entire book at **http://www.suexch .com/TSWFA**. Once you have downloaded the file, extract the folder and all contents to your desktop or an appropriate project folder (or to the TEMP folder, see Chapter 3, "Project Management").

Additional models, case studies, title blocks, scrapbooks, project models, and a discussion forum for professional users are available at **www.suexch.com**. This site complements this book and expands on advanced topics.

MENTAL PREPARATION

SketchUp is fast, fun, and intuitive—but only after a lot of practice! SketchUp is not easy. SketchUp marketing has done an excellent job of publicizing the simple use of SketchUp. It is extremely approachable in that you can open the program, click on the Line tool, and start drawing. Shortly after you create your first surface, the Push/Pull tool will enable you to quickly generate massive amounts of 3D geometry. However, once you start modeling with these simple tools, you'll quickly have more questions than answers. This lack of knowledge coupled with the desire to perform advanced operations can cause frustration.

Mentally prepare yourself to learn this software and the workflow presented in this book. Push aside any preconceived notions of "3D for everyone." Ignore your colleague's comments about SketchUp being easy to learn, simple to use, and not nearly as powerful as other 3D programs. SketchUp is similar to other CAD programs in that you need to spend a significant amount of time learning to use it in order to fully leverage it. Accept the fact that any program is easy to open and play with; but to fully understand any 3D application, including SketchUp, you'll need to fully invest your time, patience, and effort.

SKETCHUP PORTFOLIO

The examples in Figures 1.7 through 1.17 are just some of the types of models and documents you can create using SketchUp.

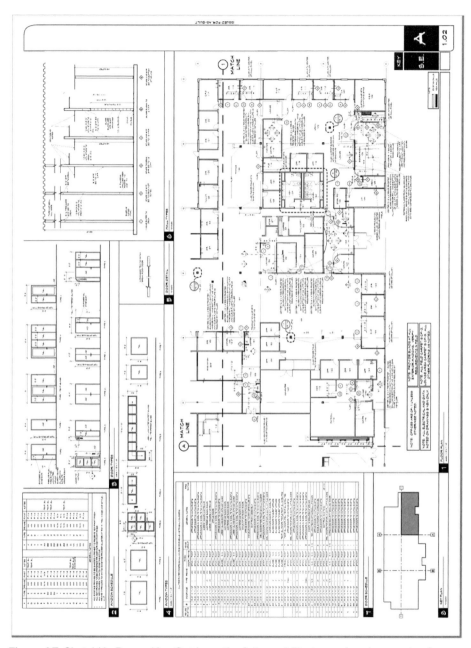

Figure 1.7 SketchUp Pro and LayOut have the full capability to produce large sets of construction documents. Office Remodel designed by Bill Morgan, Morgan Design Associates; SketchUp model and drawings by Michael Brightman

Figure 1.8 Create a winter scene by lightening and desaturating texture images. Timbercreek at Okemo House. Designed by Bensonwood Homes; model built by Michael Brightman

Figure 1.9 SketchUp is as precise as many other CAD programs, precise enough to create as-built 3D models like the one shown. Denver Loft 3D as-built model; space measured and model built by Michael Brightman

Figure 1.10 Exterior perspective. "Greenness" concept house design by Phil Lehn, Lehn Design Collaborative; model built by Michael Brightman

Figure 1.11 Modeling a house inside and out lets you fully explore the interactions of plan and elevation. "Greenness" concept house. Designed by Lehn Design; model built by Michael Brightman

Figure 1.12 Building a SketchUp model of a "model home" costs drastically less than building the real thing. "The Monticello" digital spec house. Designed by Luxury Builders; model built by Michael Brightman

Figure 1.13 By layering 2D and 3D elements, you can make expansive sites look convincing without overloading your machine. "Sterling Pointe" at Winter Park, Colorado. Designed by Wintergreen Homes LLC; model built by Michael Brightman

Figure 1.14 Timbercreek at Okemo spec house. Designed by Bensonwood Homes; model built by Michael Brightman

Figure 1.15 This lobby model was built in SketchUp and rendered in Twilight Render to add lights, soft shadows, and reflections. Design by Carol Freeman, Freeman Architecture; SketchUp model and photorealistic rendering by Michael Brightman

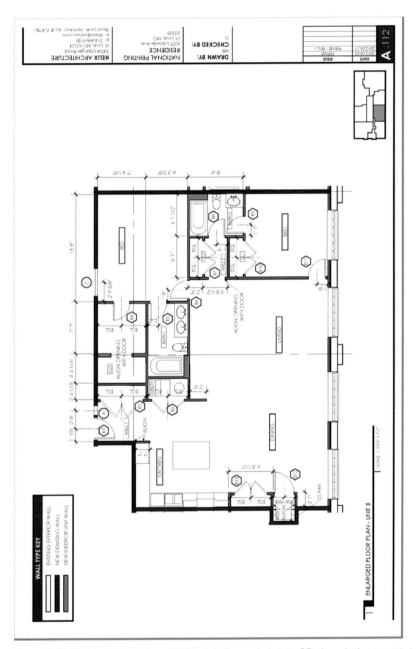

Figure 1.16 Use LayOut to turn 3D SketchUp models into 2D descriptive annotated plans. Unit plan designed by Stephen Levin, Helix Architecture; SketchUp model and drawings completed by Michael Brightman

Figure 1.17 By combining geomodeling techniques and accurate modeling strategies, you can quickly and accurately communicate realistic design possibilities. Proposed Lowry House addition. Design and model completed by Michael Brightman

CHAPTER POINTS

☑ Become familiar with SketchUp 101, SketchUp 201, and additional online content at **www.suexch.com**.

☑ Mentally prepare yourself for a rewarding challenge while completing the exercises in this book.

☑ The workflow presented in this book centers around SketchUp Pro and LayOut, but it also recognizes that many other software packages complement the design process.

☑ *The SketchUp Workflow for Architecture* is not a rigid system. It can be changed or abandoned at any stage of the design process. This workflow can be used in parts or its entirety.

Chapter 2

Building Information Modeling

Building Information Modeling (BIM) is the latest buzz in architectural design and drafting. Is BIM a revolution or just the way the industry works these days? In this chapter, you will be encouraged to contemplate and challenge the popular assumptions and standard definition of BIM. By doing so, you should realize that integrating the benefits of BIM into your workflow is easier and cheaper than you ever thought.

WHAT IS BIM?

"*Building Information Modeling* (BIM) is a digital representation of physical and functional characteristics of a facility. A BIM is a shared knowledge resource for information about a facility forming a reliable basis for decisions during its *life-cycle*; defined as existing from earliest conception to demolition." (National BIM Standard--United States) A *building information model* (BIM) is an intelligent model that integrates design, visualization, simulation, and collaboration into one process. The model is a physical representation, but it can also be informative. The model not only shows a client what a building will look like, but it also gives the client and designer a better understanding of how the building will function. A BIM is essentially a shared, digital building prototype that helps everyone on the design team make better decisions.

Stages and Uses

A building information model is intended to be used during every phase of the design process, and by every member on the team.

Architects typically create the main model and then share it with consultants who use the BIM to ensure that their trades don't interfere with the building's function or other trades. For instance, a duct physically can't run through a beam. It is better to catch issues like this on the computer rather than in the field. This BIM feature is commonly referred to as *clash detection*.

Building owners and facility managers can also use the BIM after the building is complete. For example, a BIM could help them track down the source of a stained ceiling by locating plumbing lines or by indicating possible weaknesses in the roof membrane.

TIP In reality, most building owners and facility managers won't use the building information model to solve problems—but they could. If they were to use a program, however, they'd find that the SketchUp viewer is free and very approachable.

Features

BIM is a concept not a software program. However, there are software programs that use the BIM concept to execute the design process. There is no official BIM features list, but here are a few popular features that most people expect to find in a BIM program:

- ☑ 3D modeling
- ☑ Model life-cycle use with the building, from predesign to demolition
- ☑ Interoperability with consultants and their CAD platforms
- ☑ Dynamic links between the 3D model and the construction documents. (When a change is made in a plan, that change is reflected in all other drawings, sections, elevations, and reflected ceiling plans.)
- ☑ Photorealistic rendering and raytracing
- ☑ Parametric modeling, both input and output
- ☑ Clash detection
- ☑ Energy analysis
- ☑ Cost analysis
- ☑ 4D construction phasing and schedule management

SKETCHUP AND LAYOUT AS BIM

Coming as a surprise to most, SketchUp and LayOut contain many of the most popular BIM software features. With the workflow presented in this book, SketchUp and LayOut pull the best features from each of the most popular drafting platforms (2D CAD and 3D BIM). Using this workflow, you can incorporate BIM's fundamental features into your projects. This section outlines what makes SketchUp and LayOut such a powerful design and documentation tool and explains why it is a unique design and documentation method.

Advantages

Some of the advantages of using SketchUp and LayOut as a design and documentation method are listed here:

☑ SketchUp is a *surface modeler*, which means that all objects created in SketchUp are composed of lines and surfaces. The process of drawing lines in SketchUp is very similar to the familiar process used to draw lines in 2D CAD. SketchUp could be described as a 2D CAD program that operates in a 3D environment.

☑ When you build a 3D model in SketchUp using *The SketchUp Workflow for Architecture*, you are simultaneously creating the construction documents. All 2D plans, sections, and elevations are dynamically linked to the 3D model. SketchUp allows you to think and design in 3D, which is the way your brain is wired to work. This is in sharp contrast to using other popular BIM software where you draft the construction documents, which in turn creates the 3D model. In SketchUp, you think and design in 3D; the presentation and construction documents are products of the design process. (See Figure 2.1 and Figure 2.2.)

☑ The lack of some features in SketchUp is a blessing in disguise. Because the rules for modeling and organizing are simple, there are fewer questions for the program to ask and, therefore, fewer questions for you to answer. The simplicity of SketchUp and LayOut lets you create and organize the model quickly, without interruptions. For example, to add a wall in some BIM software packages, you would have to assign several properties, such as height, thickness, material, color, and insulation. To add a wall in SketchUp, you simply draw a rectangle and pull it up—no questions asked. (In Figure 2.3 through Figure 2.5, the drafting and modeling were completed using SketchUp Pro, LayOut, and *The SketchUp Workflow for Architecture*.)

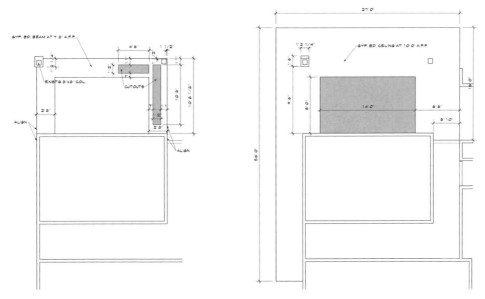

Figure 2.1 Office remodel. Enlarged ceiling plans describe the two soffit levels of the lounge area. These 2D drawings were pulled dynamically from the 3D model. All of the drafting and modeling were completed using SketchUp Pro, LayOut, and *The SketchUp Workflow for Architecture*.

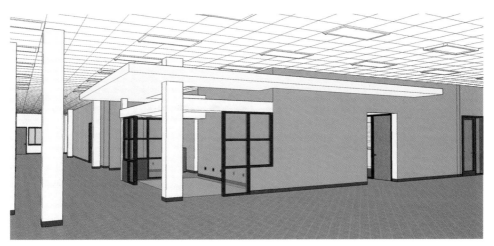

Figure 2.2 Office remodel. All 2D drawings describing this unique ceiling condition are dynamically linked to this 3D model.

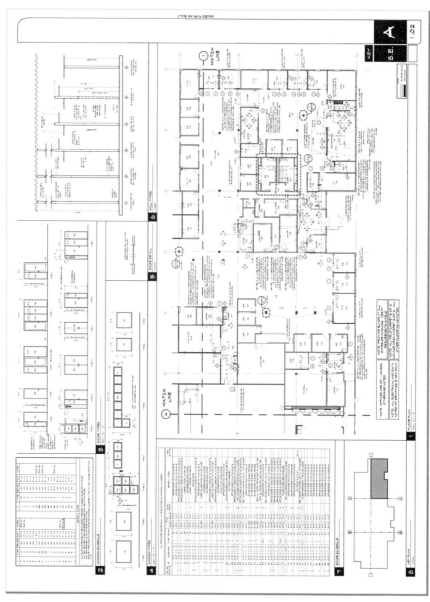

Figure 2.3 Office remodel. Sheet A1.02 contains a partial floorplan, a door schedule, door types, a window schedule, window types, wall types, and a key plan.

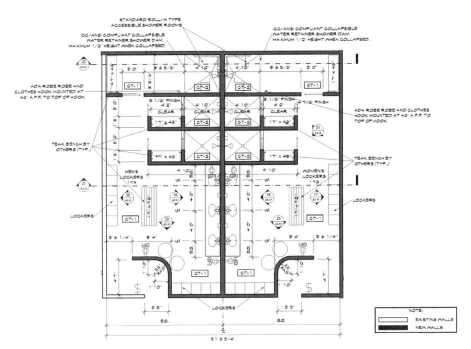

Figure 2.4 Office remodel. These enlarged plans show detailed locations of fixtures and other information that will not fit on a building plan.

☑ SketchUp offers real-time rendering, which provides infinitely better information so you can make better design decisions than you can with other software. In SketchUp, a house looks like a house, siding looks like siding, and concrete looks like concrete. In 2D CAD, a house looks like a flat collection of cyan and magenta lines. The graphical representations of most textures leave disconnects between the drawings and real-world applications of the materials. The better the 3D information is that you have during the design process, the better your design decisions will be. Figure 2.6 shows the same project in 2D CAD and in SketchUp.

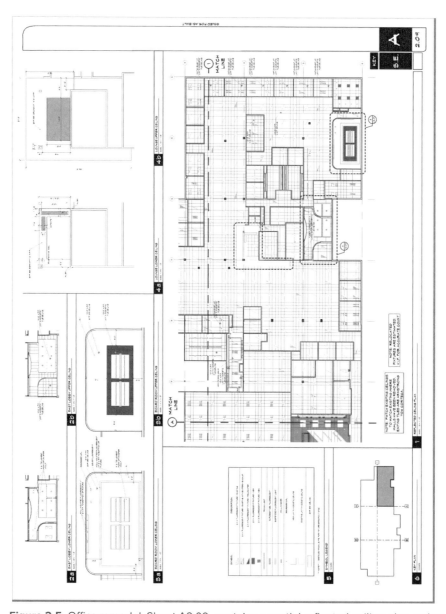

Figure 2.5 Office remodel. Sheet A2.09 contains a partial reflected ceiling plan, enlarged reflected-ceiling plans, details, and a key plan. A reflected ceiling plan is created by cutting the model similar to a plan, but looking up at the ceiling.

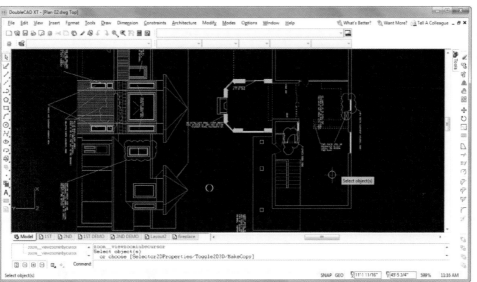

Figure 2.6 A residential project in SketchUp (top). The same residential project in 2D CAD (bottom).

Disadvantages

Some of the disadvantages of using SketchUp and LayOut as a design and documentation method include:

☑ SketchUp lacks parametric modeling features. Dynamic components can be used to compensate for some of this, but they are fairly difficult to master. Ultimately, parametric modeling attributes can be exported and viewed in spreadsheets as reports; however, changing the spreadsheet will not be reflected in the model.

☑ Scheduling is done the old-fashioned way. The door and window tags are not connected to the door and window schedules. The tags and schedules must be coordinated manually.

☑ Sheets are coordinated the old-fashioned way as well. There is no information exchange between sheets, drawings, tags, and callouts. The drawings must be coordinated manually.

☑ LayOut dimensions do not update automatically when changes are made in SketchUp. If you move a wall in SketchUp, you will need to go back and correct the dimensions in any drawings that display that wall.

☑ Entities do not attach to each other. For instance, windows and doors do not attach to walls. So, if you move the wall, you will also need to move the doors and windows separately.

FILLING IN THE BIM BLANKS

You can use plugins to extend SketchUp's BIM features. Third parties are creating plugins that expand the SketchUp universe and provide features that fill the BIM voids. Although the plugins listed in this section are not officially endorsed by or included in *The SketchUp Workflow for Architecture*, they provide a great place to begin your search to expand BIM capabilities.

Cost Analysis

☑ BimUp: **www.bimup.co.uk/**

☑ SpaceDesign: **www.renderplus.com/wk/SpaceDesign_Features_w.htm**

Energy Analysis

☑ EnergyPlus: **http://apps1.eere.energy.gov/buildings/energyplus/energyplus_about.cfm**

☑ IES V-Ware: **www.iesve.com/Software/VE-Ware**

☑ NREL OpenStudio: **http://openstudio.nrel.gov/**

HVAC

☑ 3Skeng: **www.3skeng.com/en/index.htm**

Parametric Modeling

☑ SketchUp BIM: **www.sketchupbim.com/**

☑ Instant Roof: **http://valiarchitects.com/sketchup_scripts/instant-roof**

☑ Instant Wall: **http://valiarchitects.com/subscription_scripts/instant-wall**

☑ Dynamic Components: **www.sketchup.com/intl/en/product/dcs.html**

☑ Build Edge: **www.buildedge.com/**

4D Timeline

☑ SuperPlan: **www.superplan.info/index.html**

Photorealistic Rendering and Raytracing

☑ Twilight Render: **http://twilightrender.com/**

☑ Shaderlight: **www.artvps.com**

☑ Podium: **http://suplugins.com/**

In Figure 2.7 and Figure 2.8, the drafting and modeling were completed using SketchUp Pro, LayOut, and *The SketchUp Workflow for Architecture.*

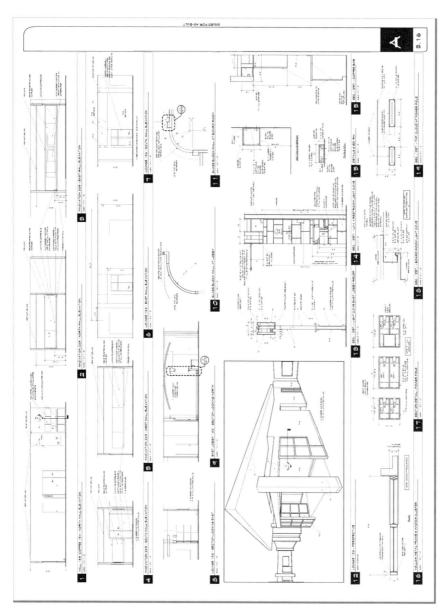

Figure 2.7 Sheet A3.16 contains interior elevations and a perspective view, all pulled from the same 3D model.

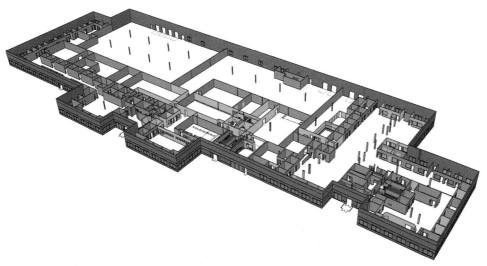

Figure 2.8 Utility styles display additional layers of information contained in a 3D model. This image represents a scope diagram, where all existing objects are shown in gray and all new objects are shown in green.

THE SKETCHUP OUTLOOK

For a few good years, Google owned SketchUp and supported it. Among other features, Google SketchUp introduced styles, the Follow Me tool, MatchPhoto, integration with Google Maps and Google Earth, and a huge leap forward with LayOut. The Google years were exciting at first, but after SketchUp 7 Google seemed to lose interest in the project and deprioritized it.

Why would such a cool company do this to such a cool program? Perhaps it was because lighter cloud programs such as Google Building Maker can create 3D models for Google Earth, which was one of the original reasons Google purchased SketchUp. Another possibility is that taking on the architectural drafting industry juggernauts didn't fit into Google's mission statement, which is to organize the world's information and make it universally accessible and useful. Either way, SketchUp was put on the back burner for several years during a period of minimal releases and minimal new features. Nobody likes a breakup, but it was time for SketchUp to tell Google, "It's not me, it's you."

Google handled the breakup with maturity and sensitivity to the loyal SketchUp community by finding a buyer who really appreciated the product. Trimble, the new owners, might not have the allure and mystique Google has, but they do have some radical hardware.

Trimble creates GPS devices for automating farm equipment and efficiently fertilizing crops. They build handheld devices for construction management. Interestingly enough, Trimble creates 3D laser scanners. These high-tech machines can be placed in a room and within minutes they can generate an accurate as-built 3D model of the space. Yet another intriguing product that Trimble owns is Tekla, a BIM program aimed toward engineering. Now, with the purchase of SketchUp, they possess a wildly popular 3D platform that architects embrace. SketchUp may have been close to extinction, but now its future looks great.

SketchUp (a fast and fun 3D design tool) + **LayOut** (a lean 2D presentation and documentation program) + **3D laser scanners** (automated creation of as-built 3D models) + **Tekla** (an established BIM software) = **WILD SPECULATION**

Figure 2.9 An equation that inspires speculation

CHAPTER POINTS

- ☑ Building Information Modeling is a loose concept open to interpretation.
- ☑ BIM is not a software program; it is a concept used by design and documentation software programs.
- ☑ There is no absolute set of features that defines BIM software.
- ☑ SketchUp is not marketed as BIM software, but it does offer several popular BIM features.
- ☑ Plugins can be used to fill in the BIM blanks.
- ☑ Most facilities managers won't touch BIM. However, if they do, they would be likely to use SketchUp.
- ☑ Google sold SketchUp to Trimble instead of a huge AEC software company with the reputation for squashing competitors with buyouts.

Chapter 3
Project Management

U nwavering, relentless organization is essential to a successful project. Just like a messy desk, a messy PROJECT folder can cause miscommunication, lost work, and ultimately cost you time and money. The techniques illustrated in this chapter will help you organize your design projects. Keep in mind that this is not a rigid system; the suggested workflow is flexible and can be tweaked to meet your specific needs. In other words, feel free to modify this method any way you see fit to meet your project type and office standards.

FOLDERS AND FILES

Approaching folders and files the same way every time will help your team collaborate efficiently. First, you need to understand some standard ground rules regarding how to organize PROJECT folders. Then you can apply the logic of this system to your PROJECT folders and further develop your own set of standards.

Naming Standards

Take a moment to invent an identifying acronym. This shouldn't be too hard; architects and designers do it all of the time—for example, HOK, RNL, and SOM. Your identifying acronym will be used to name files and many other things that you create in the digital world. This is important, not necessarily from a marketing point of view, but from an organizational point of view so that everyone knows who made the file. The acronym used for the examples in this book is BIC, which stands for Bright Ideas Consultants. Anticipate replacing the "BIC" with your own identifying acronym as you complete the exercises in this book.

Folders

Folders contain files and other folders, and they have a strong tendency to become a complete mess. Read the next sentence several times so it is etched into your memory. *The contents of a folder should present the fewest number of choices, and all choices should be self-explanatory.* That sentence thoroughly describes folder organization logic, and it is the keystone of an organized folder.

All PROJECT folder names should be in capital letters to clearly and concisely describe the folder—for example, OFFICE REMODEL. Ideally, all subfolder names within the project folder will be one word in caps; frequently, subfolder names are abbreviated. For instance, administrative files such as contracts and correspondence will be stored in a folder named ADMIN. Pictures, sketches, and diagrams will be kept in a folder named IMAGES. By capitalizing the file folder names, you are visually separating those folder names from the filenames residing in the same folder.

Files

An efficient filename gives the user as much information as possible without ever looking at the file properties (Figure 3.1).

AUTHOR_Project - File Description.extension
Figure 3.1 Clear, concise, and informative filename

For example, examine the filename `BIC_Office Remodel - Existing Conditions.skp`. This file was created by Bright Ideas Consultants, is part of the Office Remodel project, illustrates the existing conditions, and opens in SketchUp. By providing this information in the filename, you answer many questions about the file before anyone even tries to open it. Any consultant or member of your team who opens your files will immediately know where the files came from and how to use them.

Only one current version of each file should be stored in the main PROJECT folder. Avoid giving files confusing names that will make sense only at the moment you name it. Do not name files with the words `current`, `best`, `use this`, or `delete`. These types of filenames do not make it perfectly clear which file in the main PROJECT folder is actually the current file. Vague filenames provide users with ambiguous information, cause confusion, and ultimately lead to duplicated work and lost time. See Figure 3.2.

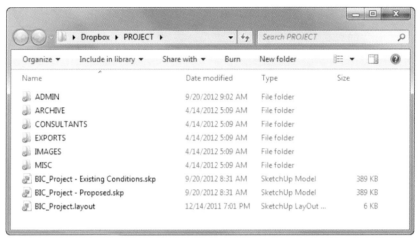

Figure 3.2 A typical PROJECT folder

Standard Folders

By placing your folders in logical places, you help your team keep track of active projects and their associated files. To start organizing your projects, you only need three basic folders: a TEMP folder, an ACTIVE PROJECTS folder, and an ARCHIVE folder. Again, this is not a rigid system; you can customize it to a system that works for you.

TEMP Folder

One way to keep junk files from accumulating on your machine is to create a place to dump them. Create a TEMP folder on your desktop.

The TEMP folder is for anything that you don't need to keep. This is a great place to save program installers, quick sketches, and email attachments. Files saved in this folder will not be missed when this folder is emptied. Every month or so, go into the TEMP folder and delete all of its contents. If you wonder whether or not you will need a file, more than likely you should save it in a PROJECT folder rather than save it in the TEMP folder.

On a side note, never save anything onto your desktop. The only items that should be on your desktop are the Recycle Bin, TEMP folder, ARCHIVE folder, ACTIVE PROJECTS folder, and possibly some application shortcuts. Never save files to your desktop. If you just need to use a file briefly, save it in the TEMP folder. If you ignore this rule, your desktop will become a mess (Figure 3.3).

Figure 3.3 A clean desktop is neater and easier to use than a messy desktop.

TIP Eliminate application shortcuts from your desktop by dragging them to the Start Bar menu, or by dragging them to the bottom of your screen and pinning them to the taskbar.

ACTIVE PROJECTS Folder

An active project is one that you access on a daily to weekly basis. The files within the ACTIVE PROJECTS folder change daily. Create a folder on your desktop and name it **ACTIVE PROJECTS**, or place it on a shared server. Save all current and active projects into your ACTIVE PROJECTS folder using the folder and file naming structures previously described.

TIP Always be aware of exactly where you are saving your active files and projects. Avoid using My Recent Documents to open files.

ARCHIVE Folder

An inactive project is a project that has already been invoiced, been paid, and probably won't be accessed again. Saving all finished work is important, just in case phase two comes around or you need to pull a piece of a model from a past project to use on a current project. Create a folder on your desktop and name it **ARCHIVE**. Inactive projects should be saved in the ARCHIVE folder on your desktop.

TIP For more information about adding completed projects to the ARCHIVE folder, see "Closing a Project" later in this chapter.

RESOURCES Folder

Within the ACTIVE PROJECTS folder, create another folder named RESOURCES. The RESOURCES folder holds all of your components, materials, plugins, scrapbooks, styles, and templates. You can also store Windows Themes, preferences.dat files, fonts, and anything else that you use across all of your machines in this folder. Add a folder for each category as shown in Figure 3.4. Consider prefixing each folder name with your identifying acronym.

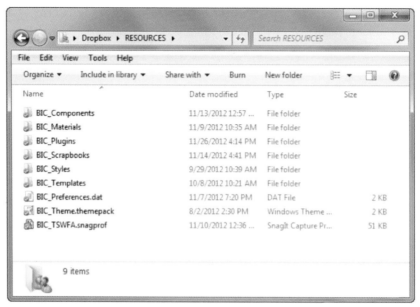

Figure 3.4 A typical RESOURCES folder

PROJECT Folders

This section suggests a starting point and system to help you organize your PROJECT folders. A PROJECT folder should contain the following subfolders: ADMIN, ARCHIVE, CONSULTANTS, EXPORTS, IMAGES, and MISC. Your particular projects can include other folders if needed.

The main project files, typically SketchUp and LayOut files, should be stored in the main PROJECT folder with the other project subfolders (Figure 3.5). This will provide easy access to the most frequently used files, which usually have the .skp and .layout filename extensions.

ADMIN Folder

The ADMIN folder should contain all administrative files. You should save contracts, time sheets, product specification sheets, correspondence, and memos that relate to the project in this folder (Figure 3.6). A safe rule of thumb is that if a file is not graphic in nature, it probably belongs in the ADMIN folder. Typical file extensions found in this folder are .doc, .xls, and .pdf.

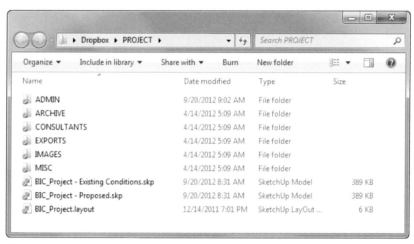

Figure 3.5 A typical PROJECT folder

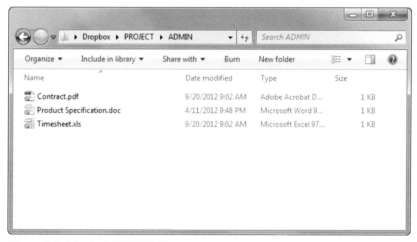

Figure 3.6 A typical ADMIN folder

ARCHIVE Folder

The ARCHIVE folder is used to preserve past versions of all important project files. Typically, you should store only zipped files and zipped folders in the ARCHIVE folder (Figure 3.7). All files should be titled with the naming convention `YYMMDD_Files.zip` or `YYMMDD_Exports.zip`.

By designating project files and exports within the .zip filename, you will be able to easily sort the archives and find any files you need. Because you will rarely access these files, they can be compressed into .zip files to save disk space.

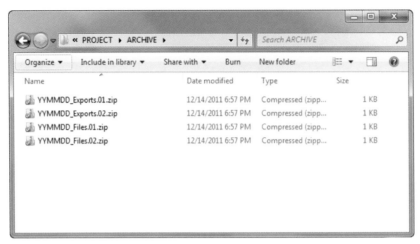

Figure 3.7 A typical ARCHIVE folder

TIP For more information on creating .zip files and backing up your work, see the "Archiving" section later in this chapter.

CONSULTANTS Folder

All of the files you receive from consultants should be saved in the CONSULTANTS folder within their respective folders. Typical subfolders include ELEC, MECH, PLUMB, and STRUCT (Figure 3.8). Each consultant you work with should have their own folder. Typically, a consultant's folder contains not only .dwg files, but also .pdf files that represent the .dwg files.

Within each consultant's folder, add subfolders with the naming convention YYMMDD. This will provide a record of when you received the files from each consultant.

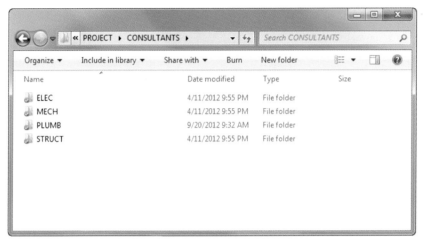

Figure 3.8 A typical CONSULTANTS folder

EXPORTS Folder

The EXPORTS folder will hold anything that you produce, or export, from your main project files. Some examples of exports are 3D models, 2D `.dwg` files, and image exports. To help you keep track of your exports, use the `YYMMDD` naming convention for subfolders. This folder naming system will also make it easy to create archive `.zip` files.

    Because you probably will be exporting several files a day, it is convenient to have one folder that always has the current backgrounds and the entire current set of files ready to print. Create a CURRENT SET subfolder. This folder should always contain all of the current `.dwg` backgrounds and `.pdf` prints associated with the project. Whenever someone needs to have a set of documents printed, or CAD backgrounds updated, you can go to this folder to access the most current set. This also means that whenever you export to a YYMMDD folder, you will need to overwrite the files in the CURRENT SET folder to keep those exports up to date. See Figure 3.9.

TIP As the project progresses, turn your EXPORTS folders into `.zip` files. The folders within the EXPORTS folder should be compressed as new, dated EXPORT folders are created. Once you are confident that these exports are not needed on a daily basis, move them to your ARCHIVE folder.

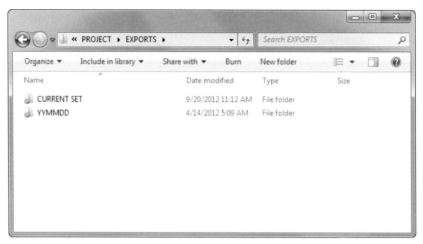

Figure 3.9 A typical EXPORTS folder

IMAGES Folder

The IMAGES folder will hold any photographs, field measurements, sketches, and diagrams relating to the project. Organize the subfolders using the YYMMDD_Description naming convention. You probably will want to separate site photos from interior photos from concept photos. The following folders will help keep them organized not only by the subject of the photographs, but also by date: YYMMDD_Site Visit, YYMMDD_Interiors, YYMMDD_Concepts (Figure 3.10).

MISC Folder

The MISC folder is the TEMP folder of a project. Save whatever you want within your MISC folder as long as it relates to the project; everyone needs a junk drawer. Subfolders of the MISC folder should be named using capitalized initials so that everyone on the team has their own junk drawer (Figure 3.11). Typically, components, sketch models, and texture images will end up in this folder. Take time every month or so to clean out the backup files and auto-save files to be sure that you don't waste space on your system.

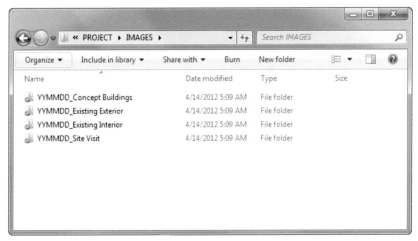

Figure 3.10 A typical IMAGES folder

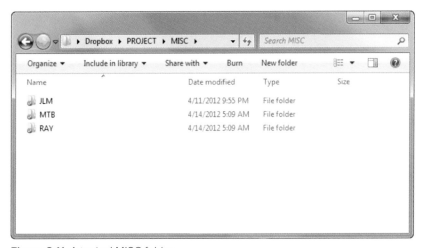

Figure 3.11 A typical MISC folder

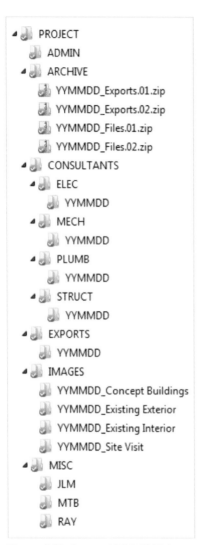

Figure 3.12 A typical PROJECT folder expanded

Refer to the chapter files to see a typical PROJECT folder that has already been created (Figure 3.12). You can copy it to your own ACTIVE PROJECTS folder and use it as a template for new projects.

CLOUD STORAGE

Consider saving your ACTIVE PROJECTS folder to the cloud for safe keeping, automatic archiving, and additional sharing options (Figure 3.13). Some standard features that many cloud storage solutions offer include:

☑ Automatic archiving

☑ File sharing without the need for an FTP site

☑ Access to previous versions of files and folders

☑ Seamless access to all of your files and folders on all of your computers

☑ File access from an Internet browser or smart phone

☑ Large file sharing without the need to email them

   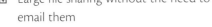

Figure 3.13 Several cloud services are available, many of which have free or very low-cost plans.

☑ Team sharing of PROJECT folders, even with team members who are not in your office

ARCHIVING

Clients change their minds. Systems crash. Data gets lost. Archiving is your free insurance policy that protects your time and work. Archiving is essential to a clean PROJECT folder and successful file management.

Archiving allows you to keep a copy of your work in case of an unexpected crash, accidental deletion, or any loss of data. Archiving also helps protect you from indecisive clients because you can revert back to previous versions without re-creating work. The techniques outlined in this section make it is easy to keep a running record of your work for a swift recovery.

Strategy

You don't need to archive everything all the time. You need to archive only the files that are constantly changing. Typically, these will be the files saved in the main PROJECT folder, the `.skp` and `.layout` files. You don't need to constantly archive the IMAGES folder or the ADMIN folder because these folders rarely change and do not reflect your time and work.

TIP You would be wise to archive before you begin making any major changes. Typically, you should archive at least once a day for an active project.

Creating a Project Snapshot

Select all of the current project files, right-click on the selections, and select Send To › Compressed (Zipped) Folder. Name the `.zip` file using the file-naming convention `YYMMDD.01_Files.zip`. Use the number at the end to track snapshots throughout the day (Figure 3.14).

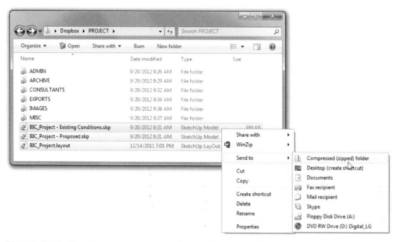

Figure 3.14 Create a project snapshot using a .zip file.

Organizing

Now drag the `.zip` file to your ARCHIVE folder in the main PROJECT folder (Figure 3.15). By naming the `.zip` archive files with the `YYMMDD` naming standard, you can easily sort them by name. Just click on the Name header in your file browser to put the files in chronological order by the date they were created and also in the proper order throughout the day. You could use the Date Modified tab within your file explorer as well; however, if you make any changes to the `.zip` file while looking for an old file, the files will no longer be in the correct order. The filename is always static and will allow you to keep archives in perfect chronological order.

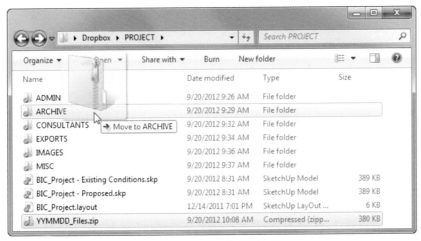

Figure 3.15 Drag the new .zip file to the ARCHIVE folder.

Closing a Project

Regardless of how long a project drags on, one day you will eventually finish. When you do, you should remove the PROJECT folder from your CURRENT PROJECTS folder to free up disk space. Once a project is complete, it is important to close the project and create a final archive in your main ARCHIVE folder.

TIP Before you archive a project, consider deleting all past archives within the project ARCHIVE folder. This may or may not be appropriate depending on the project and its potential to resurface.

Archive the entire project folder by right-clicking on the actual PROJECT folder and selecting Send To › Compressed (Zipped) Folder. This creates a separate .zip file that contains the files and folder structure of your project file in a compressed format. You can now delete the entire project folder and move the project .zip file to your ARCHIVE folder on your desktop. Here it will sit until you need to access the contents in the far and distant future.

TIP To be safe, burn these archives onto a disk, store them on a jump drive, or copy them to an external hard drive, and then store them in a safe as an additional layer of protection. You never know what can happen!

Re-opening a Project

The time may come when you need to re-open a project. To do so, right-click on the project `.zip` file within the ARCHIVE folder and choose Extract All. Click on the Browse button and choose the CURRENT PROJECTS folder on your desktop. Click Extract. All of the files will be restored to your CURRENT PROJECTS folder and maintain their original file and folder structures.

If you only need a couple of files within the archive, double-click into a zipped folder to view its contents, the same as you would a regular folder. Once in the zipped folder, drag and drop individual files into your TEMP folder for inspection. This does not actually move the file out of the `.zip` file; it makes a copy of it and leaves your archive intact.

CHAPTER POINTS

- ☑ The small amount of time you invest in organizing files will pay for itself hundreds of times over throughout the design process.
- ☑ Always know where you are opening a file from and where you are saving it. Never use My Recent Documents to open files.
- ☑ Archive often, sometimes multiple times during the day. It is better to archive too much rather than too little.
- ☑ Archive with `.zip` files to save disk space.
- ☑ For added convenience and protection from data loss, send your current files to the cloud.

PART II

SketchUp

SketchUp is an excellent design tool that gives designers the flexibility they need to sketch in a 3D digital world. SketchUp was once considered useful only for preliminary schematic designs; however, if you incorporate the organizational techniques taught in *The SketchUp Workflow for Architecture,* SketchUp is capable of much more. In this section, you'll learn about the SketchUp tools, environment, and how to use collections and ruby scripts. Before you get into the details, however, you need to make sure you are up to snuff on the basics and that your default SketchUp template is optimized for professional use.

Chapter 4

SketchUp Basics

In order to use the methods in this book, you must understand the concepts, tools, and commands presented in this chapter. Any additional knowledge you have is a plus. However, don't underestimate the usefulness of this chapter, even if you already consider yourself a SketchUp expert. It has plenty of tips, tricks, and helpful theories that will come up again later.

FIVE CORE CONCEPTS

Before you even open SketchUp, you need to understand the core concepts that make it unique. First, SketchUp is a surface modeler that is unlike most 3D modeling programs. Everything in SketchUp is composed of edges and surfaces, the basic building blocks used in SketchUp. A surface cannot exist without a closed loop of coplanar edges, and the simplest surface possible is a triangle (Figure 4.1).

Second, because it is a surface modeler, there are no true, perfect vector curves, arcs, or circles in SketchUp. However, you can still represent circles and curves with a series of small edges (Figure 4.2).

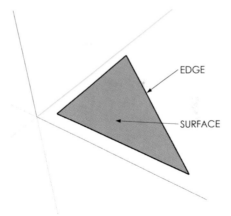

Figure 4.1 All of the endpoints (corners) of the triangle are at the same blue elevation—in other words, the edges are all on the same plane (coplanar).

Third, SketchUp geometry has a tendency to stick together. This concept is known as the "stickiness of geometry" in SketchUp. Adjoining surfaces stick together and move with each other. Connected endpoints will move with each other and stretch their corresponding lines (Figure 4.3). Even though this can be frustrating at first, once you learn to control the stickiness, you will realize how much it speeds up the modeling process.

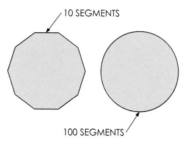

Figure 4.2 Circles and curves are represented by a series of smaller line segments. Increasing the number of segments makes a smoother circle, but can also decrease computer performance and lead to large file sizes.

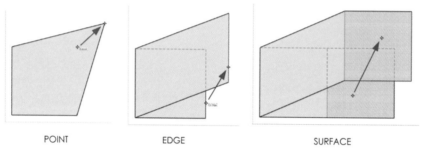

POINT   EDGE   SURFACE

Figure 4.3 Adjacent geometry sticks together in SketchUp.

Fourth, geometry does not stack in SketchUp. Only one edge or surface can exist between the same series of points. Even when multiple edges are drawn on top of each other, the edges simply combine into one. When an edge is drawn that intersects or overlaps an existing edge, the existing edge will be broken into two pieces (Figure 4.4).

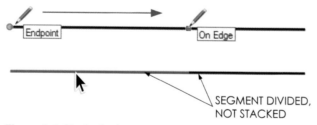

Endpoint   On Edge

SEGMENT DIVIDED, NOT STACKED

Figure 4.4 Stacked edges merge into one with edges segmented at the overlaps.

Lastly, the *inference engine* is the "brain" in SketchUp that is always working for you; it is what assumes meaningful relationships between points, edges, and surfaces. Although you can't turn off the inference engine, you can control it through the power of suggestion. There are several inferences available in SketchUp, some are shown in Figure 4.5.

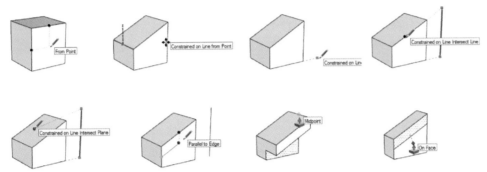

Figure 4.5 Most inferences require modifier keys or hovering on entities to "encourage" an inference.

LEVERAGING SKETCHUP

The five core concepts combine to make SketchUp a fast, fun, and unique 3D modeling program, but using it is not necessarily easy. By embracing and controlling these core concepts, you'll be able to successfully leverage SketchUp into your workflow.

Selecting a Template

When you open the SketchUp application, the first window you'll see is the Welcome to SketchUp window (Figure 4.6). You can also access it by clicking on the Help drop-down menu and choosing Welcome to SketchUp. From there, you can access learning resources, license information, and most important for now your default template. Within the Template tab, select the Plan View – Feet and Inches template and then click on Start Using SketchUp.

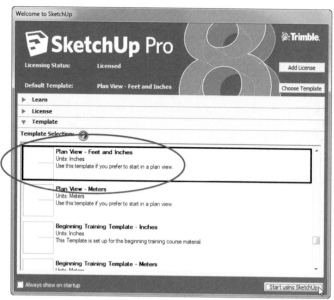

Figure 4.6 The Welcome to SketchUp window appears automatically when SketchUp is first opened.

Navigating the 3D Environment

The best way to navigate in SketchUp is to use a three-button scroll-wheel mouse, even when you're working on a laptop with a touch pad. Push down on the scroll-wheel button to orbit, hold down the Shift key with the scroll-wheel button to pan, and roll the scroll-wheel to zoom (Figure 4.7).

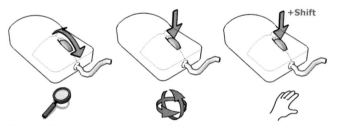

Figure 4.7 Mouse navigation diagrams

You don't need to use the Camera Tools icons on your screen because all of the Navigation tools are readily available at your fingertips (Figure 4.8). Actually, you'll be better off if you completely ignore these icons. If you use them, you'll have to search your screen outside of the work area. Every time you take your eyes off your design, you'll focus on the wrong thing. Furthermore, you'll give yourself a headache when you have to hunt around the screen for buttons.

Figure 4.8 Avoid using the Camera Tools icons. The most frequently used Navigation tools are readily available on your three-button scroll-wheel mouse.

Your cursor is the focal point of all navigation. Position it on the object you want to zoom in on, pan by, or orbit around so you will have more navigational control.

When you're completing any task in SketchUp, always navigate to a view that is strategic for the task at hand. For instance, if you are trying to work on the elevation, don't look at the model from a plan view. For any operation, you should always first determine the view that will make it easiest to perform the task. Also, be sure to utilize your large LCD monitor and really zoom in on the area you are working on.

Measurements

The Measurements dialog in SketchUp gives you complete control over any tool. Keep in mind that the Measurements dialog is always ready for your input. You never need to click in the Measurements dialog to enter a precise dimension or value; you just need to start typing.

By default, the Measurements toolbar is docked at the bottom-right corner of the SketchUp interface. You can reposition this toolbar by clicking on the View drop-down menu and choosing Toolbars › Measurements. Once the Measurements toolbar is floating, it can be repositioned or docked anywhere on the screen (Figure 4.9). The screen captures used in this chapter show a floating Measurements toolbar.

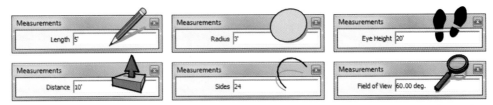

Figure 4.9 The Measurements dialog changes depending on the tool and the type of input it needs.

CREATING GEOMETRY

The most frequently used tools for creating geometry in SketchUp can be categorized into two groups: the Drawing tools and the Modification tools. To get started with any model, you must first create the geometry using the Drawing tools (the Line tool, Rectangle tool, Circle tool, Arc tool, Polygon tool, and Freehand tool). Once you've created simple 2D geometry, you can shape and change that geometry into a more complex form using the Modification tools (the Move tool, Push/Pull tool, Rotate tool, Follow Me tool, Scale tool, and Offset tool). Throughout the modeling process, you will likely go back and forth between these toolsets (Figure 4.10). Use the Drawing tools to create simple 2D geometry and make additional edges to break surfaces to set up operations for the Modification tools.

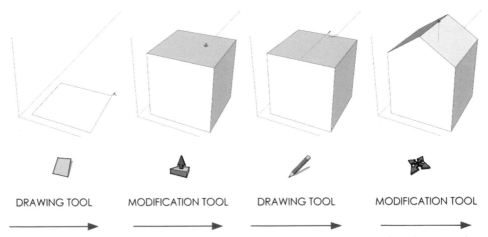

DRAWING TOOL   MODIFICATION TOOL   DRAWING TOOL   MODIFICATION TOOL

Figure 4.10 To efficiently model in SketchUp, you'll need to move back and forth between the Drawing and Modification tools. Use the Drawing tools to make additional edges and break surfaces to set up operations for the Modification tools.

Drawing Tools

The Drawing tools can be further broken down into two groups: the Surface Drawing tools and the Edge Drawing tools. A Surface Drawing tool creates a closed loop of coplanar edges, including a surface, in a specified shape. An Edge Drawing tool creates straight and curved edges (no surface). These tools provide infinite combinations to complete additive and subtractive modeling operations (Figure 4.11).

Surface Drawing Tools

The Surface Drawing tools include the Rectangle, Circle, and Polygon tools. All of these tools create a closed loop of coplanar edges and a surface. It is best to start building a model using these tools (Figure 4.12).

SURFACE | EDGE
DRAWING | DRAWING
TOOLS | TOOLS

Figure 4.11 The Drawing toolbar

Figure 4.12 Typically, you will begin a model using one of the Surface Drawing tools.

To use the Surface Drawing tools, you'll need to click twice. Click once to start, move your cursor to suggest a direction, then click again to finish. Keep in mind that you can enter precise dimensions during the command or after the command, until another command is started. The same is true for most SketchUp tools.

TIP The best way to execute most SketchUp commands is to use the click-and-release method. The click-and-drag method will get you into trouble because it is easy to accidentally perform small unnoticeable commands with many of the tools. Typically, you should click once to start, move your cursor, click again to finish, and then enter a precise dimension.

Rectangle Tool

The Rectangle tool is a very effective tool for creating surfaces, and it certainly is one of the most frequently used tools in SketchUp. One of its great features is that the geometry it creates is always aligned with the axes. This means that you can create four edges and a surface, all squared up, with just two clicks (Figure 4.13).

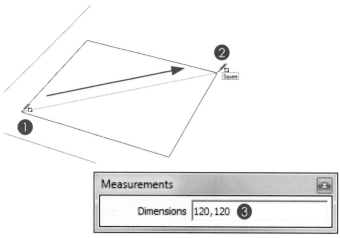

Figure 4.13 The Rectangle tool in action

1. Activate the Rectangle tool and click once to start.
2. Move your cursor to suggest a direction and click again to finish.
3. At this point, you can enter precise dimensions such as **120,120**, then press Enter.

TIP You can override the alignment with axes by starting a rectangle on an off-axis edge. The Rectangle tool will align new geometry with the edge on which it is started.

Circle and Polygon Tools

Because SketchUp is a surface modeler—meaning that the basic building blocks are edges and surfaces—there are no "true" circles in SketchUp. All circles are represented by a series of connected edges. The more sides a circle has, the smoother it looks (Figure 4.14). The default number of sides for a circle is 24 sides, and this number works for just about any circle you will need to create. Keep in mind that when you extrude a circle into a 3D form, every edge will become a surface with three additional edges. As a result, the more edges you have, the more 3D surfaces you create, and ultimately the slower your model will perform, which can be problematic.

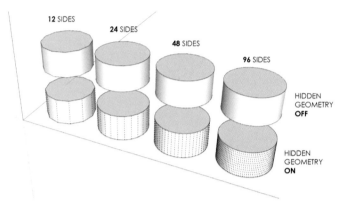

Figure 4.14 Two cylinders with different side counts. At what point are more segments unnoticeable?

Be aware of what you are modeling and how many sides you will need to achieve the quality you want. If you are creating a close-up rendering of a column, it would be appropriate to increase the number of sides before you create the circle base of the column. If you are rendering several columns for a building off in the distance, you could decrease the number of sides used to create the circle bases of the columns. There are times when a drastically lower number of sides is not noticeable. When you activate the Circle tool, you can change the default number of sides used to represent a circle (Figure 4.15).

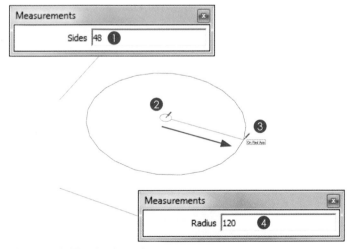

Figure 4.15 The Circle tool in action

To create a circle, follow these steps:

1. Activate the Circle tool, then immediately type **48** and press Enter to change the default number of sides on a circle to 48 sides.

2. Click once to define the center point of the circle.

3. Move your cursor away from the center point on axis, click again to finish.

4. At this point, you can enter a precise radius such as **120**, then press Enter.

The Polygon tool works the same way the Circle tool does. The difference between the two is that a polygon's edges are not softened when extruded (Figure 4.16).

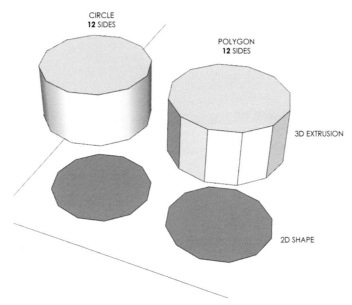

Figure 4.16 A circle and polygon in 2D; a circle and polygon extruded into 3D

Edge Drawing Tools

The Edge Drawing tools include the Line, Arc, and Freehand tools (Figure 4.17). These tools only create edges, not surfaces. You can use the Edge Drawing tools to make small additive and subtractive adjustments to existing surfaces. Although they aren't the most efficient tools for creating surfaces from scratch, you can use them to actually draw the sides of a closed loop of coplanar edges.

Line Tool

The Line tool is the most basic Edge Drawing tool in SketchUp, and it is the tool with which most designers begin. Although it has many uses, surprisingly, using it is not the most effective way to create geometry. The Line tool is best used to make small adjustments and modifications.

Figure 4.17 The Edge Drawing tools

When you're drawing in 3D with the Line tool, you can draw on axis by locking the Line tool on an axis.

To lock an axis, first find the axis and then hold down the Shift key to lock it. Finish the operation by clicking on a point to define the distance, and then release the Shift key. You can also lock an axis by tapping an arrow key while drawing a line. The Right arrow key locks the red axis, the Left arrow key locks the green axis, and the Up and Down arrow keys lock the blue axis.

Locking an axis eliminates two of the three dimensions, so all you need to do is define a distance along the specified locked axis (Figure 4.18). You can do this by using the inference engine to snap to a point, edge, or surface. Also, you can enter precise dimensions into the Measurements dialog.

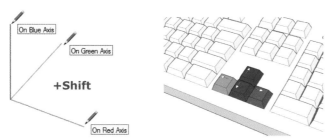

Figure 4.18 Use either the Shift key or arrow keys to lock the Line tool on an axis.

The Line tool can also be used to heal surfaces (Figure 4.19). Right-click on an edge of a surface and choose Erase. When you erase an edge, you break the closed loop of coplanar edges and, in turn, lose the surface. Redraw the line from point to point and you will have the edge and surface back.

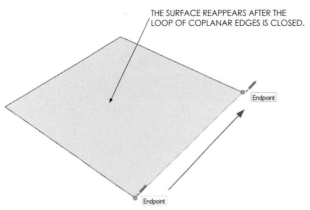

THE SURFACE REAPPEARS AFTER THE
LOOP OF COPLANAR EDGES IS CLOSED.

Endpoint

Endpoint

Figure 4.19 Redraw a deleted edge using the Line tool to recreate the edge and surface at the same time.

Now, right-click on the surface and choose Erase to delete only the surface. Use the Line tool to retrace any edge around the closed loop of coplanar edges. The surface is now healed (Figure 4.20). Keep in mind that because geometry does not stack in SketchUp, there is only one edge remaining where you traced the edge.

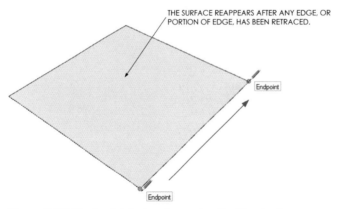

THE SURFACE REAPPEARS AFTER ANY EDGE, OR
PORTION OF EDGE, HAS BEEN RETRACED.

Endpoint

Endpoint

Figure 4.20 Heal a deleted surface using the Line tool.

Arc Tool

Use the Arc Tool to create precise curves. 1. Click once to define the starting point of the arc. 2. Click again to define the endpoint of the arc, or enter a precise dimension into the measurements dialog. 3. Click once more to define the bulge (Figure 4.21). Using the Measurements dialog, you can also enter a specific distance for the bulge.

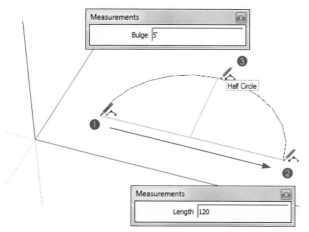

Figure 4.21 To use the Arc tool you'll need to make three clicks: one for the start point, one for the endpoint, and one for the bulge.

When you're using the Arc tool to round the corners of a rectangle, look for the magenta Equidistant and Tangent to Edge inferences (Figure 4.22). When you're continuing an arc, look for the cyan Tangent at Vertex inference to make a smooth transition between the two arcs (Figure 4.23).

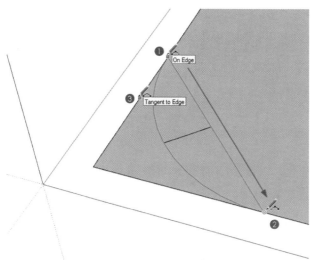

Figure 4.22 Rounding the corners of a rectangle

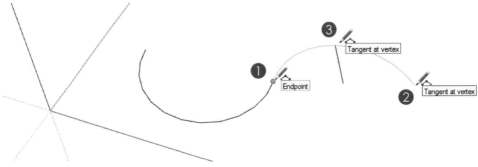

Figure 4.23 Continuing an arc

Freehand Tool

The Freehand tool is one of the few tools that require you to click and drag (Figure 4.24). You can use it to draw loose, sketchy lines. 1. Click and drag to draw a line. Release on the starting point to finish and create a surface.

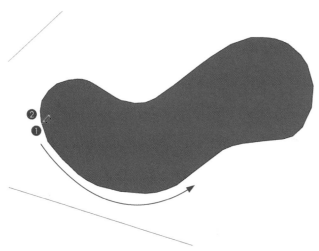

Figure 4.24 When using the Freehand tool, be sure to finish on the starting point to create a surface.

TIP To learn how to draw more accurate loose curves, read about the Bézier curve plugin in Chapter 8, "Ruby Scripts."

Modification Tools

Once you've created the geometry using the Drawing tools, you can change it using the Modification tools (Figure 4.25). The Modification tools can quickly transform 2D geometry into 3D objects and quickly create complex geometry by scaling, stretching, moving, and copying.

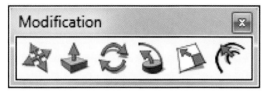

Figure 4.25 The Modification tools

The Select Tool

The Select tool is included in the Principal tools, but it is critical for using the Modification tools. Of all the tools you need to master, this one is by far the most underestimated and the most important. You will use the Select tool before you use most of the other SketchUp tools. Typically, you will default back to the Select tool after issuing a command. All modification operations are complemented by the Select tool. It is best to preselect an entity before you use the Modification tools. Some of the Modification tools have a hot spot that auto-selects entities, but you will find that you can obtain complete control by first preselecting an entity with the Select tool.

Click once on an edge or surface to select it. Double-click on a surface to select the surface as well as the bounding edges. Triple-click on a surface to select all of the connected geometry (Figure 4.26).

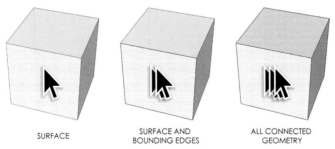

SURFACE   SURFACE AND   ALL CONNECTED
                       BOUNDING EDGES   GEOMETRY

Figure 4.26 Single-click, double-click, or triple-click to quickly select individual or multiple entities.

To perform a window selection, click and drag from left to right over the entities you want to select (Figure 4.27). Only the entities that are completely in the selection window will be selected. A window selection is represented by a solid selection window.

To perform a crossing selection, click and drag right to left over the entities you want to select. A crossing selection will select the entities that are completely within the selection window as well as any entity that the selection window touches. A crossing selection is represented by a dashed selection window.

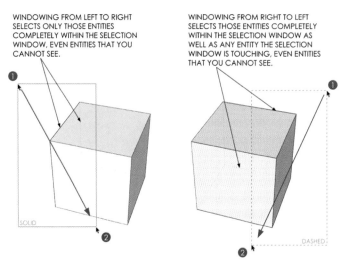

WINDOWING FROM LEFT TO RIGHT SELECTS ONLY THOSE ENTITIES COMPLETELY WITHIN THE SELECTION WINDOW, EVEN ENTITIES THAT YOU CANNOT SEE.

WINDOWING FROM RIGHT TO LEFT SELECTS THOSE ENTITIES COMPLETELY WITHIN THE SELECTION WINDOW AS WELL AS ANY ENTITY THE SELECTION WINDOW IS TOUCHING, EVEN ENTITIES THAT YOU CANNOT SEE.

Figure 4.27 Click and drag with the Select tool to create selection windows.

Hold down the Ctrl key (Option on Mac) while you are using the Select tool to add entities to the selection. Hold down the Ctrl (Option on Mac) and Shift keys while you are using the Select tool to remove entities from the selection. Hold the Shift key while you are using the Select tool to inverse the selection. All of these modifier keys work with selection windows, too (Figure 4.28).

ADD (CTRL) SUBTRACT (CTRL + SHIFT) INVERSE (SHIFT)

Figure 4.28 You can alter a selection by using modifier keys.

TIP Before starting any command it is best to clear all selections. You can deselect all of the entities in a model by clicking on the Edit drop-down menu and choosing Deselect All, or by right-clicking on the model background.

To see additional selection options, right-click on an edge or surface (Figure 4.29). From this menu, you can select Bounding Edges, Connected Faces, All Connected, All on Same Layer, or All with Same Material. These unique selection options can help you make complex selections faster.

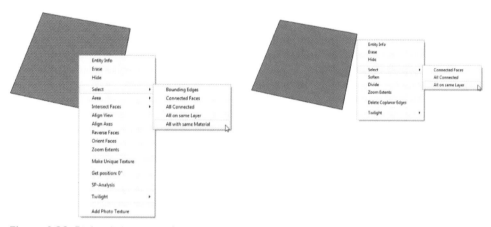

Figure 4.29 Right-click on a surface or an edge for additional selection options.

If you find yourself tediously picking through a model, keep in mind that there is always a fast and easy way to make the selection you need. Use a combination of all of the selection techniques to select only what you need in the most effective manner. Approach the selection process just as you do the modeling process; the process can be additive or subtractive. Before starting the selection, ask yourself if it would be easier to select several entities and then deselect what you don't need, or would it be better to add each piece individually. Perhaps using a combination of the two techniques would be the most effective. Every selection is different, so be sure to keep your approach flexible.

The Move Tool

The Move tool's efficiency relies heavily on the stickiness of the geometry. You can move points, edges, and surfaces using the Move tool. Moving each of these entities has a different effect on the entity, as well as the adjacent, connected entities (Figure 4.30). The Move tool's hot spot is right in the middle of the icon. Place your cursor on an edge or a surface, and note that the Move tool will auto-select entities. Click once to pick an entity up, then click again to put it down.

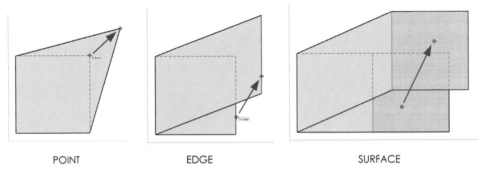

POINT   EDGE   SURFACE

Figure 4.30 Move a point and the connecting edge will follow. Move an edge and the connecting edges will follow. Move a surface and all the bounding edges of the surface will move as well.

TIP Beware! The Move tool is the number one destroyer of models. Be careful about what you are selecting and what is beyond your selection. You can select entities that are visibly blocked by other geometry, which makes it very easy to move entities accidentally and "blow out" the back of a model.

Precise Move

A *precise move* is executed by preselecting entities and then moving the selection from a specific spot on the selection to another specific spot in the model (Figure 4.31). A *precise move* can be started and ended on an edge, endpoint, midpoint, or surface, depending on the desired final location.

To make a precise move, follow these steps:

1. Using the Select tool, preselect the entity you want to move.

2. Activate the Move tool. Hover on the front-bottom corner of the cube until you see the Endpoint inference notification. Click once to pick up the cube.

3. Move your cursor, and the cube, to the front-bottom of the large cube. Hover on the corner until you see the Endpoint inference notification and click to place the cube.

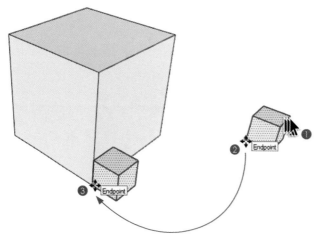

Figure 4.31 A precise move

TIP Don't "eyeball it" when you can be precise. When performing a precise move, be sure to snap to other entities in your model.

Linear Copy and Array

The Move tool is also the "copy tool." To toggle the Copy command on and off, tap the Ctrl key (Option on Mac). As you are moving any entity, tap the Ctrl key (Option on Mac) to leave a copy of it behind.

To make a copy, follow these steps (Figure 4.32):

1. Using the Select tool, preselect the entity that you want to copy.
2. Activate the Move tool and click once on the entity (you could start the copy from anywhere in the model).
3. Tap the Ctrl key (Option on Mac) to toggle on the Copy command while you move the cursor along an axis, then click again to finish.
4. At this point, enter a precise distance into the Measurements dialog, such as 20′, then press Enter.

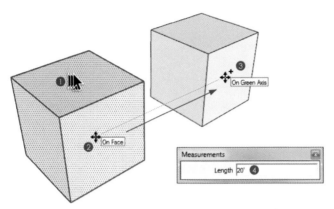

Figure 4.32 To create a copy of any entity, use the Move tool and the Copy toggle.

5. To create multiple copies at a specified distance, immediately after you complete the Move/Copy command, enter the number of copies you want to make—for example, type **4x**, then press Enter. This will create four copies of the selection in addition to the original, just as a copy machine would (Figure 4.33).

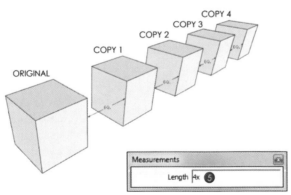

Figure 4.33 Create multiple copies at set intervals using the multiply array.

Another way to array using the Move tool is to divide the distance between the copies (Figure 4.34). After you complete a copy, specify the number of divisions between the two copies within the Measurements dialog, as follows:

1. Using the Select tool, preselect the entity that you want to copy.

2. Activate the Move tool and click once on the entity (you could start the copy from anywhere in the model).

3. Tap the Ctrl key (Option on Mac) to toggle on the Copy command while you move the cursor along an axis, then click again to finish.

4. At this point, enter a precise distance into the Measurements dialog—for example, type **100'**, then press Enter.

5. Immediately after entering the distance, enter the desired number of divisions between the two copies—for instance, type **5/**, then press Enter.

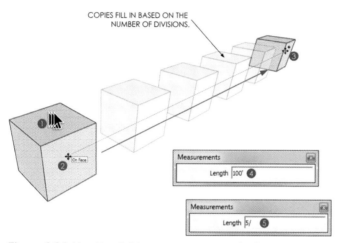

Figure 4.34 Use the divide array to create multiple copies at set intervals.

You can continue to modify the copy and array until you start another command. Try entering different numbers of copies and different distances, and switch between using multiply and divide arrays. Once you click on another tool, you will lose the ability to modify the array (Figure 4.35). At that point, the new geometry will be just that, geometry. You will need to delete or reposition geometry to change the array.

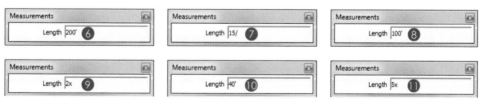

Figure 4.35 You can continue to modify the copy and array until you invoke another command.

Auto-fold

If a surface does not have the proper lines, or breaks, to fold the surface and allow the selection to move on all axes, it can stick to another surface. The Auto-fold command automatically draws all the lines needed to break a surface and allow the selected surface to move in any direction (Figure 4.36). While performing a move, tap the Alt key (command key on Mac) to toggle the Auto-fold command on.

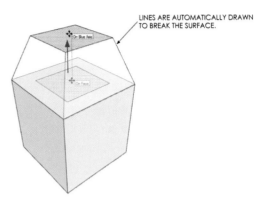

Figure 4.36 Auto-fold in action

TIP Don't use the Auto-fold command as a crutch. Sometimes it can appear to help make an entity move where you want it to, but it can actually create off-axis geometry that will be problematic later.

Push/Pull Tool

The Push/Pull tool is one of the fastest and easiest ways to generate large amounts of geometry. The Push/Pull tool extrudes 2D surfaces into 3D forms, perpendicular to the starting face. This means that geometry is typically on axis, or at least perfectly square with the starting surface. The Push/Pull tool affects only surfaces. Just follow these steps:

1. Position the Push/Pull tool on a surface; it will auto-select the surface. The hot spot of the Push/Pull tool is at the tip of the red arrow on the icon. Click on the surface to start the operation.

2. Move your cursor to push or pull the surface. The surface will extrude perpendicular to the starting surface (Figure 4.37). Click again to finish.

3. At this point, you can enter a precise dimension, type **5'**, then press Enter.

Tap the Ctrl key (Option on Mac) before or during any Push/Pull operation to leave a copy of the starting face (Figure 4.38). This is a toggle, so tap the Ctrl key (Option on Mac) again and the starting face will disappear. In Chapter 17, "Site Analysis: Documenting an Existing Building," you will see how valuable this function is for creating floorplans.

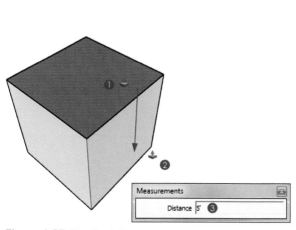

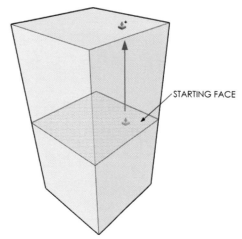

STARTING FACE

Figure 4.37 The Push/Pull tool in action

Figure 4.38 The Push/Pull tool can leave a copy of the starting face behind if desired.

TIP The Push/Pull tool has a memory. Once you have completed a Push/Pull operation, you can double-click on another surface to reproduce the last push/pull.

Follow Me Tool

The Follow Me tool generates massive amounts of complex geometry with very few clicks. This tool works by extruding a 2D profile along a path (Figure 4.39). A path can be a series of connected edges, or a surface which defines the path with its bounding edges. Follow these steps:

1. Using the Select tool, preselect the path, in this example a surface.
2. Activate the Follow Me tool.
3. Click on the profile to finish.

TIP The profile does not have to touch the path for the Follow Me tool to work, although the operation and results make more sense and are easier to predict if it does touch the path.

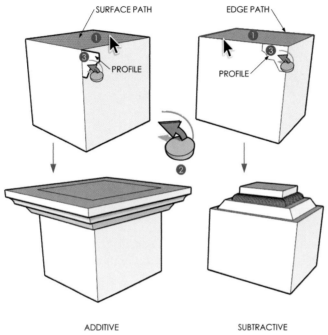

SURFACE PATH

EDGE PATH

PROFILE

PROFILE

ADDITIVE

SUBTRACTIVE

Figure 4.39 The Follow Me tool in action

Rotate Tool

The Rotate tool spins entities around a defined center point of rotation at a specified angle (Figure 4.40). To use it, follow these steps:

1. Using the Select tool, preselect the entity you want to rotate.

2. Activate the Rotate tool. Click and hold at the desired center point of rotation, and drag away to set the axis of rotation. Look for the inference line to turn red, green, or blue. Release once you have found the desired axis of rotation—for this example, rotate about the red axis.

TIP Use guides or encourage an inference to specify a meaningful center point of rotation.

3. Move your cursor around and notice that it is locked at the defined center point of rotation. Click to define the reference angle. The reference angle can be arbitrary for most rotations, unless you are trying to align one object with another.

4. Move your cursor and click again to define the degree of rotation away from the reference angle. You can click at a random angle, or

5. At this point let go of the mouse and enter a precise angle into the Measurements dialog—for example, type **90**, then press Enter. This will rotate the object 90 degrees off the reference angle around the defined center point of rotation.

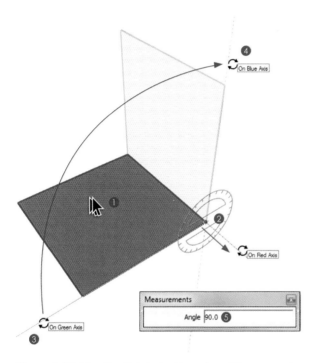

Figure 4.40 Use the Rotate tool to spin entities around a specified axis.

Similar to the Move tool, during any rotation, tap the Ctrl key (Option on Mac) to toggle on the Copy command. This will leave a copy of the selected object behind (Figure 40.41). To perform a polar copy and array, follow these steps:

1. Pre-select the entity you wish to rotate and copy. Activate the Rotate Tool, hover on a point to encourage an inference and use a meaningful starting point.

2. Click and drag and release on the blue axis.

3. Move your cursor to the right and click once to set the reference line. Tap the Ctrl key (Option on Mac) to toggle on the Copy command while you move your cursor down the screen.

4. Click to place the copy.

5. Immediately type a precise degree of rotation, such as **90**, then press Enter.

6. To make three copies, immediately type the number of copies as **3x**, then press Enter. You can continue to change both the degree of rotation and the number of copies until you invoke another command.

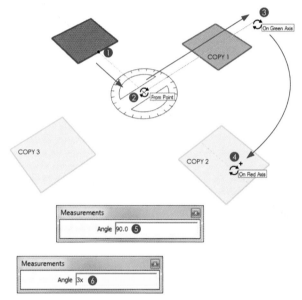

Figure 4.41 The Rotate tool can create copies and polar arrays.

TIP Similarly to the way you use the Move tool, you can also enter the overall copy rotation and specify divisions. For example, after making a copy type **180,** then press Enter, immediately type **5/,** then press Enter. This will make the original copy at 180 degrees and fill the space between with five divisions.

Scale Tool

The Scale tool distorts entities based on a scale factor or a "hard" dimension. The hot spot of the Scale tool is at the tip of the red arrow, but it usually is best to preselect entities before scaling. Follow these steps:

1. Using the Select tool, preselect the entity you want to scale.

2. Activate the Scale tool and click on the top center grip.

3. Move your cursor to scale the object and click to finish the command.

4. Immediately enter a scale value, such as **1.5**, then press Enter.

5. You can also type a precise dimension into the Measurements dialog—for example, **20'**, then press Enter. Be sure to specify feet or inches because the Scale Tool defaults to a scale value rather than the models default units (Figure 4.42).

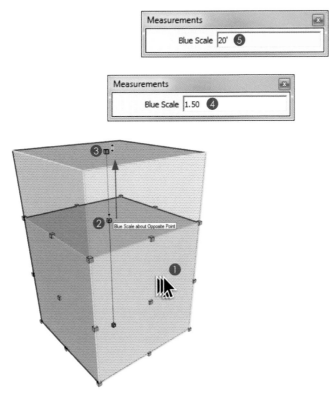

Figure 4.42 The Scale tool distorts entities based on a scale factor or set dimension.

TIP The Scale tool also has modifier keys to help you achieve the desired scaling effect. Hold the Shift key to toggle between a uniform and nonuniform scale. Hold the Ctrl key (Option key on Mac) to scale about the center of the entity.

Offset Tool

The Offset tool concentrically copies a series of connected edges or a surface's bounding edges (Figure 4.43). Follow these steps:

1. Use the Select tool to preselect a series of connected coplanar edges, or use the tool's hot spot at the tip of the red arrow to auto-select a surface and offset its bounding edges. Hover on an edge to set the starting point.

2. Move your cursor to suggest the direction of the offset and let go of the mouse.

3. At this point, you can type a precise dimension, such as **2'**, then press Enter.

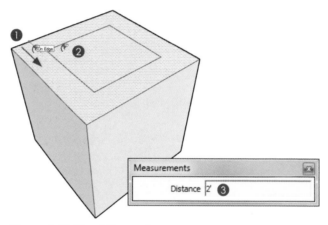

Figure 4.43 The Offset tool in action

TIP The Offset tool also has a memory. You can double-click on another surface or series of coplanar lines to reproduce the last offset.

ADVANCED INFERENCING

The inference engine is always running in the background and is there to help keep your geometry aligned in accurate and meaningful ways. Mastering inferences is essential to fast and efficient drafting in SketchUp. The inferences discussed in this section are advanced techniques; becoming familiar with each of these inferences will make you much faster at drawing in SketchUp. Try to think of ways to eliminate clicks from your own modeling techniques. Often, inferences can eliminate guides and clicks. Many of the following inferences work with both the Drawing tools and the Move tool.

TIP The inference engine cannot be turned off, but why would you want to? Once you master the available inferences, you will wonder how you ever lived without advanced inferences.

Multiple Points

You can encourage an inference from a point, a midpoint, or even two points (Figure 4.44). Follow these steps:

1. With the Line tool active, hover on an endpoint until you see the Endpoint notification. When you see the notification, the edge is loaded into the inference engine. Move your cursor away from the point and you will see a dotted inference line representing the axis it is on.

2. Hover on another endpoint until you see the Endpoint notification. When you see the notification, the edge is loaded into the inference engine. Move your cursor away from the point and you will see two dotted inference lines projecting from the two inferenced points.

3. Click where the inference lines meet to start the line at a meaningful point. Now you can go on to encourage more inferences and click to finish.

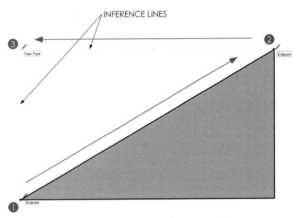

Figure 4.44 Encouraging two inference points to use a meaningful starting point

Parallel to Edge

Draw parallel to an existing edge by encouraging a Parallel to Edge inference (Figure 4.45). Follow these steps:

1. Click once to start a line.

2. Position your cursor on the edge to which you want to draw a line parallel. Wait for the On Edge inference to appear; this lets you know that SketchUp loaded that edge into the inference engine.

3. Position you cursor roughly parallel to the edge. The active line will turn magenta and you will see the Parallel to Edge notification appear. At this point you can hold down the Shift key to lock the inference.

4. Position your cursor over a point, edge, or surface to specify the distance and click to finish.

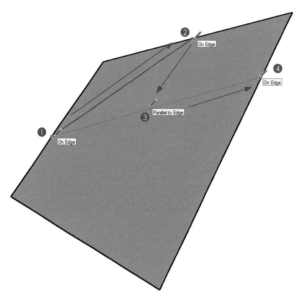

Figure 4.45 A Parallel to Edge inference

Constrained on Line

The Edge Constrained inference allows you to either start or finish an operation along a specific edge (Figure 4.46). Follow these steps:

1. Using the Line tool, hover on an edge. When you see the On Edge inference, hold down the Shift key.

2. Move your cursor off of the existing geometry and notice that the starting point is constrained on the edge. Click to start the line.

3. Hover on another edge. Once you see the On Edge inference, hold down the Shift key to constrain the next point along that edge.

4. Click to finish the line.

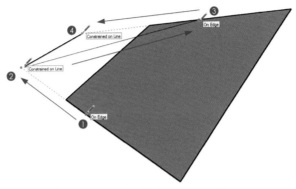

Figure 4.46 A constrained inference on a line

TIP You can also constrain an operation on a surface by first hovering on the surface and then holding the Shift key. This will limit any line that you draw to be coplanar with the inferred surface. Constrained inferences, both edge and surface, are especially helpful when you're working out complex roofs in three dimensions.

Line Intersect

Use the Line Intersect inference to take the place of guides and project intersections between lines (Figure 4.47). Follow these steps:

1. To encourage the inference, use the Line tool to hover on an endpoint until you see the Endpoint inference notification.

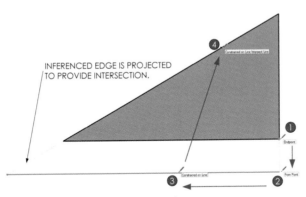

Figure 4.47 The Line Intersect inference

2. Move your cursor down away from the Endpoint on the green axis and click to set the starting point.

3. Move your cursor to the left until you find the red axis. Once the active line turns red, hold down the Shift key to lock the axis.

4. Position you cursor on the angled line. The endpoint of the line has been projected to the intersection of the locked axis and the inferenced edge. Click to finish.

ORGANIZING GEOMETRY WITH CONTAINERS

SketchUp has two basic containers for geometry: groups and components (Figure 4.48). These containers not only separate edges to control stickiness, but also organize entities and geometry to make more efficient models. Groups are unintelligent containers that have no connection between copies. Groups simply hold geometry. Components on the other hand have intelligence in that each instance is connected. If any instance of a component is modified, all instances of the same component reflect those changes as well.

Figure 4.48 Components are intelligent; groups are not.

TIP In this book, the term *container* refers to both groups and components.

Groups

Groups are unintelligent containers that simply hold geometry (Figure 4.49). If you make a copy of a group, there will be no connection between the original and the new copy. Almost every object should be made into a group. It is almost impossible to make too many groups.

Groups are mainly used to contain entities, form a hierarchy of layers, and control the stickiness of geometry.

The organization techniques utilized during *The SketchUp Workflow for Architecture* require advanced layering and organization of groups. Model organization diagrams (Figure 4.50) are used to complement the text and further explain layering and grouping.

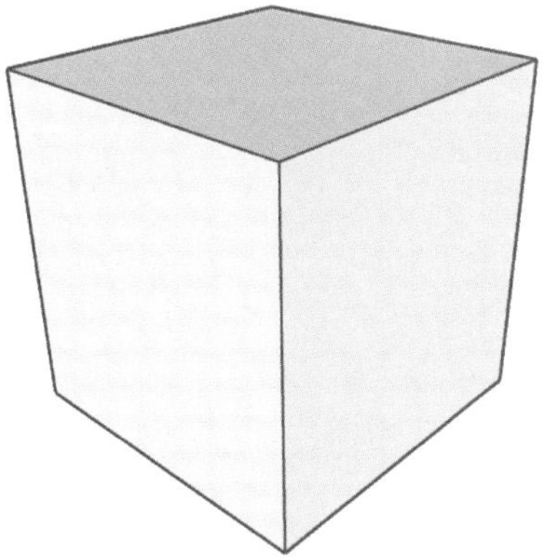

Creating a Group

To create a group, follow these steps:

1. Using the Select tool, select at least two entities (edges, surfaces, groups, or components).

2. Right-click on the selection and choose Make Group, or click on the Edit drop-down menu and choose Make Group.

Figure 4.49 Groups can hold any entity created in SketchUp. When selected, both groups and components highlight with a blue bounding box.

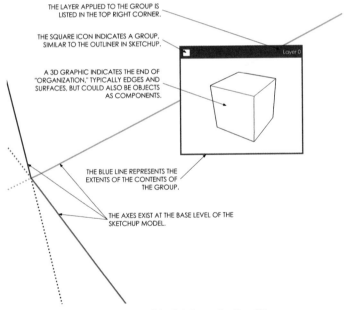

THE LAYER APPLIED TO THE GROUP IS LISTED IN THE TOP RIGHT CORNER.

THE SQUARE ICON INDICATES A GROUP, SIMILAR TO THE OUTLINER IN SKETCHUP.

A 3D GRAPHIC INDICATES THE END OF "ORGANIZATION," TYPICALLY EDGES AND SURFACES, BUT COULD ALSO BE OBJECTS AS COMPONENTS.

Layer 0

THE BLUE LINE REPRESENTS THE EXTENTS OF THE CONTENTS OF THE GROUP.

THE AXES EXIST AT THE BASE LEVEL OF THE SKETCHUP MODEL.

Figure 4.50 A simple group Model Organization Diagram

Components

Unlike groups, components are intelligent containers. They hold geometry just as groups do, but there is a linkage between all copies of a component. Suppose you make a component and then copy it several times throughout a model. If you edit any one instance of a component, all instances of that component will update simultaneously to reflect those changes (Figure 4.51).

Components are used to make extremely efficient models. When you see repeating elements, similar elements, and lines of symmetry, you should think component.

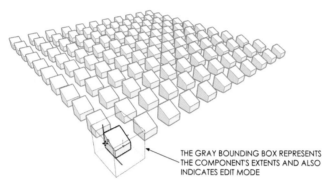

THE GRAY BOUNDING BOX REPRESENTS THE COMPONENT'S EXTENTS AND ALSO INDICATES EDIT MODE

Figure 4.51 Any changes to the contents of a component are reflected in all instances of that component.

TIP A component's behavior is similar to a block in CAD, or a smart object in Adobe Photoshop.

Creating a Component

To create a component, follow these steps (Figure 4.52):

1. Using the Select tool, select at least two entities.

2. Right-click on the selection and choose Make Component.

3. In the Create Component dialog, assign the desired properties and choose Create.

Figure 4.52 The Create Component dialog

TIP If you are making a copy of a group, it should most likely be made into a component first. To change a group into a component, right-click on the group and choose Make Component. It is easier to make a group first, and then choose Make Component because this method bypasses the often unnecessary Create Component dialog.

Making Unique Components

The Make Unique command is used for similar elements. It is similar to a Save Copy As command in other programs. The original component instance(s) are left connected and intact, and a new component instance is created based on the selected component (Figure 4.53). To make a component, or multiple components unique, select them, then right-click on the selection and choose "Make Unique."

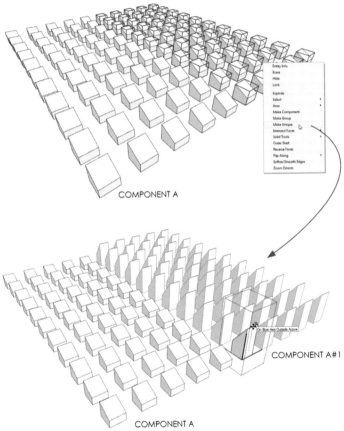

Figure 4.53 Once a component or selection of components is made unique, the components are independent of the original instance and are connected only to each other.

Navigating Containers

The ability to quickly move in and out of containers is essential to fast and efficient modeling in SketchUp. The first way to navigate containers is slow and methodical. Use this method when you're first learning to navigate containers; it is easy to understand which container level of the model you are in. Follow these steps:

1. Right-click on a container and choose Edit Group or Edit Component, depending on which type of container you are editing.

2. To close the container, right-click outside of the container bounding box and choose Close Group or Close Component.

A much faster method for navigating containers utilizes the Select tool. Use the Select tool method for navigating containers after you have a solid understanding of which container level of the model you are in. Follow these steps:

1. Using the Select tool, double-click on a container to move in one level (Figure 4.54).

2. To close the container, press the Esc key to back out while the Select tool is active. You can also click outside the bounding box of the container to back out one level.

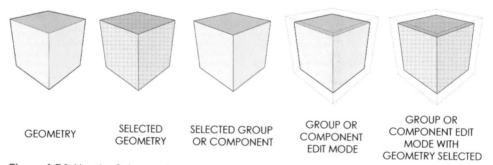

GEOMETRY SELECTED GEOMETRY SELECTED GROUP OR COMPONENT GROUP OR COMPONENT EDIT MODE GROUP OR COMPONENT EDIT MODE WITH GEOMETRY SELECTED

Figure 4.54 Use the Select tool to select entities and navigate quickly in and out of containers.

The Outliner shows a file-structure-type diagram of the contents of your model to help you find your way through the various container levels (Figure 4.55). To open the Outliner, click on the Window drop-down menu and choose Outliner. Click on entity names in the Outliner to select them. Double-click or right-click on containers within the Outliner to navigate in and out of the container.

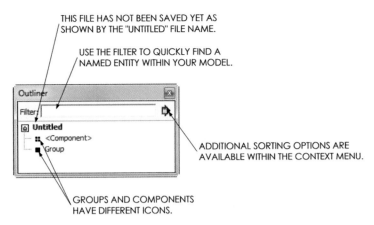

THIS FILE HAS NOT BEEN SAVED YET AS SHOWN BY THE "UNTITLED" FILE NAME.

USE THE FILTER TO QUICKLY FIND A NAMED ENTITY WITHIN YOUR MODEL.

ADDITIONAL SORTING OPTIONS ARE AVAILABLE WITHIN THE CONTEXT MENU.

GROUPS AND COMPONENTS HAVE DIFFERENT ICONS.

Figure 4.55 The Outliner

The Outliner is very helpful when all the groups and components in your model are accurately named. Groups and components can be named using the Entity Info dialog. To open the Entity Info dialog, click on the Window drop-down menu and select Entity Info (Figure 4.56). Then, use the Select tool to select an entity; its properties will be displayed in the Entity Info dialog where they can be edited. Make sure to assign logical names. For instance, if a group contains walls, name the group WALLS.

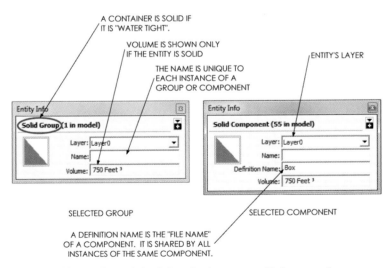

A CONTAINER IS SOLID IF IT IS "WATER TIGHT".

VOLUME IS SHOWN ONLY IF THE ENTITY IS SOLID

THE NAME IS UNIQUE TO EACH INSTANCE OF A GROUP OR COMPONENT

ENTITY'S LAYER

SELECTED GROUP

SELECTED COMPONENT

A DEFINITION NAME IS THE "FILE NAME" OF A COMPONENT. IT IS SHARED BY ALL INSTANCES OF THE SAME COMPONENT.

Figure 4.56 The Entity Info dialog displays any entity's properties.

Modifying Containers

Containers in SketchUp, including groups and more importantly components, can be modified without affecting the contents of the container. For instance, you can move and rotate a container without affecting the contents of the container. Remember, if you were to move or rotate the contents of a component, all instances would reflect that change. Rotating and moving are fairly easy concepts to grasp, but there are also more abstract ideas related to modifying containers covered in this section. In this section, you will learn to make components (and groups) different without actually affecting the contents of the component.

Move Tool

Use the Move tool to reposition containers exactly the same way you would reposition edges and surfaces. The Move tool also auto-selects entire containers and offers a rotate option (Figure 4.57). Just follow these steps:

1. Deselect all entities by right-clicking on the background, activate the Move tool and hover over a container. The Move tool auto-selects the container and displays red crosses on each side that you hover on.

2. Hover on one of the red crosses and you will see the Rotate tool positioned at the center of the container. Click once to start the rotation.

3. Move your cursor to rotate the container, then click again to define the actual rotation of the container.

4. At this point, you can enter a precise degree of rotation by typing **135**, then press Enter.

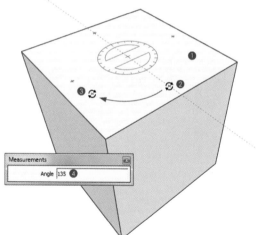

Figure 4.57 Auto-select a component with the Move tool and rotate. The contents of the container will not be modified.

Scale Tool

The Scale tool allows you to stretch and distort geometry, as well as containers. Scaling a container does not affect the contents of the container, so these changes will not be reflected in all instances of the component (Figure 4.58).

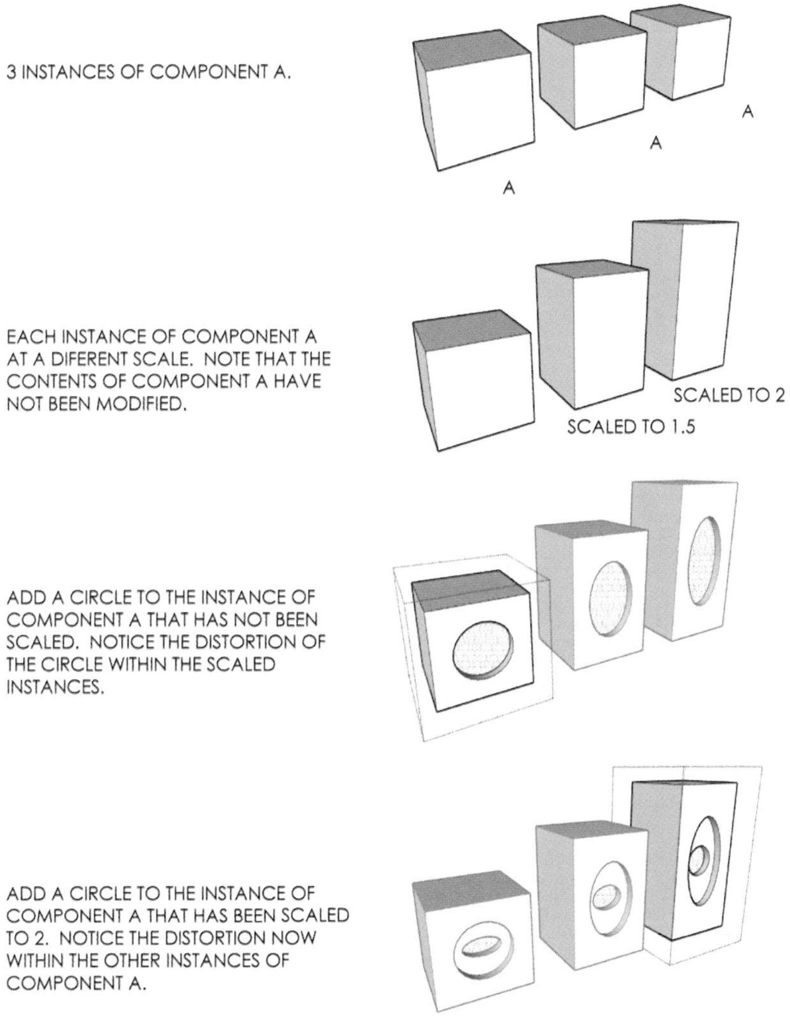

3 INSTANCES OF COMPONENT A.

EACH INSTANCE OF COMPONENT A AT A DIFERENT SCALE. NOTE THAT THE CONTENTS OF COMPONENT A HAVE NOT BEEN MODIFIED.

SCALED TO 2

SCALED TO 1.5

ADD A CIRCLE TO THE INSTANCE OF COMPONENT A THAT HAS NOT BEEN SCALED. NOTICE THE DISTORTION OF THE CIRCLE WITHIN THE SCALED INSTANCES.

ADD A CIRCLE TO THE INSTANCE OF COMPONENT A THAT HAS BEEN SCALED TO 2. NOTICE THE DISTORTION NOW WITHIN THE OTHER INSTANCES OF COMPONENT A.

Figure 4.58 The effects of scaling on the component container

To create a line of symmetry, use the Scale tool and assign a scale factor of −1 to mirror the component (Figure 4.59).

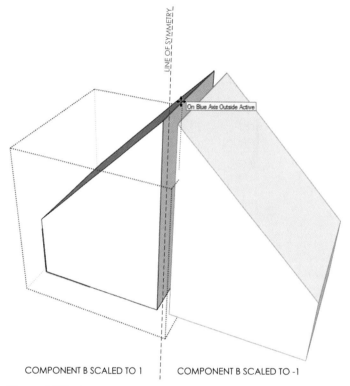

COMPONENT B SCALED TO 1   COMPONENT B SCALED TO -1

Figure 4.59 Copying and mirroring a component creates a line of symmetry, but does not modify the contents of the container.

TIP Scaling to −1 does the same thing as the Flip Along command; however, the Scale tool is more visual and therefore easier to use. If you do choose to use the Flip Along command, you can access it by right-clicking on an entity and choosing Flip Along. Then you will have to define the axis along which you want to flip.

Default Material

Any surface in a container that has the default material applied to it will take on the material of its parent (Figure 4.60). In other words, suppose there is a cube (six surfaces) in a container that has the default material applied to each surface. If you paint the outside of the group with a material, all the surfaces in the group will take on that material. This default material can be overridden by applying a different material to the actual surface in the group.

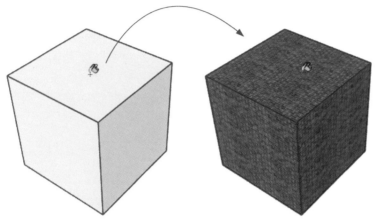

Figure 4.60 The default material is applied to every edge and surface that is created. Any surfaces in a container with the default material applied to them will take on the material applied to the "outside" of the container.

By leveraging the default material behaviors, you can have components that have efficiently linked geometry but display different materials. This characteristic can come into play when you use repeating elements that need to be slightly different. For example, you could have a chair component that is efficiently linked, but has a different colored cushion.

TIP At some point, you may try to right-click on a surface with a material applied to it and not see the Texture menu. If this happens, you are probably actually clicking on a surface that has the default material applied to it, within a group that has a texture image material applied to the outside of it. You can fix this by applying the desired texture image material directly to the surface.

Nested Containers

Nested containers are containers within containers within containers (Figure 4.61). There is virtually no limit to the number of "levels" deep your model can be. Mastering the concept of nested containers is essential to organizing for *The SketchUp Workflow for Architecture*.

Select any two containers, right-click on the selection and choose Make Group or Make Component, depending on the desired container.

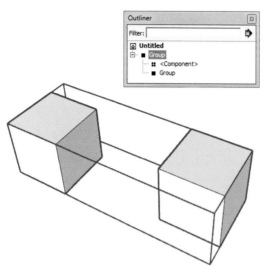

Figure 4.61 A group and a component are shown nested within a group.

The need for nested containers depends on layering, repeating elements, and lines of symmetry. The organization techniques utilized during *The SketchUp Workflow for Architecture* require advanced layering and organization of nested containers, groups, and components. Model organization diagrams (Figure 4.62) are used to complement the text and further explain these layering and grouping strategies.

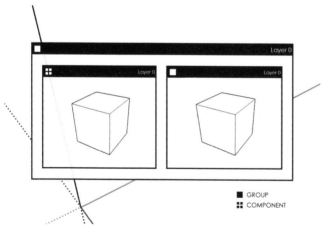

Figure 4.62 Nested containers are graphically displayed in this book using this diagram.

Explode

The Explode command could also be called the "Un-Container" tool. Right-click on a group or component and choose Explode to remove the container. Keep in mind that when a container is exploded, all entities previously within the container take on the layer previously applied to the exploded container.

SECTION PLANES

The best way to open up a model and look inside is to use section planes. A section in SketchUp does not delete or modify geometry in any way; it simply hides geometry in front of the section plane. Follow these steps:

1. Activate the Section Plane tool.

2. Position the section plane on a face that is parallel to the desired section's cut direction (Figure 4.63a).

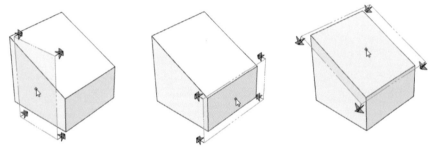

Figure 4.63a The section plane orients itself parallel to the face you are hovering on.

3. Once you find the proper section orientation hold the Shift key to constrain it.

4. Continue holding the Shift key until you click again to place the section cut. You will now see the section plane hiding all geometry in front of it (Figure 4.63b).

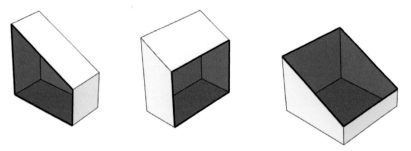

Figure 4.63b An active section plane hides all entities behind it.

Once a section cut is placed, it can be reversed, moved, rotated, copied, deleted, activated, and deactivated. Right-click on a section plane to access a helpful context menu. The Reverse command will flip the section plane to point the opposite direction. Check Active Cut on and off to activate and deactivate the section plane. Select Create Group from Slice to generate a group containing the 2D linework of the section cut.

Only one section plane can be active at a time in each level of a model. If you want to have multiple section cuts, you must separate them into containers (Figure 4.64, Figure 4.65).

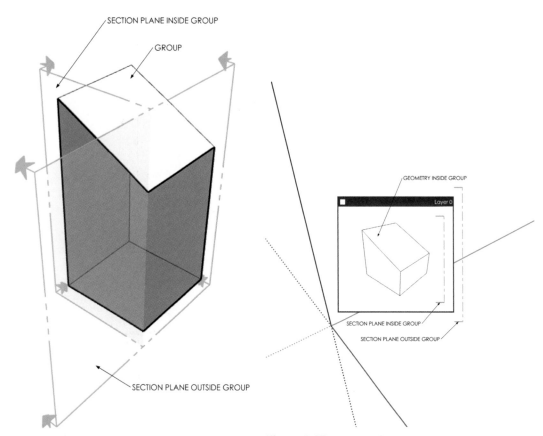

Figure 4.64 You can have more than one active section planes by separating them into containers.

Figure 4.65 A Model Organization Diagram representing two active section planes separated by a container

LAYERS, STYLES, AND SCENES

Layers, styles, and scenes are all related. Layers control the visibility of entities within SketchUp. Styles control the way in which entities are displayed in SketchUp. Layers and styles attach to scenes. So, by clicking on a scene, you can jump to a preset state for layers and styles, as well as several other properties that can be attached to scenes.

By mastering layers, styles, and scenes, you will gain full control over any drawing you want to create and you will become a faster modeler. In this section, you will learn the basic functions and operations of these features, and how they relate to each other. Later in this book, you will flex these features and leverage them to make more efficient models, presentations, and construction documents.

Layers

SketchUp *layers* are different than layers in many other 3D and 2D programs—but in a good way. SketchUp layers are simple. There is no stacking of layers in SketchUp, so the order in which layers are displayed in the Layers dialog has nothing to do with the way in which geometry is displayed in your SketchUp model. Layers can be assigned to any entity in SketchUp, including edges, surfaces, groups, and components. You are only able to control whether or not a layer is visible and the color of the layer when on a color-by-layer style. That's it!

Click on the Window drop-down menu and choose Layers. The Layers dialog is where you set the current layer, visible layers, and layer colors; it is also where you add, delete, and rename layers (Figure 4.66).

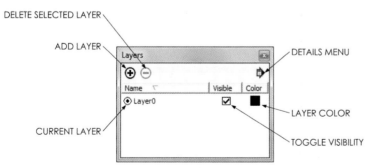

Figure 4.66 The Layers dialog

The current layer, defined by the dot to the left of the layer name, should always be set to Layer0. Layer0 cannot be deleted or renamed. Any entity created within or added to the model will be assigned to the current layer, Layer0. It is possible to change the current layer, but doing so is not advisable. The workflow presented in this book requires that all edges and surfaces be drawn on Layer0. So, it is best to always leave Layer0 as the current layer. To work with layers, follow these simple guidelines:

☑ To add a layer, click on the plus sign (+) in the top-left corner of the Layers dialog. Once a new layer is created, you can immediately rename the layer by typing over the blue highlighted text and pressing Enter to finish.

☑ To rename a layer, double-click on the layer name and type over the blue highlighted text, then press Enter to finish.

☑ To delete a layer, first click on the layer name to select it. Then, click on the minus sign (−) in the top-left corner of the Layers window to delete it. If there are entities on the layer you are deleting, you will be asked "What to do with the entities."

☑ Click on a layer's color swatch to change it. A layer's color will only show when on a color-by-layer style.

☑ Click on the check box next to a layer in the *Visible* column to toggle the layer's visibility on and off.

☑ To organize the list of layers by name, visibility, or color, click on the headings at the top of the columns.

☑ To assign an entity to a layer, right-click on the entity and choose Entity Info. Within the Entity Info dialog box, click on the Layers drop-down menu and choose a different layer. A Layers toolbar is available by clicking on the View drop-down menu and choosing Toolbars › Layers. The Layers toolbar works the same way as the Layer drop-down menu in the Entity Info dialog (Figure 4.67).

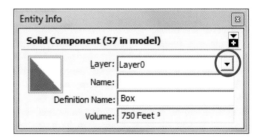

Figure 4.67 Entity Info and the Layers toolbar

Once the Entity Info dialog and the Layers toolbar are open, you can simply select an entity and adjust its layer in one of these dialogs. There is no need to right-click on the entity every time.

Styles

Styles provide a different way to look at your model. Styles do not affect geometry; they are simply a unique set of lenses for looking at your model. You can make the model edges sketchy, change the color of the sky, make all faces render as the same color, and use many other attractive visual settings without actually affecting any edges or surfaces.

To open the Styles browser, click on the Window drop-down menu and choose Styles. Within the Styles browser, you can select from preloaded styles by clicking on the Libraries drop-down menu (Figure 4.68). Once you find a style you like, click on it.

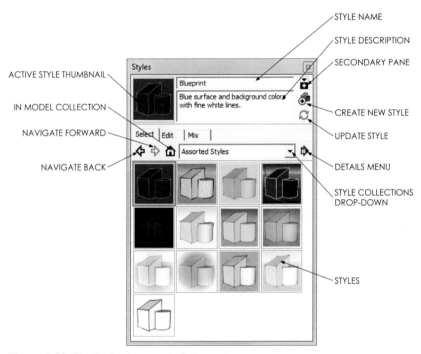

Figure 4.68 The Styles browser's Select tab

To change the properties of a style, click on the Edit tab. Five boxes in the Edit tab represent Edge, Face, Background, Watermark, and Modeling settings (Figure 4.69). Try changing a few of the settings and see how the display properties of the geometry in your model are affected.

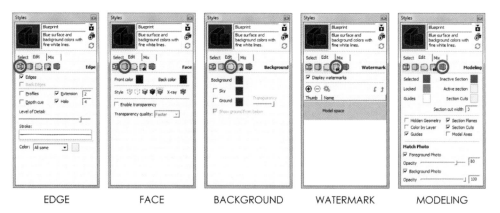

EDGE   FACE   BACKGROUND   WATERMARK   MODELING

Figure 4.69 The Styles browser's Edit tab with all five views

Changing any of the Style properties means that the style is now out of date. A "recycle" watermark will appear on the active style's thumbnail image. In order to save any changes you've made, you must update the style by clicking on the Style thumbnail or on the Refresh button in the Style browser (Figure 4.70). If any property of a style is changed, the style must be updated to save the changes.

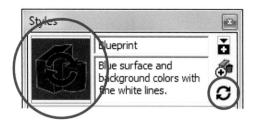

Figure 4.70 Update a style by clicking on the active style's thumbnail, or by clicking on the Update Style button.

Use the Mix tab to make your own unique Style creations. See "Chapter 7: SketchUp Collections" for more information on using the Mix tab.

TIP It is possible to change many of the Style settings using drop-down menus. For instance, if you click on View › Axes and turn off the Axes, that is actually a Style setting. You must be aware and update the style within the Styles browser if you want to save that change.

Scenes

Scenes are most often associated with a camera. In other words, most people assume that a scene is just like a bookmark for a specific view of your model. This is true, but scenes also save many other properties in addition to the camera location. Scenes can also save hidden geometry, visible layers, active section planes, style and fog, shadow settings, and axes locations. By creating complex scenes, you can create any rendering, drawing, or diagram that you need.

Take a look at the Scenes browser by clicking on the Window drop-down menu and selecting Scenes. The Scenes browser is where you will add, name, delete, and update the scenes in your model (Figure 4.71).

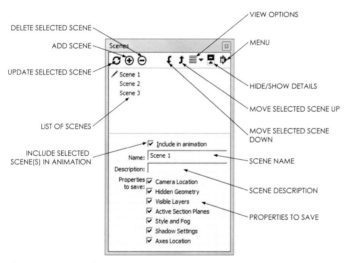

Figure 4.71 The Scenes browser

In the Scenes browser, you can see that scenes have a name, description, and properties to save. The name of a scene will appear in the Scene browser as well as on the corresponding Scene tab at the top of the screen. The description of a scene, which is usually unnecessary, is displayed in the Scene browser and also when you hover your cursor over a Scene tab. The Properties to Save are the critical attributes of scenes (Figure 4.72). The check boxes next to the properties control whether or not the selected scene will hold onto the named settings. For example, if the Camera Location property is not checked on to be saved, there will be no camera location information associated with that scene.

Frequently, the Properties to Save are confused with the Properties to Update. Remember, 99 percent of the time you will want all of the Properties to Save checked on, and you will never need to touch them again once the scene is created. When you want to modify the scene, click on the Refresh button and check and uncheck the desired Properties to Update.

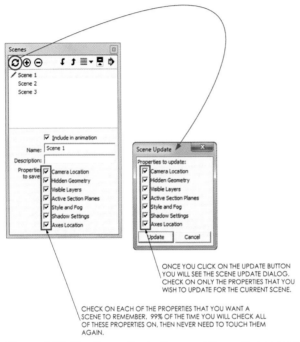

ONCE YOU CLICK ON THE UPDATE BUTTON YOU WILL SEE THE SCENE UPDATE DIALOG. CHECK ON ONLY THE PROPERTIES THAT YOU WISH TO UPDATE FOR THE CURRENT SCENE.

CHECK ON EACH OF THE PROPERTIES THAT YOU WANT A SCENE TO REMEMBER. 99% OF THE TIME YOU WILL CHECK ALL OF THESE PROPERTIES ON, THEN NEVER NEED TO TOUCH THEM AGAIN.

Figure 4.72 The Properties to Save and Properties to Update are easily confused. Make sure you understand the function of each.

Similar to styles, scenes also need to be updated if you want to save any changes to the scene. The tricky thing about scenes is that there is no visual cue that that tells you the scene needs to be updated.

Typically, the only time you would uncheck certain properties within the Properties to Update dialog is when you are applying aspects of one scene to another scene. For instance, to match the camera view from one scene to another, first go to the scene with the desired camera view by clicking on its scene tab. Then click on the scene you want to have the same camera view within the Scenes dialog. Click on the Update Scene button and uncheck everything but the Camera Location in the Properties to Update dialog. Click on Update and the two scenes will have the same camera location.

Combining Layers, Styles, and Scenes

By combining layers, styles, and scenes, you can completely control a model. Experiment with all of the settings shown in the following diagrams until you have fully mastered them (Figure 4.73, Figure 4.74).

Keep these tips in mind when you're working with layers, styles, and scenes:

☑ When you're creating scenes, it is usually best to change all of the desired settings so that your screen looks the way you want the scene to look. Then you add the scene to take a digital "snapshot" of the settings that make the screen look that way.

☑ If you decide to change a property that is saved within a style, you will need to update the style. You do not need to update the scene after making changes to a style if the style is already attached to the scene.

☑ When you're creating a scene, most of the time you will want to have all of the Properties to Save checked on. After checking them on, there is almost never any reason to go back and uncheck them.

☑ If a Property to Save is unchecked, that property won't be saved with the scene. For instance, if the camera location is unchecked, then no matter how many times you click on that scene or update it, it will not take you back to a camera view. The camera location must be checked on in Properties to Save in order for the scene to remember the camera location.

☑ If you decide to change a property that is saved by a scene, and you want the scene to reflect those changes, you will need to update the scene. Typically, it is safest to make the adjustments, click on the Update button, then uncheck all properties in the Properties to Update dialog, except the properties that you have changed.

☑ If you need to modify the properties of a scene, you'll be better able to keep track of what you're doing if you first click on the Scene tab to see all of the Scene settings visually presented on your screen. Make only the changes that you want, and then right-click on the Scene tab and choose Update to update all of the properties at the same time. This can be dangerous if you don't completely understand how to use scenes, but it will ultimately save you time because you'll avoid the Properties to Update dialog and all of the checking and unchecking.

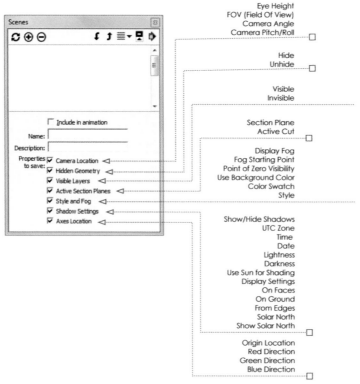

Figure 4.73 A scene's properties are stored with the scene. To save any changes you make to the listed properties, you must update the scene.

CHAPTER POINTS

☑ SketchUp is a surface modeler, which means its basic building blocks are edges and surfaces. All shapes in SketchUp are composed of edges and surfaces; there are no true solid shapes such as spheres, cubes, and cylinders.

☑ Inferencing and axis locking allow you to interact with the 3D SketchUp environment effectively through your 2D computer screen.

☑ Typically, you should start with a Drawing tool that adds surfaces, such as the Rectangle tool, Polygon tool, or Circle tool.

☑ Use Drawing tools that only add edges to set up slight additive and subtractive adjustments.

☑ Use the Modification tools to turn simple forms into complex geometry.

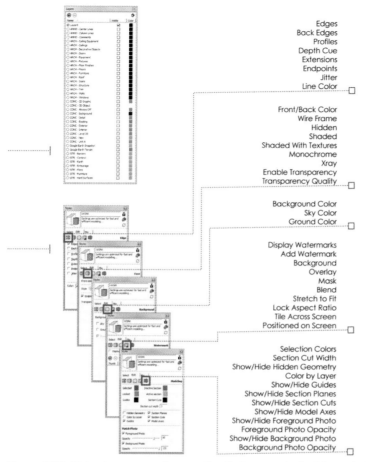

Figure 4.74 Styles have several properties that are controlled through the Styles browser. If a property of a style is changed, the style must be updated.

☑ When you're creating components, look for repeating elements. If you need a similar element, use the Make Unique command. Mirror a component container using the Scale tool or Flip Along command to create lines of symmetry.

☑ Layers, styles, and scenes are absolutely necessary for creating a useful SketchUp model. To avoid frustration in later chapters, you should explore these combined concepts until you completely understand how they work before you proceed.

☑ The best way to learn about layers, styles, and scenes is to review this chapter while playing around with their settings. Don't be afraid to make a copy of a model and mess it up by experimenting.

Chapter 5
The Professional's SketchUp Template

SketchUp provides several default templates that are excellent to use for learning, but ultimately not fit for professional use. Your default template in SketchUp should do more than just paint a pretty picture; it should also make modeling easier and reveal deeper levels of information stored within your model. You can customize your own SketchUp template by optimizing the model settings, creating utility scenes and styles, and adding default layers that will fit any design project.

BASE TEMPLATE

Start by opening SketchUp. If you see the Welcome to SketchUp window, uncheck the Always Show on Startup box in the bottom-left corner of the window (Figure 5.1). The Welcome to SketchUp window is designed to introduce first-time users to SketchUp and is not necessary for a professional. Close the Welcome to SketchUp window by clicking on the Start Using SketchUp button.

To select a template, click on the Window (SketchUp on Mac) drop-down menu and choose Preferences, then click on the Template tab. Find the Plan View – Feet and Inches template, click on it, and choose OK.

Click on the File drop-down menu and choose New to start a new model using the Plan View – Feet and Inches template. To see the new template, you will always need to start a new file. This template starts off in a clean white background, and the default units are inches. Now that you have selected a stock default template, you are going to customize it and save it as your own default template. Click on the File drop-down menu and choose save, navigate to your RESOURCES/TEMPLATES folder and name the file BIC_Default Template.skp.

Figure 5.1 The Welcome to SketchUp Window offers links to learning resources, licensing information, and the default template. All of this information and more is available in the Help menu and at SketchUp.com.

MODEL INFO

The Model Info settings travel with your model. In this section, you will modify only the settings that will help make your modeling faster and more efficient. Keep in mind that all of the Model Info settings can be changed once a new model is started. To get started, click on the Window drop-down menu and choose Model Info.

Animation

Unless you are creating an animation, you won't need to see scene transitions while you're designing in SketchUp. Sure, they look cool, but they also kill a couple of seconds every time you change to a different scene. As a professional, you need instant information, so go to the Animation tab and uncheck the Enable Scene Transitions check box (Figure 5.2).

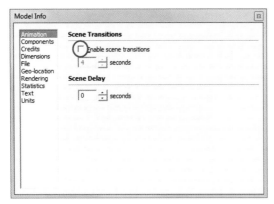

Figure 5.2 The Animation tab in the Model Info window

Dimensions

Dimensions are best shown in LayOut, where you have full control of placement, size, scale, font, and style. In some instances, you may find it help ful to add dimensions to a quick sketch in SketchUp. When you're adding dimensions in SketchUp, make sure to apply your own style to set your presentations apart from other SketchUp users. Choose your font style and size from the Dimensions tab (Figure 5.4). Also choose your favorite arrow type and alignment.

When there is not enough room to clearly display the dimensions, you can use the Expert Dimension settings to control whether or not to display them. Typically, there is no "best" default setting for the Expert Dimension settings. You should modify the settings on a case-by-case basis.

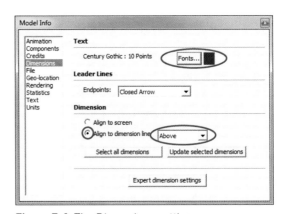

Figure 5.4 The Dimensions settings

Rendering

Enabling anti-aliased textures may speed up SketchUp's performance (Figure 5.5).

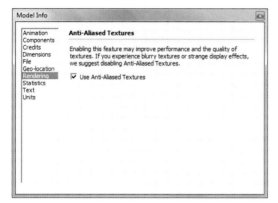

Figure 5.5 The Rendering settings

Text

Similar to dimensions, text annotations are preferably added within LayOut; although they are not used nearly as much within SketchUp, you can still customize the text style within SketchUp. Set your favorite font within the Text tab, which will probably match the Dimensions Text settings (Figure 5.6).

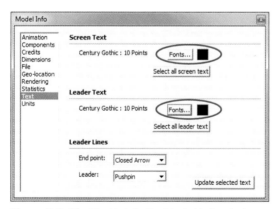

Figure 5.6 The Text tab in the Model Info window

Units

The default units are set to inches in the Plan View – Feet and Inches template. By thinking in terms of inches, you can save time while you are modeling. For example, to draw a line at five-feet-six-inches long, rather than typing **5′6″** and pressing the Enter key, you can just type **66** and press Enter. In this case, by thinking in inches, you cut the number of keystrokes in half. Saving three keystrokes may not seem significant, but think of the hundreds of commands you perform in an hour when you are using SketchUp.

The Model's Precision setting indicates the number of units that will display in the Measurements dialog box. The Model's Precision setting can be overridden by entering a precise dimension into the Measurements dialog box during an operation. For example, if the model's accuracy is set to 1/8″, and you enter a dimension that ends in 1/64″, that line will actually be drawn to the 1/64″, but when measured will be rounded to the nearest 1/8″ because of the precision setting. Typically, a Model's Precision is set to the most accurate setting of 1/64″.

TIP Professionals should always have the model accuracy set to the highest tolerance of 1/64g (Figure 5.7). It is important that the model itself has the most precise dimensions possible. Then, if necessary, you can use less precise dimensions in LayOut to clean up fractional dimensions for schematic presentations. Once you begin a model, do not change the Precision setting.

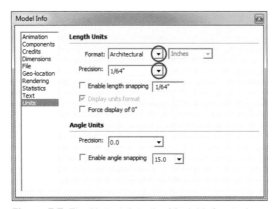

Figure 5.7 The Units tab in the Model Info window

Length snapping limits the dimensions of an object drawn in SketchUp to predefined intervals. Enabling length snapping is the best way to keep your dimensions clean. For example, when designing on a very loose preliminary sketch of a site plan or building footprint, you might set the length snapping to 6″ or 12″ to keep the dimensions round and clean. If you are designing with masonry block, set the length snapping to 8″ to design within the limitations of the material. By entering precise dimensions in the Measurements dialog box, you can override length snapping during any operation.

STANDARD LAYERS

A logical set of layers will help you keep a model organized, which will prove helpful when you are exporting backgrounds for consultants, moving to other CAD programs, rendering with a photorealistic plugin, and creating construction documents in LayOut. Figure 5.8 displays a list of standard layers used to create SketchUp models with these tasks in mind. These are the official layers of *The SketchUp Workflow for Architecture*. Note that the layers are organized into three categories: CONCEPTUAL, ARCHITECTURAL, and SITE. ARCHITECTURAL and SITE layers are nouns, often named after actual physical objects. CONCEPTUAL layers are adjectives that describe the ARCHITECTURAL and SITE layers. CONCEPTUAL layers are more abstract and intangible.

You'll learn more about how and where to apply these layers later in this book. Right now it is important to create your customized default template and workspace so that later everything will flow easily. Add these layers to your template now. Assign a green to the CONC - New layer and assign a gray to the CONC - Existing layer. All other layers can be assigned the color black, or disregarded.

Now save your SketchUp model into the ACTIVE PROJECTS/RESOURCES/Templates folder. These new files need to be saved shortly after you first start them. SketchUp's auto-save feature will not kick in until you have saved the model once yourself.

STANDARD LAYERS		
CONCEPTUAL	**ARCHITECTURAL**	**SITE**
CONC - New	ARCH - Ceiling Equip	SITE - Barriers
CONC - Existing	ARCH - Ceilings	SITE - Context
CONC - Interior	ARCH - Decorative	SITE - Earth
CONC - Exterior	ARCH - Doors	SITE - Entourage
CONC - 3d Object	ARCH - Equipment	SITE - Furniture
CONC - 2d Graphic	ARCH - Fixtures	SITE - Flora
CONC - Detail	ARCH - Floor Finishes	SITE - Hard Surfaces
CONC - Always Off	ARCH - Floors	Google Earth Snapshot
CONC - Backgrounds	ARCH - Furniture	Google Earth Terrain
CONC - Option A, B, C...	ARCH - Roof	
CONC - Building 1, 2, 3...	ARCH - Stairs	
CONC - Phase 1, 2, 3...	ARCH - Structure	
CONC - Level 00, 01, 02...	ARCH - Trim	
CONC - Unit A, B, C...		

Figure 5.8 *The SketchUp Workflow for Architecture*'s standard SketchUp layers

STYLES

If you have used SketchUp for even a small amount of time, you probably have explored the enticing visual effects offered by styles. Styles allow you to completely alter the appearance of your model without affecting the underlying geometry. For instance, you can add sketchy lines, blueprint colored faces, canvas watermarks, and different color backgrounds without modifying any geometry or materials. These are all great visual effects you can use for presentations, but you'll pay the price by slowing down your computer when using complex styles.

What if a style could also do the opposite, increase computer performance by turning off the resource-hogging visual features? In this way, styles can also be used as a tool rather than just an attractive visual effect. Styles control properties that can make your models easier to work on, optimize your system's performance, and visually communicate deeper levels of information stored within the model (Figure 5.9). In the next section, you will explore styles by creating several utility and presentation styles, including DESIGN, LINE DRAWING, PRESENTATION, COLOR BY AXIS, COLOR BY FACE, and COLOR BY LAYER. After you create the styles, you will combine them with the power of scenes to make your time-saving default template complete.

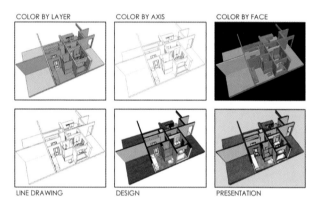

Figure 5.9 Styles being used as Modeling and Presentation tools

DESIGN Style

The DESIGN style turns off all of the bells and whistles that make SketchUp models look great but at the same time heavily tax the processor and graphics card, thereby slowing the system. When working on a model, you want to be fast and effective. It is important to have a default state where you know your machine is going to perform its best. This optimized default state will utilize the DESIGN utility style.

Click on the Create New Style button to add a new style to your template model and name it "DESIGN". Click on the Edit tab and adjust the settings as shown in Figure 5.10. Click on the Update button to save the changes and the watermark will go away, indicating that everything has been saved. The DESIGN utility style is complete.

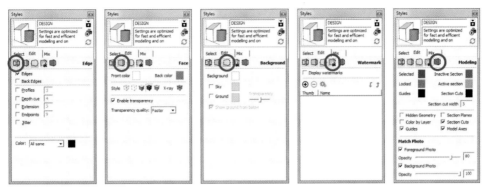

Figure 5.10 The DESIGN style settings

LINE DRAWING Style

The LINE DRAWING style presents all geometry in simple black lines on a white background. This style is ideal for creating CAD-type 2D output as typically seen in construction documents.

Click on the Create New Style button to add a new style to your template model and name it LINE DRAWING. Click on the Edit tab and adjust the settings as shown in Figure 5.11. Click on the Update button to save the changes and the watermark will go away, indicating that everything has been saved. The LINE DRAWING utility style is complete.

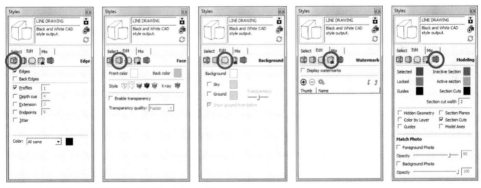

Figure 5.11 The LINE DRAWING style settings

PRESENTATION Style

The PRESENTATION style is the opposite of the DESIGN style in that it turns on all of the desired visual bells and whistles. The PRESENTATION settings typically utilize sketchy edges and more complicated effects for a final rendering. Start with what is shown here, then get creative and make your own PRESENTATION style.

Click on the create new style button to add a new style to your template model and and name it PRESENTATION. Click on the Edit tab and adjust the settings as shown in Figure 5.12. Click on the Update button to save the changes and the watermark will go away, indicating that everything has been saved. The PRESENTATION utility style is complete.

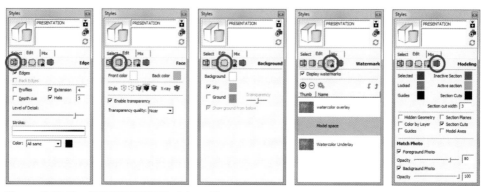

Figure 5.12 The PRESENTATION style settings

TIP You can also use the Mix tab to drag and drop your favorite properties into the current style. Once you are satisfied, be sure to click on the Update button to update the style. See Chapter 7 "SketchUp Collections", Creating a Style section, for more information on using the Mix tab..

COLOR BY AXIS Style

The COLOR BY AXIS style can help you troubleshoot a problematic model. If you are tracing lines and a surface will not reheal, often the problem is an edge that is off axis. By switching to the COLOR BY AXIS utility style, all of the edges will be colored by the same as the axis the edge is parallel to and all surfaces will be white. It will become immediately clear which lines are causing the problem because any off axis edge will be black.

Click on the create new style button to add a new style to your template model and name it COLOR BY AXIS. Click on the Edit tab and adjust the settings as shown in Figure 5.13. Click the Update button to save the changes and the watermark will go away, indicating that everything has been saved. The COLOR BY AXIS utility style is complete.

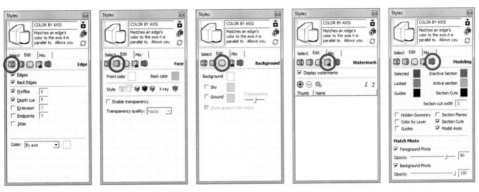

Figure 5.13 The COLOR BY AXIS style settings

COLOR BY FACE Style

The COLOR BY FACE utility style displays the geometry of the side of the surface that is showing, the front or the back. Viewing geometry in this way will help you prepare a model for photorealistic rendering.

Click on the create new style button to add a new style to your template model and name it COLOR BY FACE. Click on the Edit tab and adjust the settings as shown in Figure 5.14. Click on the Update button to save the changes and the watermark will go away, indicating that everything has been saved. The COLOR BY FACE utility style is complete.

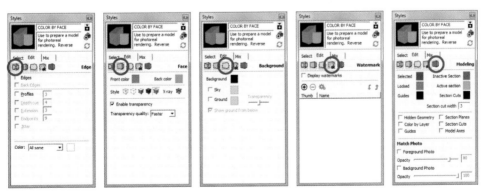

Figure 5.14 The COLOR BY FACE style settings

COLOR BY LAYER Style

The COLOR BY LAYER utility style displays geometry according to the color assigned to the geometry's layer. Viewing geometry in this way will visually show you deeper levels of information stored in your model's layers.

Click on the create new style button to add a new style to your template model and name it COLOR BY LAYER. Click on the Edit tab and adjust the settings as shown in Figure 5.15. Click on the Update button to save the changes and the watermark will go away, indicating that everything has been saved. The COLOR BY LAYER utility style is complete.

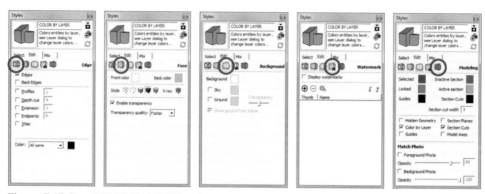

Figure 5.15 The COLOR BY LAYER style settings

ACTIVITY

See **www.suexch.com** for additional styles that you might want to make, but don't necessarily want to attach to a utility scene—for example, Hatch-50, Hatch-25, Hatch-75, Hatch-100, Line Drawing-50, Line Drawing-Red, and Mask.

UTILITY SCENES

Styles are helpful by themselves, but the ability to attach a style—along with layer states and many other settings—to a scene, means that all of these settings are readily available through the Scene tabs at the top of your screen. Utility scenes are the core of a professional's template. Utility scenes are included in a template and used as a tool, rather than merely a visually attractive presentation view (Figure 5.16).

Figure 5.16 The utility scenes

Using scenes, you have the ability to control properties such as camera location, hidden geometry, visible layers, active section planes, fog, shadow settings, axes locations, and most importantly styles. You can combine the best features of both scenes and styles to make an extremely useful and efficient template and get the most out of your model.

TIP In the Scenes window, you can determine whether or not to use thumbnail images. Click on the context arrow at the top-right corner of the Scenes window and uncheck Use Scene Thumbnails. Scene thumbnails can be helpful at times, but generating them requires extra rendering time and computer resources and you do not need them.

Layer State Scenes

Layer state scenes save only the visible layers within scene's properties to save. They are the switches that turn on and turn off the information you want to view. Click on the Add Scene button in the scenes dialog, then adjust the settings for each of the utility scenes.

The ALL ON utility scene makes all layers visible (Figure 5.17).

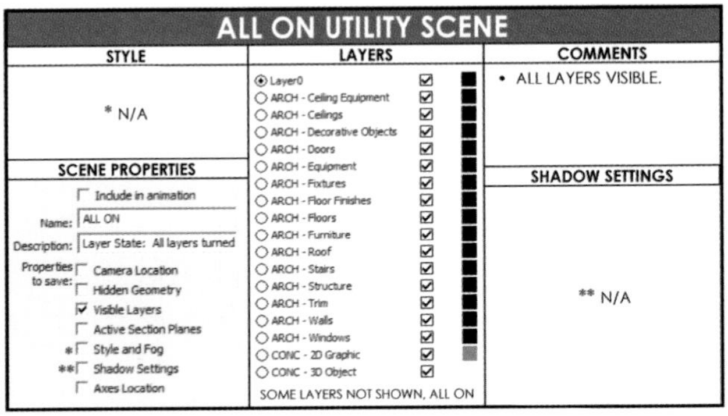

Figure 5.17 The ALL ON scene properties and layers

The ALL OFF utility scene makes all layers invisible (Figure 5.18).

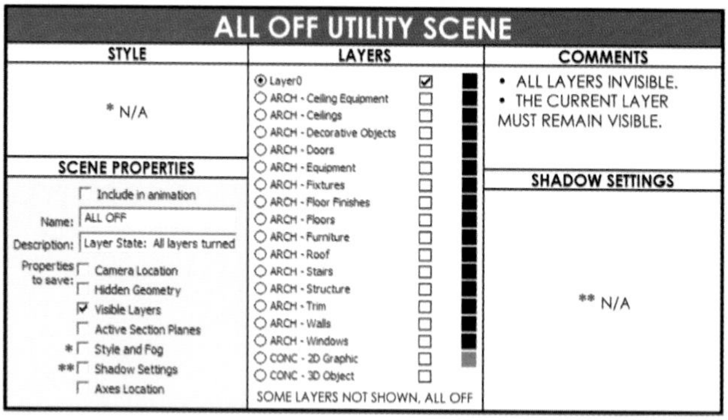

ALL OFF UTILITY SCENE		
STYLE	**LAYERS**	**COMMENTS**
* N/A	⦿ Layer0 ☑ ■ ○ ARCH - Ceiling Equipment ☐ ○ ARCH - Ceilings ☐ ○ ARCH - Decorative Objects ☐ ○ ARCH - Doors ☐	• ALL LAYERS INVISIBLE. • THE CURRENT LAYER MUST REMAIN VISIBLE.
SCENE PROPERTIES	○ ARCH - Equipment ☐ ○ ARCH - Fixtures ☐ ○ ARCH - Floor Finishes ☐	**SHADOW SETTINGS**
☐ Include in animation Name: ALL OFF Description: Layer State: All layers turned Properties to save: ☐ Camera Location ☐ Hidden Geometry ☑ Visible Layers ☐ Active Section Planes *☐ Style and Fog **☐ Shadow Settings ☐ Axes Location	○ ARCH - Floors ☐ ○ ARCH - Furniture ☐ ○ ARCH - Roof ☐ ○ ARCH - Stairs ☐ ○ ARCH - Structure ☐ ○ ARCH - Trim ☐ ○ ARCH - Walls ☐ ○ ARCH - Windows ☐ ○ CONC - 2D Graphic ☐ ■ ○ CONC - 3D Object ☐ SOME LAYERS NOT SHOWN, ALL OFF	** N/A

Figure 5.18 The ALL OFF scene properties and layers

The INTERIOR utility scene turns on the layers and, in turn, the geometry that relates to the inside of a building (Figure 5.19). This is helpful for working on the plan without having exterior walls blocking your view of the interior.

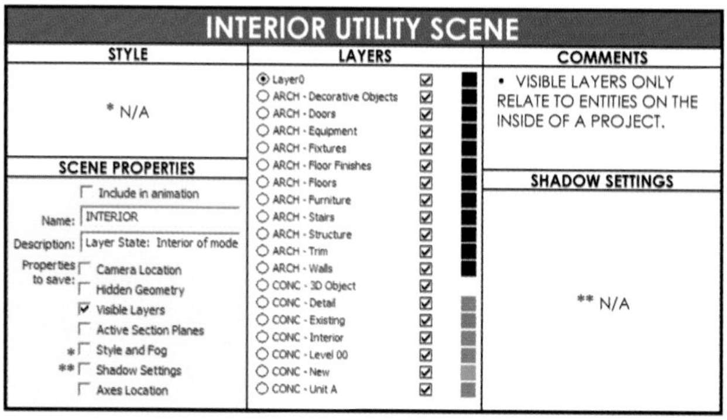

INTERIOR UTILITY SCENE		
STYLE	**LAYERS**	**COMMENTS**
* N/A	⦿ Layer0 ☑ ■ ○ ARCH - Decorative Objects ☑ ■ ○ ARCH - Doors ☑ ■ ○ ARCH - Equipment ☑ ■ ○ ARCH - Fixtures ☑ ■	• VISIBLE LAYERS ONLY RELATE TO ENTITIES ON THE INSIDE OF A PROJECT.
SCENE PROPERTIES	○ ARCH - Floor Finishes ☑ ■ ○ ARCH - Floors ☑ ■ ○ ARCH - Furniture ☑ ■	**SHADOW SETTINGS**
☐ Include in animation Name: INTERIOR Description: Layer State: Interior of mode Properties to save: ☐ Camera Location ☐ Hidden Geometry ☑ Visible Layers ☐ Active Section Planes *☐ Style and Fog **☐ Shadow Settings ☐ Axes Location	○ ARCH - Stairs ☑ ■ ○ ARCH - Structure ☑ ■ ○ ARCH - Trim ☑ ■ ○ ARCH - Walls ☑ ■ ○ CONC - 3D Object ☑ ■ ○ CONC - Detail ☑ ■ ○ CONC - Existing ☑ ■ ○ CONC - Interior ☑ ■ ○ CONC - Level 00 ☑ ■ ○ CONC - New ☑ ■ ○ CONC - Unit A ☑ ■	** N/A

Figure 5.19 The INTERIOR scene properties and layers

The EXTERIOR utility scene turns on the layers and, in turn, the geometry that relates to the outside of a building (Figure 5.20). This is helpful for designing the exterior elevations without having the site and interior of the model turned on, thereby slowing your computer.

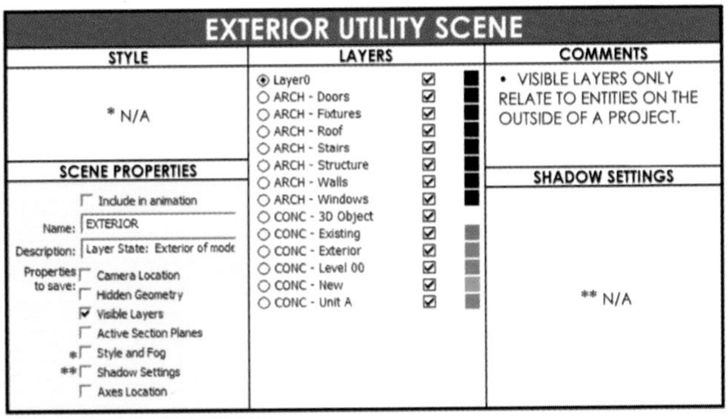

Figure 5.20 The EXTERIOR scene properties and layers

The SITE utility scene turns on the geometry that relates to the outside of a building and the site (Figure 5.21). This is helpful for working on the landscape plan without having the interior of the model turned on, thereby slowing your computer.

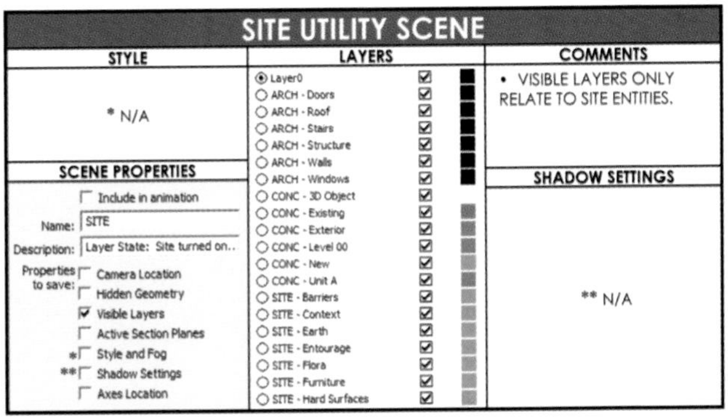

Figure 5.21 The SITE scene properties and layers

Presentation Scenes

Presentation scenes are used to display the model in a final format, either in print or on screen. Typically, you will use these scenes before you create additional scenes to send to LayOut.

The DESIGN utility scene combines the settings of the DESIGN utility style with additional performance-enhancing settings of scenes (Figure 5.22). Use this utility scene when you're working on the model and navigating a model in real time for on-screen presentations.

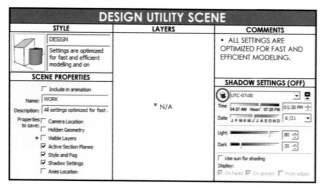

Figure 5.22 The DESIGN utility scene properties

The 3D PERSPECTIVE utility scene sets the view to the desired final-presentation state (Figure 5.23). Typically, this scene is determined by your personal presentation preferences. Don't hesitate to modify the suggested settings.

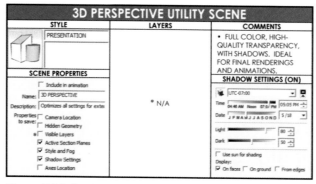

Figure 5.23 The 3D PERSPECTIVE scene properties, layers, and active style

TIP When you're creating an interior scene, brighten up the ceilings with Shadow settings. Set the Light slider to 20 and the Dark slider to 100. Set the time of day to noon and make sure the Use Sun for Shading check box is checked. These settings eliminate the "gray ceiling effect" often seen in interior SketchUp renderings.

The 2D DRAWING scene switches to the LINE DRAWING style to display the geometry as black lines on a white background (Figure 5.24). This scene is also determined by your personal preference for creating CAD-type output.

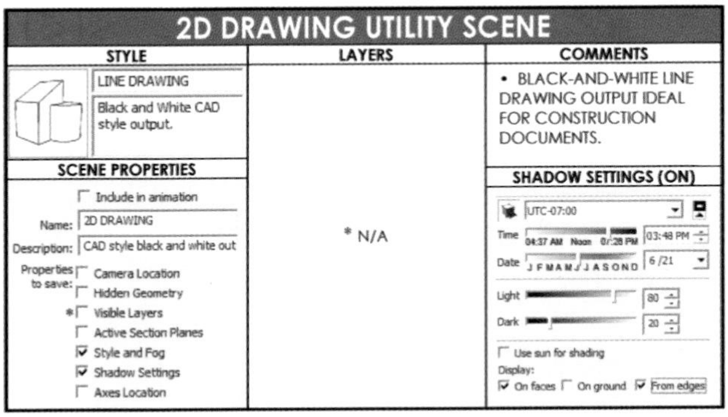

Figure 5.24 The 2D DRAWING scene properties, layers, and active style

Diagrammatic Scenes

Diagrammatic scenes display the model in ways that visually communicate more information.

The AXIS CHECK utility scene can help you troubleshoot a problematic model (Figure 5.25). If you are tracing lines and a surface will not reheal, the problem is frequently an edge that is off axis. When you switch to the AXIS CHECK utility scene, all of the edges will be colored by axis and all of the surfaces will be white. It will become immediately apparent which lines are causing the problem because they will be black.

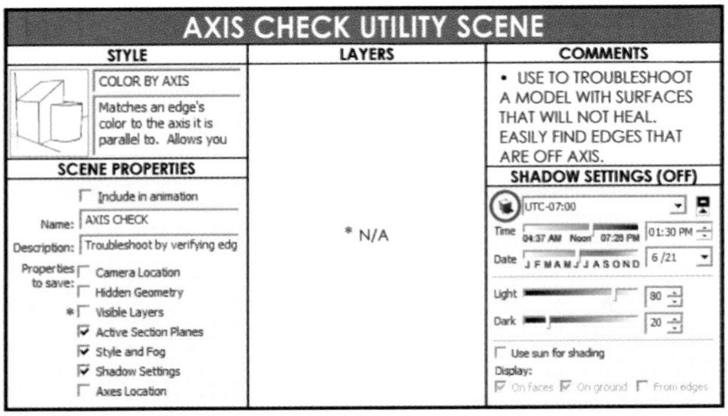

Figure 5.25 The AXIS CHECK scene properties, layers, and active style

The SCOPE utility scene displays the model colored by new and existing objects based on the CONC - New and CONC - Existing layer's assigned color (Figure 5.26). The type of diagram that is generated is perfect for explaining the scope of a project to a new team member. This diagram gives an overall snapshot of the amount of demolition and construction to be completed.

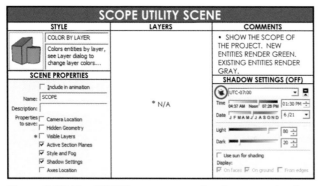

Figure 5.26 The SCOPE scene properties, layers, and active style

The ORIENT FACES utility scene displays the model colored by faces (Figure 5.27). Using the diagram, you can easily right-click on the faces and reverse them until all of the fronts are facing out. Your entire model should be pink, which means that all fronts are facing out and is best for photorealistic rendering.

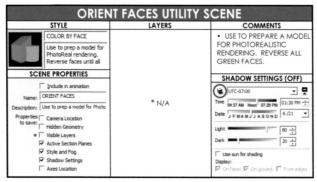

Figure 5.27 The ORIENT FACES scene properties, layers, and active style

The 45 and 90 utility scenes make it easier for you to create plans that follow two or more grids (Figure 5.28). These types of scenes save the location and rotation of the axes. Keep in mind that in this example you are switching the grid to 45 degrees, but you could use any angle of grid shift.

90 UTILITY SCENE		
STYLE	**LAYERS**	**COMMENTS**
*** N/A		• LEAVE AXES AT THE DEFAULT 0 DEGREE ROTATION.
SCENE PROPERTIES		**SHADOW SETTINGS (OFF)**
☐ Include in animation Name: 45 Description: Set axis to 45 degrees... Properties to save: ☐ Camera Location ☐ Hidden Geometry * ☐ Visible Layers ☐ Active Section Planes *** ☐ Style and Fog ** ☐ Shadow Settings ☑ Axes Location	* N/A	** N/A

Figure 5.28 The 90 utility scene properties, layers, and active style

Now create the 45-degree scene. First, right-click on any axis and select Move. Go to the Move Sketching Context dialog box and change the Z rotation to **45**. This will rotate the axes around the blue axis to a 45-degree angle. See Figure 5.29 and Figure 5.30.

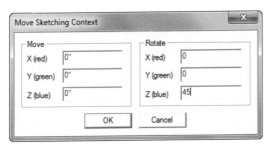

Figure 5.29 Use the Move Sketching Context dialog box to accurately modify the drawing axes.

45 UTILITY SCENE		
STYLE	**LAYERS**	**COMMENTS**
*** N/A		• SET ROTATION TO 45 ON THE BLUE AXIS.
SCENE PROPERTIES		**SHADOW SETTINGS (OFF)**
☐ Include in animation Name: 45 Description: Set axis to 45 degrees... Properties to save: ☐ Camera Location ☐ Hidden Geometry * ☐ Visible Layers ☐ Active Section Planes *** ☐ Style and Fog ** ☐ Shadow Settings ☑ Axes Location	* N/A	** N/A

Figure 5.30 The 45 utility scene properties, layers, and active style

Saving as a Template

Now that you have added utility scenes, styles, and default layers to the base template, save it as your own custom template. Before saving, click on the ALL ON Utility Scene, then Click on the DESIGN Utility scene to set your template to the ideal default state. Click on the File drop-down menu and select Save to update the saved version in your RESOURCES/ Templates folder. Now, click on the Window (SketchUp on Mac) drop-down menu and choose Preferences. Click on the Template tab, click the Browse button, and navigate to your templates in the RESOURCES/Templates folder. Select the `BIC_Default Template.skp` and click Open.

When you choose a new template, you must always start a new document to see the template activate. Click on the File drop-down menu and select New. You will see the new active default template with all of the custom layers, styles, and scenes.

CHAPTER POINTS

☑ The Bright Ideas Consultants default template is available for download at **www .suexch.com**.

☑ Not all styles need to have a scene. Some of the hatching and 2D drawing styles will be selected when the scene is created. This is up to the user's discretion based on the type of design you do, whether or not you need each of these utility scenes.

☑ The utility styles and utility scenes created in this chapter are only a few possibilities. Experiment with other properties attached to styles and scenes to determine how to make your SketchUp workflow even more efficient.

☑ All utility styles, scenes, and layer states should be modified to fit your project type. A default template is a constant work in progress.

Chapter 6
The Professional's SketchUp Environment

A professional's work environment is streamlined, logical, and organized. SketchUp provides a default environment that is great for learning but is ultimately not fit for professional use. Customize the SketchUp environment to make it work best for you. Optimize system resources, remove visual clutter, and access all commands with a keystroke by adding your own set of shortcuts to enhance your SketchUp experience.

TOOLBARS

Toolbars generally clutter screen space with static icons taking up space that should be used for exciting 3D graphics (Figure 6.1, Figure 6.2). Using toolbars and icons takes your eyes off of the design. It's like texting while driving: it's very distracting and can be disastrous. That might be an exaggeration, but seriously, you should keep your eyes on the road and model at all times by minimizing your use of toolbars. Instead of having all those buttons and icons, a better solution is to have an extensive collection of keyboard shortcuts. If you can't completely eliminate toolbars and go full-screen full-time, try to limit yourself to the following settings.

☑ A pixel is a valuable commodity. Maximize your 3D workspace by minimizing your toolbar footprint. Select View › Toolbars › Large Buttons to toggle the large icons on and off.

☑ Monitors are enormous these days, so it is reasonable to allow yourself one row of toolbars across the top of your screen. Select View › Toolbars and open the following toolbars: Construction, Drawing, Layers, Measurements, Modification, Principal, Sections, and Walk-through (Figure 6.3). These toolbars are worth keeping open all the time. When you're performing specific tasks, you'll need to open other toolbars briefly, but you don't need to have them open at all times. Once you start working with your favorite tools, you'll be able to determine which toolbars you prefer to have open and accessible at all times.

☑ Dock the toolbars to organize your workspace. Click and drag an undocked toolbar to the top, bottom, or side of the screen. The toolbar will lock itself to the SketchUp window. To undock a toolbar, click and drag on the line at the left of the toolbar, move it away from the perimeter of the SketchUp workspace, and release the toolbar to place it where you want.

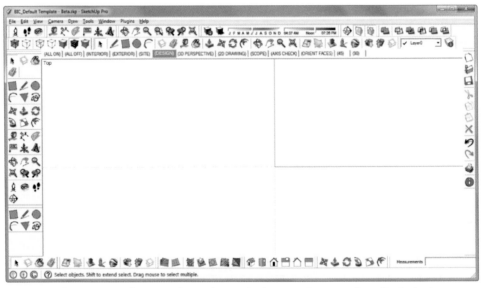

Figure 6.1 Excessive toolbars are distracting and take attention away from the task at hand, which is designing.

Figure 6.2 Utilize a sleek toolset by limiting yourself to one row of toolbars. This will encourage the use of keyboard shortcuts.

Figure 6.3 Suggested toolbars

TIP Once you have all of your toolbars in place, select View › Toolbars › Save Toolbar positions. Now, you can undock and reposition the toolbars, and always be able to get back to the original positions by choosing View › Toolbars › Restore Toolbar Positions.

DIALOGS

All dialog boxes and windows are available from the Window drop-down menu. You can collapse all dialogs by clicking on the window heading. While they are collapsed, the dialog boxes can be docked to other dialogs. Typically, it is best to keep open only the dialogs that you'll need to use regularly—such as Entity Info, Materials, Components, Styles, Layers, Scenes, and Shadows. The other dialogs are not used as often, so it is fine to open them on an as-needed basis.

You can hide all of the dialogs at once by clicking on the Window drop-down menu and choosing Hide Dialogs. Unhide the dialogs by going to the same menu and choosing Show Dialogs. See Figure 6.4 and Figure 6.5.

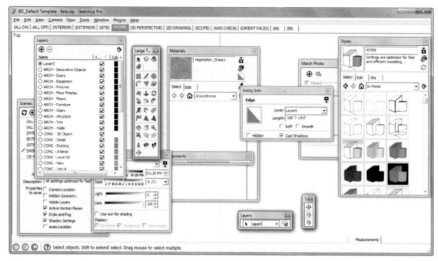

Figure 6.4 A cluttered screen is distracting and takes attention away from the task at hand, which is designing.

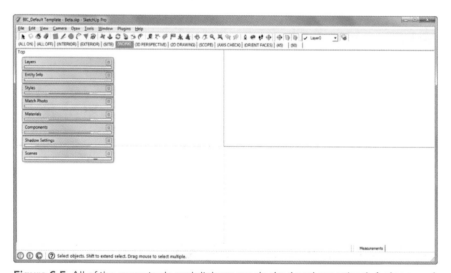

Figure 6.5 All of the same tools and dialogs are docked and organized. A clean workspace leads to productivity.

SYSTEM PREFERENCES

SketchUp has additional settings you can use to tweak your system and make it more streamlined and efficient. Use the Preferences dialog to adjust these settings. System preferences do not travel with the model; they are local SketchUp settings that are the same for every model you open. You will need to adjust these settings on every computer you work on. To access system preferences, click on the Window (SketchUp on Mac) drop-down menu and choose Preferences.

Drawing

The easiest way to draw in SketchUp is to use a three-button, scroll-wheel mouse utilizing click-move-click. SketchUp's default settings provide both the click-drag-release and click-move-click style of drawing. Change the Drawing settings to allow only Click-Move-Click and Continuous Line (Figure 6.6). This will prevent you from clicking and dragging, which makes it very easy to accidentally move objects by tiny increments or accidentally draw tiny, almost-unnoticeable unwanted geometry. Drawing style is a personal preference, so feel free to adjust to the one that works for you.

Figure 6.6 System Preferences – Drawing

Files

By specifying file locations, you can save time because you won't have to navigate through multiple folders to perform common SketchUp tasks (Figure 6.7). When you import, export, and open collections, SketchUp will already know where you want to look first. Select Window › Preferences and then select the Files menu at the left. Set your default file locations as follows:

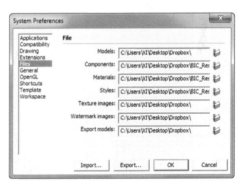

Figure 6.7 System Preferences – Files on Windows. This feature is not available on Mac.

☑ In the Models field, define the starting point for all open and save operations. Designate the directory path as `\Desktop\ACTIVE PROJECTS\` or your office's shared network drive.

☑ In the Components field, set the default location to use when you open or create a collection in the Components browser. Set the directory path to `\Desktop\ACTIVE PROJECTS\RESOURCES\Components\`.

☑ In the Materials field, set the default location to use when you open or create a collection in the Materials browser. Set the directory path to `\Desktop\ACTIVE PROJECTS\RESOURCES\Materials\`.

☑ In the Styles field, set the default location to use when you open or create a collection in the Styles browser. Set the directory path to `\Desktop\ACTIVE PROJECTS\RESOURCES\Styles\`.

☑ The Texture Images field is where you can set the default location for all images that can be used as textures. SketchUp will use this location as the starting point for all File › Insert › Image as Texture operations. Set the directory path to `\Desktop\TEMP\`.

☑ In the Watermark Images field, set the default location for all images that can be used as a watermark. Set the directory path to `\Desktop\ACTIVE PROJECTS\`.

☑ In the Export Models field, set the default location for all models that are to be exported out of SketchUp. SketchUp will use this location as the starting point for all File › Export › 3D Model operations. Set the directory path to `\Desktop\ACTIVE PROJECTS\`.

General

Within the General settings, make sure the Auto-Save box is checked, and allow SketchUp to automatically save your model every 5 minutes (Figure 6.8). Auto-saving can take a long time if your model is large; however, by applying the model lightening techniques explained in this book you will minimize the problem. Remember, SketchUp will not auto-save a new model until you have first saved it yourself.

Creating a backup file is pretty much a necessity—just in case! A backup file is saved in the same folder as the original `.skp` file and given the extension `.skb`. In the rare event that a model becomes unusable, change the file extension of the backup from `.skb` to `.skp` and you will be able to open the file in SketchUp.

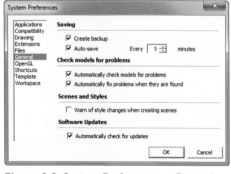

Figure 6.8 System Preferences – General

Open GL

Open GL settings can be used to troubleshoot your graphics card if strange things happen in your model (Figure 6.9). Uncheck the Use Hardware Acceleration box to disable your graphics card and take it out of the equation. If this fixes the problem, you know that your graphics card needs to be replaced or is incompatible, or the driver needs to be updated.

Use Maximum Texture Size is not necessary and will actually slow down your computer performance; leave this option unchecked. The maximum texture size improves the appearance of what you see on your screen but does so at the cost of system performance. This setting will not improve printing or exporting resolution.

The Use Fast Feedback option is necessary; leave it turned on. SketchUp typically controls this setting on its own. If your graphics card supports this feature, SketchUp will use it.

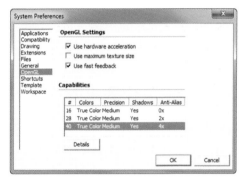

Figure 6.9 System Preferences - Open GL

In the Capabilities section, choose the best options for your graphics card. *Anti-aliasing* smooths out the jagged edges that result from a diagonal line of pixels. Pick a setting with the highest amount of anti-alias your monitor can handle, so your model will look its best on your screen.

Shortcuts

Keyboard shortcuts allow you to access any SketchUp command with the press of a key. Use shortcuts to help you work faster and relieve a huge amount of strain on your eyes and mouse hand. Every time you take your eyes off your design, you are slowing down. Take the time to focus on your keyboarding technique and set up your own custom keyboard shortcuts.

Adding Shortcuts

Modify your keyboard shortcuts in the Preferences dialog box by clicking on the Window (SketchUp on Mac) drop-down menu and choosing Preferences › Shortcuts (Figure 6.10).

1. Type a command, such as **hide**, into the Filter window to parse through all of the options and quickly find a command.

2. Click on a command in the Function box—for example, Edit/Hide.

3. Click in the Add Shortcut box and press the H key.

4. Click on the plus sign (+) to lock in the assigned keyboard shortcut.

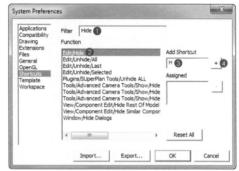

Figure 6.10 The Shortcuts tab in the System Preferences window

TIP If you try to assign a key that is already associated with another command, you will be prompted to reassign the key to the new command. Don't worry. You can always use the Reset All button to restore the keyboard shortcuts to the default state.

TIP By using shortcuts to interact with the Windows operating system, you will be able to work faster and more efficiently in any program. Hold down the Alt key and tap the Tab key to scroll through all the open applications. Once you are in an application, hold down the Ctrl key and tap the Tab key to scroll through the open files within that application. Hold down the Windows key and tap the Tab key to see a 3D scrolling effect that displays all open applications.

Now that you've assigned the keyboard shortcut H to the command Hide Geometry, the H key is taken; however, several helpful hide commands are left unassigned. You may have trouble remembering them if they don't have an "H" associated with them. Fortunately, you can use combinations of modifier keys such as Ctrl, Shift, and Alt to add more shortcut options in the Add Shortcut text box. To assign a modifier key to a shortcut command, simply press and hold the modifier key while you enter the desired key in the text box. For example, to hide the rest of the model when you're editing a group or component, assign the keyboard shortcut Ctrl+H. To unhide all, assign the keyboard shortcut Shift+H. Assign the shortcut Alt+H to show/hide hidden geometry. For a less-frequently used command such as Hide Similar Components, try to assign a combination of the modifier keys such as Ctrl+Shift+H.

In addition to the common commands and tools, it is helpful to have shortcuts assigned to just about every command you use. Figure 6.11 lists some less-frequently used commands that will help you expedite modeling every day.

You can use the Shortcuts tab to export and share a list of your shortcuts and file locations. Click on the Export button to save a .dat file containing all of your shortcuts. You can email this file to colleagues and even use this file to set up standard shortcuts and file locations on your other machines. Simply click the Import button and select the preferences.dat file.

HELPFUL SHORTCUTS

KEY	COMMAND
Ctrl + D	Show/Hide Dialogs
Shift + E	Zoom Extents
Ctrl + 1	Top View
Z	Zoom Window
Ctrl +R	Reverse Faces
F9	Toggle Parallel Projection/Perspective
Ctrl + Q	Toggle Shadows On/Off
Ctrl +E	Delete Guides
Ctrl + Shift + V	Paste in Place

Figure 6.11 Take the time to add additional shortcuts. If you constantly access a command using an icon or a drop-down menu, take the time to assign a keyboard shortcut to that command.

Download the official BIC_Shortcuts list at **www.suexch.com/TSWFA**. Save the file to your TEMP folder. Next, in the Shortcuts window, click on Import. Select the BIC_Shortcuts file from your TEMP folder and click Import. You may be prompted to reassign some of your current shortcuts, so be sure to archive your current settings first!

ACTIVITY

Ready Stance

To stay nimble, keep your left hand in the standard typing position with your thumb on the spacebar. This is an excellent default three-point stance for tackling SketchUp. If you already have a comfortable stance, stick with it—but at the same time, don't be afraid to try something new. Just be sure to always use the keyboard shortcuts and practice using keys without looking, even if it seems slower at first. Keyboard shortcuts will make you faster.

CHAPTER POINTS

☑ A clean screen will encourage efficiency and ultimately increase productivity.

☑ Keep your eyes on the model by using keystrokes without looking at the keyboard. Even if this technique takes longer at first, it will make you much faster in the long run.

☑ Customize your keyboard shortcuts in a way that makes sense to you.

☑ Try using keyboard shortcuts in other programs too.

Chapter 7

SketchUp Collections

When using SketchUp, people frequently miss the opportunity to fully organize and even use collections. That is a big mistake. Collections are notoriously messy. Whether you're working with a collection of components, styles, or textures, it is easy to be lazy and not keep the collections clean and organized—but now there is no excuse for laziness. This section will show you all of the rules and resources you need to build extensive, high-resolution, organized collections. Adhering to these standards will ensure that you always have the files you need right when you need them.

MATERIAL COLLECTION

You may have noticed that almost every amateur SketchUp model has the same shingles, bricks, and grass. Avoid using the materials that are preloaded in SketchUp. These materials are easily recognizable and will make your models look elementary. Diligently search for texture images to find ones that best represent the materials you have chosen for your design. This section contains several strategies for finding, creating, and organizing your professional material collection.

The Materials Browser

Before you begin in earnest, take a moment to explore the Materials browser. Launch it by activating the Paint Bucket tool, or by clicking on the Window drop-down menu and choosing Materials. The Materials browser has two separate tabs: Select and Edit (Figure 7.1). The Select tab displays preloaded collections, favorite collections, and the materials in your model. This is where you find materials to apply to surfaces within your model. The Edit tab is where you can change the many properties of a material already added to your model (Figure 7.2). Use the Edit tab to change the color, scale, texture image, and opacity of the active material.

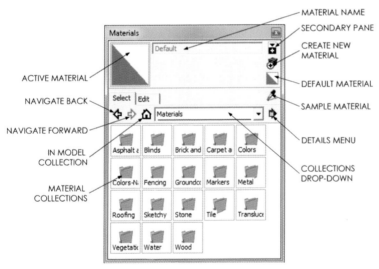

Figure 7.1 The Materials Browser's Select tab allows you to choose materials from preloaded collections and see the materials already in your model.

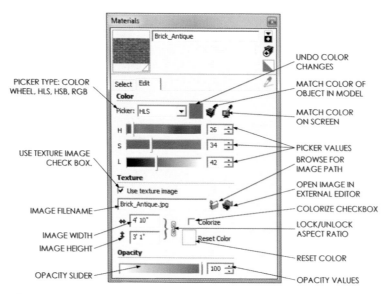

Figure 7.2 The Materials Browser's Edit tab allows you to modify the properties of a material.

TIP The Material Browser is very different on the Mac, but the underlying concepts are the same. This book does not contain Mac screenshots, but it is not hard to apply the directions from Windows to Mac.

Creating a Material

Texture images are relatively small, optimized images that can repeat infinitely without seams, and they are essential for creating professional-quality SketchUp materials. Professional-quality materials are essential for creating convincing 3D models that accurately represent your design.

An enormous number of texture images are available online for free. To begin collecting textures, perform a Google image search for "tileable grass." You can sort the results from a Google image search by many filters, most importantly size. For this exercise, click Medium to view images that are at a high enough resolution to look great, yet still maintain a reasonable file size. When searching for images, you can find the most valuable images by adding the words "tileable," "texture," or "material" to the query (Figure 7.3).

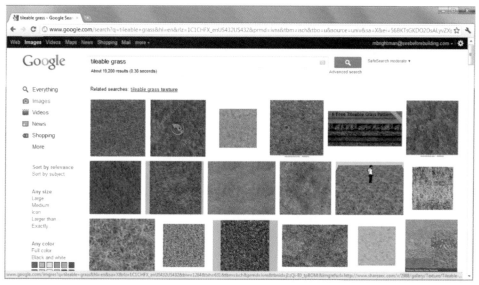

Figure 7.3 A Google image search

Click on an image thumbnail to navigate to the site that hosts the image. From there, you can right-click on the image and choose Save Image As. Save the image to your TEMP folder. Raw texture images should be saved in the TEMP folder because you won't need the original image once it is imported into a SketchUp material.

Now, add the texture image to a new material in SketchUp. To do that, follow these steps:

1. In the Materials browser, click the Create Material button to add a new material (see Figure 7.4). When you create a new material, the Create Material dialog opens and creates a copy of the active material.

2. Name the material **Grass 01**.

3. Click on the folder icon to add a texture image. Navigate to your TEMP folder and select the Grass Texture material. Click the Open button.

4. Click OK to finish creating the material.

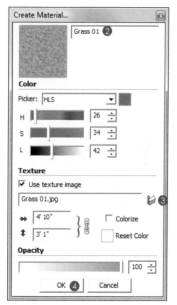

Figure 7.4 Use the Create Material dialog to modify the properties of a new material.

Once a texture is created, it resides in the current model only. You will need to add the new material to a collection to access it while working on other models. To do that, follow these steps:

1. Click on the In Model Collection (house icon) to see the materials that are in your model.

2. Right-click the Grass 01 material thumbnail and choose Save As.

3. Navigate to the RESOURCES/MATERIALS folder and save the material in the appropriate material folder. If you set your default folders as described in Chapter 6, "The Professional's SketchUp Environment," you will be taken there immediately.

Other excellent free and commercial sources for textures are available. Try searching Google for "free textures" and see what you can find. When you use an image search and find an image you like, the site hosting it will usually have other collections and textures available. Click on the Website for this image link to view more offerings from the site hosting the image. Access more materials in SketchUp by clicking on the Details menu and choosing Get More to see a SketchUp blog post about sources for free texture images. Lastly, FormFonts.com has an extensive library of texture images available at a very reasonable price. Regardless of where you get your textures, just be sure that you keep them organized.

Adding the Collection to Favorites

Now that you have added a material to your collection, you need to add that collection to your favorites within the Materials browser. This will give you access to the collection every time you open SketchUp.

1. In the Materials browser, click the Details menu and choose Add Collection to Favorites (Figure 7.5).

2. Navigate to the RESOURCES/MATERIALS folder and select OK.

3. Click the Material Collections dropdown menu and select the MATERIALS folder. The new Materials collection will be at the bottom of the list. Once a collection is added to your favorites, you can always access the collection from the Collections dropdown menu in the Materials browser.

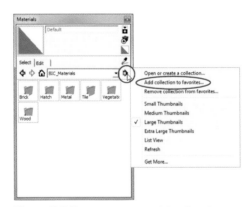

Figure 7.5 To manage material collections and favorites, use the Details menu in the Materials browser.

TIP Manage your collection from the secondary pane or from a file browser such as Windows Explorer. Under the BIC_Materials folder, add logical subfolders such as Hard Surfaces, Textiles, Metals, Roofing, Stone, Tile, Glass, Water, Wood, Cladding, and Ground Cover.

COMPONENT COLLECTIONS

Components have several useful applications, one being prebuilt SketchUp models of common objects that will save you an immense amount of time. Everyone can use objects such as lamps, plants, cars, and furniture, but no one wants to build these complex objects from scratch every time they are needed. Fortunately, component collections allow you to save and organize all of these objects for easy access and reuse.

The Components Browser

The Components browser is where you can view component collections, access the 3D Warehouse, and see which components are in your model. To access the Components browser, click on the Window drop-down menu and choose Components (Figure 7.6).

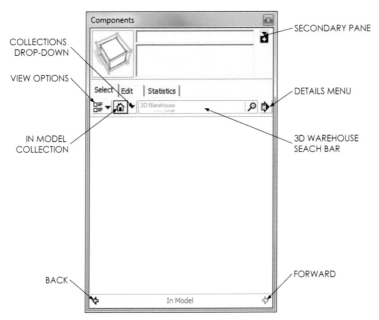

Figure 7.6 Use the Components browser to find components and organize them into collections.

Finding Components

Hundreds of thousands, if not millions, of components are immediately available for free within the Trimble 3D Warehouse. This is a huge repository of user-created, user-submitted, and user-rated models. Buyer beware, though. You get what you pay for, and when you pay nothing you should not expect much. Many of the models on the 3D Warehouse need to be optimized, correctly scaled, or even completed. This is not to say that it is not a good place to look. Just keep in mind that most of the models in the 3D Warehouse are not plug-and-play; they will require some work to make them useable.

To search the 3D Warehouse, enter your query directly into the search box in the Components browser. You can search for object titles, such as chair, table, car, and people. You can also search for brand names, such as West Elm, Pella, and Mercedes; brand searches typically return more favorable results. Once your search is complete, use the arrows at the bottom left and right to navigate through the search results (Figure 7.7).

At this point, you can click on a model thumbnail in the Components browser and then click again in your model to place the component. The selected component will be copied into your model.

Searching within the Components browser is a quick way to grab models from a minimalist interface. You can also access the 3D Warehouse through the Web, which provides significantly more model information and search options. Click the Details menu and select View in Trimble 3D Warehouse. This will launch the web version of the Trimble 3D Warehouse, which will be larger and easier to view; but most important, it will be sortable by ratings and popularity to help you filter the best models to the top. You can access search results in the 3D Warehouse web interface from the Details menu or by clicking on the component name in the search results (Figure 7.8).

Figure 7.7 The results of a West Elm search

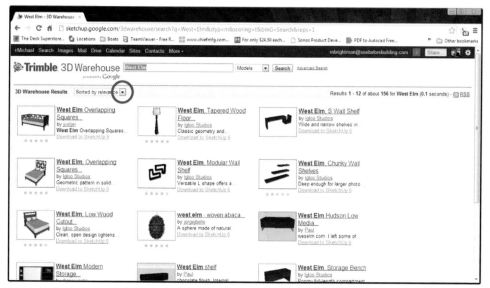

Figure 7.8 To get more options and information than the Components browser provides, view the 3D Warehouse search results in a web browser.

Click the Download Model button to save a component to your ACTIVE PROJECTS/ RESOURCES/COMPONENTS collection.

A better solution for building a component collection is to pay for the models. Form-Fonts.com offers an extensive collection of excellent professionally built, commercially available models. All of the models at FormFonts.com are properly scaled, textured, and optimized, making them easy to use "right out of the box." For professionals, paying for models is worth the small monetary investment to have perfect models in seconds.

Adding a Collection to Favorites

Once you have created a collection, you will want to access it every time you open SketchUp. To do that, follow these steps:

1. Click the Details menu and choose Open or Create a Local Collection.

2. Navigate to your RESOURCES folder, select the COMPONENTS folder, and then click OK.

3. Click the context arrow again and choose Add to Favorites. The COMPONENTS collection will be available every time you open SketchUp under the Component Collections drop-down menu.

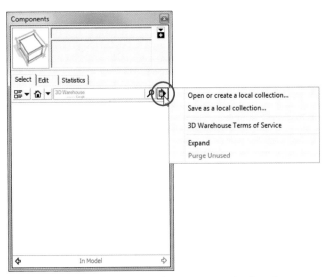

Figure 7.9 In the Components browser, use the Details menu to manage component collections and favorites.

TIP Manage your collection from a file browser such as Windows Explorer. Add logical subfolders to the Components folder—for example, Landscape, Furniture, Entourage, Doors, Windows, etc. You might even consider organizing your components by project.

STYLES COLLECTION

Currently, styles are not as widely available as materials and components are; this is probably because the preloaded libraries are more than enough to get you started.

Creating a Style

Use the Mix tab in the Styles browser to combine your favorite styles into new creations. To do that, follow these steps:

1. In the Styles browser, click on the Mix tab. This automatically launches the secondary pane.

2. In the secondary pane, choose your favorite collection.

3. Drag a style to one of the properties in the Mix tab. The current style will inherit the specified properties from the style that you dragged up.

4. Click the Style icon to update and save the changes made to the current style. The watermark will disappear upon updating.

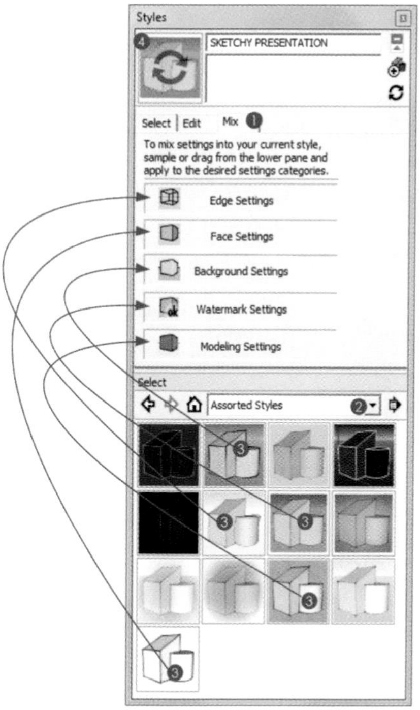

Adding a Style to a Collection

Not every style needs to be a part of the default template, so you will need a style collection to hold additional useful styles. Any style that you create should be saved in your Styles collection. To save a style, follow these steps:

1. Click the In Model Collection (house icon) to see which styles are in your model; you will see the styles that you created in Chapter 5, "The Professional's SketchUp Template."

Figure 7.10 The Mix tab in the Style browser gives you creative license to take your favorite styles and blend them.

2. Right-click on a style and choose Save As.

3. Navigate to your RESOURCES/STYLES folder, select it, and click Save. If you set your default folders as described in Chapter 6, you will be taken there immediately.

Adding a Collection to Favorites

So that this collection is always available when you need it, click on the Details menu and select Add Collection to Favorites. Navigate to and select the RESOURCES/STYLES folder and choose OK. The collection will be available every time you open SketchUp under the Style Collections drop-down menu (Figure 7.11).

TIP In addition to any new styles you create, add all of the styles from the default template to your Styles collection.

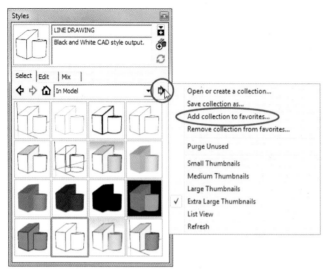

Figure 7.11 Use the Details menu in the Styles browser to manage style collections and favorites.

CHAPTER POINTS

☑ Collections are most valuable when they are kept current and organized. Organize material and component collections in a way that works for you. Consider organizing your collections by types, project, client, or even design style—for example, modern or traditional.

☑ All browsers have a secondary pane and a drag-and-drop interface that makes managing collections easier. You can also manage collections from a file browser.

☑ When you use a collection to add materials, components, and styles to your current model, you are creating a copy of the original from the collection and placing that copy in the model. When you edit the materials, components, or styles, you are editing only the copy in the model, not the original in the collection.

Chapter 8
Ruby Scripts

Ruby scripts are the original apps. Before apps were extreme fajitas and potato poppers, and even before apps allowed you to digitally chug a beer on your phone, there were ruby scripts. These little pieces of code expedite the tedious and repetitive tasks in SketchUp that drive you crazy. If you find that a certain task is taking entirely too long, take a step back and start looking for a ruby script. In this section, you will review several useful ruby scripts and learn how to find and install some others.

FIND RUBY SCRIPTS

Some rubies are free and some aren't. Just as with the 3D Warehouse, you get what you pay for. When you purchase a ruby, typically you can expect to receive support and clear instructions. If you grab a free ruby, you should probably expect to put in a little extra effort figuring it out. A great place to buy rubies and grab a few freebies is at **www.smustard.com**. Huge collections of free ruby scripts are available at the Ruby Library Depot (Google it), **www.sketchucation.com**, and **www.sketchup.com**.

INSTALLING RUBY SCRIPTS

Once you have downloaded your ruby, save it to the Plugins folder (for example, `C:\Program Files\Google\Google SketchUp 8\Plugins`). Keep in mind that the path could vary, depending on your drive name and operating system. If a ruby is zipped, you must extract the contents to this location. After the `.rb` file is saved in the Plugins folder, you will need to close SketchUp and re-open it in order to load the new ruby.

TIP Sometimes one ruby depends on another to operate properly. Read through any instructions and documentation thoroughly before you try to use a ruby. For example, many rubies will not work without the sketchup.rb and progressbar.rb rubies installed in the Plugins folder.

Newer ruby scripts that are written specifically for SketchUp 8 are packaged as .rbz files. The compressed one-file format makes it much easier to install the ruby scripts. To unzip a compressed ruby, follow these steps:

1. Click on the Window drop-down and choose Preferences › Extensions.
2. Click the Install Extensions button.
3. Navigate to and select the `.rbz` file and click the Open button.

USING RUBY SCRIPTS

You'll frequently encounter ruby scripts that don't have any directions or documentation explaining exactly how to use the ruby. Once a ruby is installed, you may have to access it from different locations, depending on how the author designed the user experience. The first place to look is in the drop-down menus (such as Draw, Tools, and Plugins) at the top of the screen. If you still can't find it, open the ruby script in a text editor to gather some clues. Authors frequently include a few notes about how to get started (Figure 8.1).

RECOMMENDED RUBY SCRIPTS

Listed here are a few ruby scripts that will come in handy when you're using this book and also when you're modeling in general. Don't stop here, there are infinite more rubies out there!

Bézier Spline Tool

Once you've mastered the Bézier Spline tool, you will have almost no need to use the Arc tool to draw continuous arcs. Furthermore, with this tool, you will have no need for the Freehand tool, which is completely inaccurate. You can download the Bézier Spline tool and other tools at

http://www.sketchup.com/intl/en/download/rubyscripts.html

Figure 8.1 The author's notes and instructions displayed in a text editor.

Dashed Lines Ruby

The Dashed Lines ruby will segment a selected line into several different line types. It is great for creating dashed lines to represent 2D graphics and for creating rare annotations in SketchUp (for example, center lines and column lines). You can find the Dashed Lines ruby at

http://www.smustard.com/script/DashedLines

Scale and Rotate Multiple

Select a few shrubs or trees and run the Scale and Rotate Multiple ruby to randomly scale and rotate the objects. This ruby is great for quickly making landscape elements look more natural rather than computer generated. You can download it at .

http://sketchucation.com/forums/viewtopic.php?t=17507#p139946

Add Hidden Layer Ruby

When you're adding a layer in SketchUp, the default is to turn on the layer in all existing scenes. The Add Hidden Layer ruby does the opposite and turns it off, which is typically more desirable. You can download this ruby at

http://rhin.crai.archi.fr/rld/plugin_details.php?id=6

Zorro Tool

The Zorro tool is helpful when transitioning a sketch model to a refined design, or when breaking a model into levels. With the Zorro tool, you draw a line across geometry that slices through all the geometry, even the groups and components. Typically, a head-on parallel projection view is the best view to use for full control of this ruby. You can download the Zorro tool at

http://rhin.crai.archi.fr/rld/plugin_details.php?id=498

Instant Road Plugin

The Instant Road plugin expedites the creation of realistic roads in SketchUp. This plugin picks up where the Sandbox tool falls short. You can download it at

http://valiarchitects.com/sketchup_scripts/instant-road

Flatten Tool

The Flatten tool takes any 3D object and reduces it to a 2D symbol. This ruby script will come in handy when a 3D object does not quite render the way you wanted it to render in a plan. You can download it at

http://www.smustard.com/script/Flatten

CHAPTER POINTS

- ☑ If you are performing a task that is repetitive, tedious, and taking entirely too long, stop immediately and look for a ruby script.
- ☑ Paying for rubies is absolutely worth it. They are usually inexpensive and will save you hours of labor working on mind-numbing, repetitious tasks and searching for freebies.

PART III

LayOut

Like Kevin from *Home Alone,* LayOut is easily overlooked and very much underestimated. More often than not, LayOut is an afterthought—if it is even considered at all—yet this program is the keystone of an effective SketchUp workflow. LayOut turns 3D SketchUp models into stylized print and screen presentations—presentations that ultimately sell your ideas and produce the instructions to build the spaces you envision in SketchUp. In Part III you will receive a complete education in all that is LayOut, from theory to the toolset.

Chapter 9
Introduction to LayOut

Sketch Up Pro is a software suite that includes the unrestricted version of SketchUp, as well as the invaluable presentation application LayOut—and StyleBuilder, which is not covered in this book. Although SketchUp Pro is undeniably excellent by itself, SketchUp Pro becomes truly radical when it is paired with LayOut (Figure 9.1).

Figure 9.1 The free version of SketchUp is for hobbyists; SketchUp Pro is for professionals.

WHAT IS LAYOUT?

In short, LayOut is a multifaceted Presentation tool. It is a page-creation program that has 3D presentation capabilities coupled with 2D Drafting tools (Figure 9.2). In LayOut, you arrange 3D perspective views and scaled 2D orthographic views on a sheet of paper to graphically explain a design. When you're done, you can use LayOut's sleek drawing toolset to add informative annotations on top of those views and provide an additional layer of information for your audience (Figure 9.3). With LayOut's tools, you can quickly and easily add dimensions, text, leader text, callouts, and custom line types.

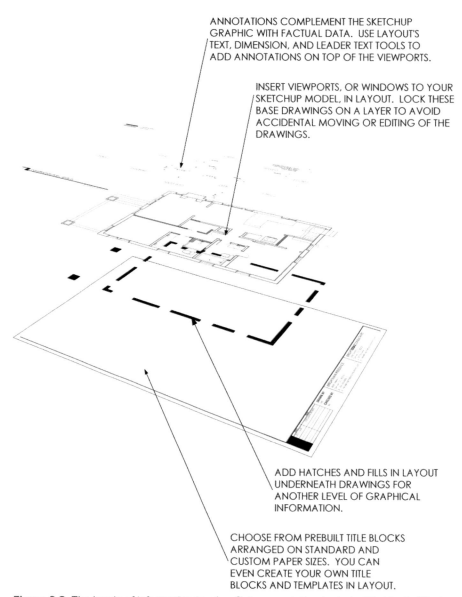

ANNOTATIONS COMPLEMENT THE SKETCHUP
GRAPHIC WITH FACTUAL DATA. USE LAYOUT'S
TEXT, DIMENSION, AND LEADER TEXT TOOLS TO
ADD ANNOTATIONS ON TOP OF THE VIEWPORTS.

INSERT VIEWPORTS, OR WINDOWS TO YOUR
SKETCHUP MODEL, IN LAYOUT. LOCK THESE
BASE DRAWINGS ON A LAYER TO AVOID
ACCIDENTAL MOVING OR EDITING OF THE
DRAWINGS.

ADD HATCHES AND FILLS IN LAYOUT
UNDERNEATH DRAWINGS FOR
ANOTHER LEVEL OF GRAPHICAL
INFORMATION.

CHOOSE FROM PREBUILT TITLE BLOCKS
ARRANGED ON STANDARD AND
CUSTOM PAPER SIZES. YOU CAN
EVEN CREATE YOUR OWN TITLE
BLOCKS AND TEMPLATES IN LAYOUT.

Figure 9.2 The levels of information in a LayOut presentation include title block, 3D viewport, and annotation.

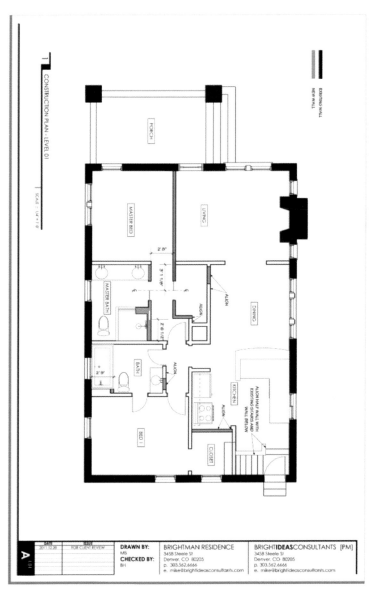

Figure 9.3 When all of the graphics and annotations are flattened, you have an architectural drawing.

Design in SketchUp. Present in LayOut. That is the basic concept. For a more in-depth explanation, read on to learn about paper space, model space, and the dynamic link between the two that makes LayOut such a valuable tool.

Paper Space and Model Space

Now for the longer, technical answer: LayOut is SketchUp's equivalent to CAD's paper space. Take a moment to fully grasp the concept of designing in model space and presenting in paper space.

Model Space

SketchUp's *model space* is where your design comes to life. Everything built in SketchUp 3D is drawn at a 1:1 real-world scale. This means that if a wall is to be built 10 feet tall in the real world, you draw the wall 10 feet tall in your SketchUp model. You don't need to crunch the numbers into an architectural scale while working in model space. Everything in SketchUp is built to the size it is intended to be built to in the real world (Figure 9.4).

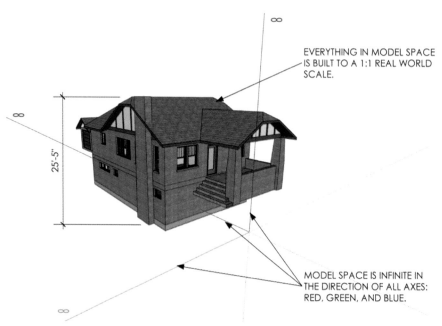

EVERYTHING IN MODEL SPACE IS BUILT TO A 1:1 REAL WORLD SCALE.

MODEL SPACE IS INFINITE IN THE DIRECTION OF ALL AXES: RED, GREEN, AND BLUE.

Figure 9.4 Model space is where you design and build a model representing your design. Model space contains mostly 3D objects rather than graphics and annotations.

Paper Space

LayOut's *paper space* is where your presentation comes to life (Figure 9.5). Place the *viewports* (windows looking into your SketchUp model) on a standard paper size. Arrange the viewports on the sheet and set the orthographic views to architectural scales. In other words, LayOut will very quickly do the math so you can present your life-sized designs at a reduced architectural scale. This is where you will determine what sheet size you need to present your design at a specific architectural scale.

PAPER SPACE IS LIMITED TO A SET PAPER SIZE, IN THIS CASE 11" X 17" TABLOID, ORIENTED LANDSCAPE. LAYOUT HAS STANDARD PAPER SIZES INCLUDED, AND ALSO GIVES YOU THE OPTION OF CREATING CUSTOM PAPER SIZES.

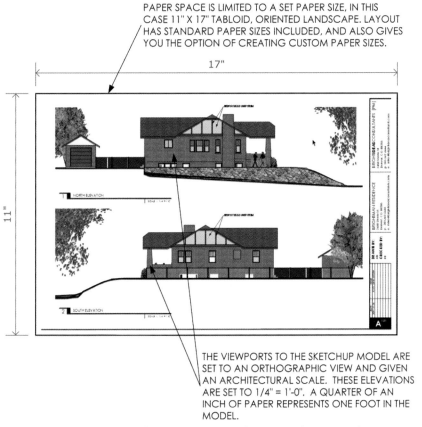

THE VIEWPORTS TO THE SKETCHUP MODEL ARE SET TO AN ORTHOGRAPHIC VIEW AND GIVEN AN ARCHITECTURAL SCALE. THESE ELEVATIONS ARE SET TO 1/4" = 1'-0". A QUARTER OF AN INCH OF PAPER REPRESENTS ONE FOOT IN THE MODEL.

Figure 9.5 Paper space is where you create and organize the pages of your presentation based on a specific paper size. Paper space contains only 2D annotations and text overlayed on static 2D views of the 3D SketchUp model.

Dynamic Link

The 3D SketchUp model space and the 2D LayOut paper space are connected. The dynamic link between them is critical to the efficiency of the SketchUp workflow for architecture. After you modify and save the SketchUp model, LayOut will let you know that the link needs to be updated. When you update or refresh the model within LayOut, all of the linked 2D drawings in your presentation will reflect the most current design (Figure 9.6). This dynamic link eliminates the need to re-export every time you make a presentation. This feature also gives you the freedom to make last-minute design changes in 3D and then simply update your presentation before a meeting. This dynamic link gives you the power to progressively build your presentation in small, one-at-a-time pieces leading up to the final presentation and construction documents. This type of process is much more manageable than tackling a large presentation or an entire set of construction documents all at once.

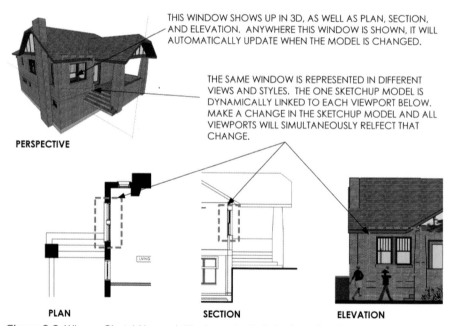

THIS WINDOW SHOWS UP IN 3D, AS WELL AS PLAN, SECTION, AND ELEVATION. ANYWHERE THIS WINDOW IS SHOWN, IT WILL AUTOMATICALLY UPDATE WHEN THE MODEL IS CHANGED.

THE SAME WINDOW IS REPRESENTED IN DIFFERENT VIEWS AND STYLES. THE ONE SKETCHUP MODEL IS DYNAMICALLY LINKED TO EACH VIEWPORT BELOW. MAKE A CHANGE IN THE SKETCHUP MODEL AND ALL VIEWPORTS WILL SIMULTANEOUSLY RELFECT THAT CHANGE.

PERSPECTIVE

PLAN   SECTION   ELEVATION

Figure 9.6 When a SketchUp model is dynamically linked to a LayOut presentation, all drawings are derived from one model and updated simultaneously.

WHY LAYOUT?

After you've worked in SketchUp, you may find it difficult to go back into the cyan and magenta world of 2D CAD or the tedious world of BIM. SketchUp and LayOut are much faster, more fun, and more colorful to work with than other drafting programs. If you can accomplish the same goals and so much more with SketchUp and LayOut, why not use LayOut?In addition to being fun and colorful, there are a few purely utilitarian reasons for using LayOut. It has a few professional design features that should convince you—or your boss—to pull the trigger on SketchUp Pro.

Expanded Export Options

SketchUp Pro and LayOut offers several export options for presenting, sharing with consultants, and moving the project into other software packages. You can export a `.pdf` from LayOut to produce large format prints and deliverables to pass out at a meeting. You can also export the LayOut presentation paper space or SketchUp model space as a CAD file in `.dwg` or `.dxf` format. To finish the job, you can then open the LayOut file in your familiar 2D drafting program. Finally, you can export all pages as `.jpg` files or `.png` files from LayOut. This option replaces the need for exporter plugins within SketchUp, and it expedites the entire export process.

Professional Renderings

If you are a professional designer building a SketchUp model, you probably want others to see it. Because it is limited to your screen resolution, the free version of SketchUp does not have the export capabilities required by professionals. SketchUp Pro, mainly LayOut, gives you all of the tools and rendering settings you'll need to maximize your SketchUp model for presentation and sharing.

Exporting from SketchUp Pro allows you to create extremely high-resolution raster images and also gives you several vector file formats (Figure 9.7). Exporting from LayOut combines the best of raster and vector into one hybrid view. This concept will be covered in detail later in Chapter 10, "The LayOut Interface."

EXPORTING FROM SKETCHUP (FREE) LIMITS YOU TO THE SCREEN RESOLUTION. LINES ARE PIXELATED, BULKY, AND BLURRY. THIS IS THE BEST YOU WILL EVER GET WITH SKETCHUP (FREE).

EXPORTING FROM SKETCHUP PRO GIVES YOU NEARLY UNLIMITED RESOLUTION FOR EXPORTS. THIS IS GOOD, BUT THE LINES START TO FADE OUT AT HIGHER RESOLUTIONS.

EXPORTING FROM LAYOUT GIVES THE OPTION FOR HYBRID RENDERING. THIS SETTING COMBINES HIGH-RESOLUTION RASTER IMAGE WITH VECTOR LINEWORK LAID ON TOP. WHEN PRINTING HIGH-RESOLUTION OR LARGE FORMAT, YOU WILL GET EXPONENTIALLY BETTER RESULTS.

Figure 9.7 SketchUp Pro can create much better images that you can use for large-scale presentations.

Software Replacement

When you render and export images from your 3D model, you have to insert those images into page-creation software to create the deliverables. Then if you want to make a slideshow, you need to insert those same images into slideshow software to create the presentation. Then you have to use another application to create a completely separate set of construction documents. If you need to make any changes, you need to re-export, reinsert, re-export, reinsert…. LayOut gives you the ability to link one 3D model to a program that can create all these drawings and presentation materials at the same time, and simultaneously update all the drawings and renderings.

LayOut can replace the page-creation software normally used to develop print presentations. For example, with LayOut, you don't need to export from SketchUp and use programs such as InDesign, Photoshop, and Illustrator to arrange those images on a sheet. LayOut can do all of this and do it better because of the dynamic link to SketchUp and the expanded rendering settings optimized for SketchUp models.

SketchUp Pro and LayOut together can replace all of your CAD drafting software. The techniques provided in this book pull the best strategies and features from BIM and 2D drafting into one efficient workflow centered around SketchUp Pro. SketchUp Pro and LayOut can replace Architectural Desktop, Revit, and VectorWorks, as well as any other 2D or 3D BIM vector drafting programs.

LayOut replaces slideshow software such as PowerPoint. When it's time for you to present at a meeting, you can use LayOut's Presentation mode to display your 2D LayOut presentation on a projection screen. LayOut's Presentation mode enables you to present each page as a slide, and it has a red Line tool you can use to mark up a set of drawings while you're giving your presentation in front of an audience (Figure 9.8). The red lines are conveniently added to a time-stamped layer for easy review, revision, and deletion later. LayOut doesn't offer any transitions or sound effects, but animated page curls and swoosh noises really don't do much to sell a design.

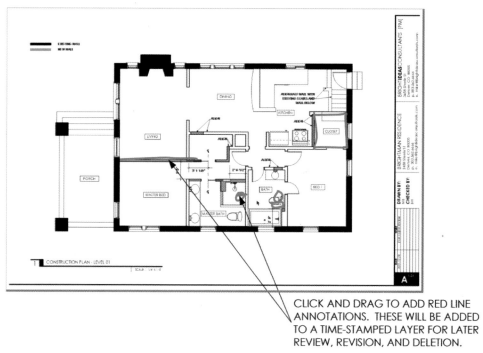

CLICK AND DRAG TO ADD RED LINE
ANNOTATIONS. THESE WILL BE ADDED
TO A TIME-STAMPED LAYER FOR LATER
REVIEW, REVISION, AND DELETION.

Figure 9.8 Red lines in LayOut's Presentation mode allow you to mark up a set in front of an audience.

Line Control

SketchUp's Profiles, Depth Cue, and Section Cuts settings give you some ability to control line weights. They offer everything you need to make compelling 3D views and animations. LayOut gives you full control over line weights even when you're working with scaled 2D drawings that require several line weights to align with industry graphic standards.

Each viewport within LayOut can be set to a specific line weight independent of other viewports. This flexibility allows you to thicken large detail drawings and thin out smaller scaled plans.

The annotation lines and shapes you add in LayOut can be set to any line weight. You can assign several different line types and arrowheads to any line you draw in LayOut (Figure 9.9), and you can adjust the color of those lines. The combination of these settings gives you the ability to create any symbol or annotation in the graphic style you choose.

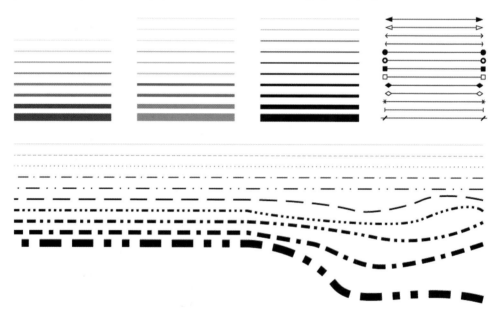

Figure 9.9 Line weights, line types, and arrows are abundant in LayOut.

CHAPTER POINTS

☑ SketchUp Pro is a necessity for professional designers. SketchUp (free) offers just enough of the program for hobbyists to learn how to build 3D models.

☑ SketchUp Pro can replace many popular software packages, which will save you money and make creating all-inclusive presentations easier.

☑ Design, think, and explore in 3D SketchUp's model space.

☑ Present, annotate, and explain in 2D LayOut's paper space.

Chapter 10
The LayOut Interface

This chapter explains the intricacies of the LayOut interface and introduces all of the settings, toolbars, and features you'll need to use LayOut. Use it now as a roadmap, while you tour LayOut and become familiar with the interface. Even after you've mastered the concepts explained here, you'll be able to use it as a helpful resource to answer any questions you have about individual menus, settings, and dialogs.

GETTING STARTED

To open LayOut, click the icon on your desktop. The Getting Started window will appear, allowing you to access new templates, recent files, and recovered presentations.

New Tab

Initially, you will be taken to the New tab by default (Figure 10.1). Preloaded templates that you can use to create new presentations will appear in the right pane. From the Default Templates library, select either a title block or a plain piece of paper. To select a default template (a template you will always start with), check the Always Use Selected Template box. Typically, you won't need to use this feature because you will need different sizes of paper and title blocks for each presentation you create.

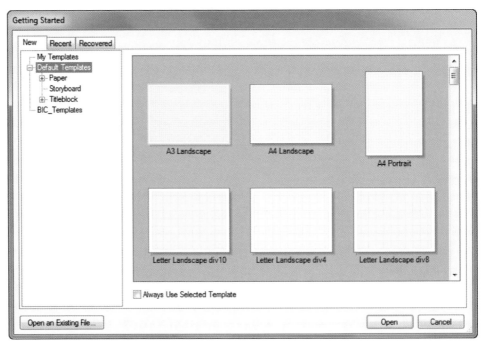

Figure 10.1 The New tab in the Getting Started window

Recent Tab

The Recent tab displays all of the documents you have worked on in the not-so-distant past. When you use this tab, be careful because it is similar to My Recent Documents. Even though a file is shown there today, it might not be shown there tomorrow if you open other LayOut presentations. If you are using the Recent tab, you may not be aware of where you are saving the actual file.

The best way to open a file that you have already created is to click the Open an Existing File button at the bottom-left corner of the Getting Started window. Make sure you know where you are saving files so you can navigate to the appropriate project folder when you need them. To open a file, you can either double-click on its thumbnail or select the thumbnail and choose Open.

Recovered Tab

The Recovered tab at the top of the Getting Started window appears when files need to be recovered; you can use the recovery feature to help you get back work that was lost during a crash. LayOut does crash at times if you overload it, but it also does a great job of recovering files. Don't worry, though; the techniques you'll learn in this book will drastically reduce the number of crashes you experience. If LayOut does crash, re-open LayOut and look for your recovered document in the Recovered tab.

MAIN TOOLBAR

The Main toolbar in LayOut contains the most commonly used and basic tools (Figure 10.2). Undock a LayOut toolbar by clicking and dragging on the line at the far left of the toolbar. Dock a toolbar by dragging the header to the top, bottom, or side of the screen.

Figure 10.2 The Main toolbar

TIP See Chapter 11, "The Professional's LayOut Environment," for more information on creating and customizing the LayOut toolbars.

DOCUMENT SETUP

The Document Setup settings apply to the currently open document; they are not global settings for LayOut. In other words, these settings can travel with a template or a presentation file, but they will not change globally for every document you open in LayOut. To open the Document Setup dialog, click on the Window drop-down menu and choose "Document Setup."

General Tab

The General tab has fields where you can give credit to the author of the file and describe the contents of the file (Figure 10.3). These fields are rarely used. However, if you are sharing a template with others and would like to receive authorship credit, you might want to fill out this section.

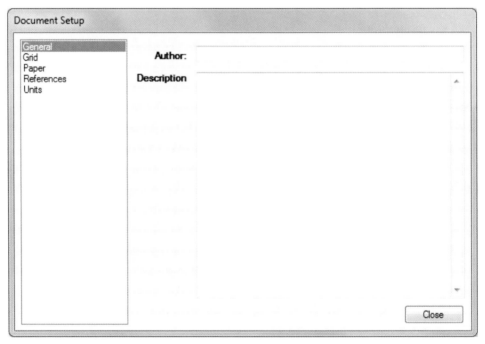

Figure 10.3 The General tab

Grid Tab

The Grid tab is where you can adjust the size and visual properties of the grid (Figure 10.4).

TIP The numerals in the diagrams refer to the keyed notes and do not represent any order of operation.

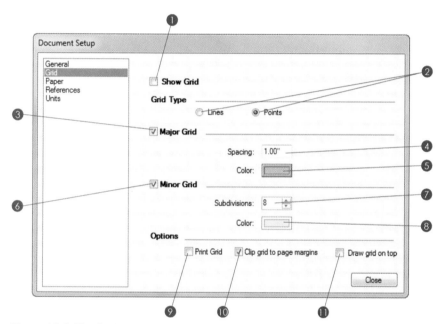

Figure 10.4 The Grid tab

1. You can check and uncheck the Show Grid check box to toggle between making the grid visible and invisible.

2. You can use the radio buttons to set the grid type to lines or points. Typically, a traditional line grid is the most useful option (Figure 10.5).

3. Click the Major Grid check box to toggle the visibility of the thicker grid lines on and off.

4. To adjust the major grid spacing, click in the Spacing text field, enter the grid spacing you want, and then press Enter. You can use decimal format or you can use a space to separate inches (the default units) from fractions.

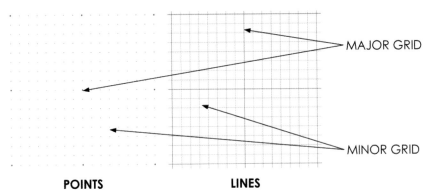

POINTS   LINES

Figure 10.5 The Grid options in LayOut

5. To change the color of the major grid, click on the color block. This automatically opens the Color Inspector, where you can select a color from several different tabs: Wheel, RGB, HSB, Grays, Image, and List. Typically, the first three tabs offer the easiest way to make the color selection you want.

6. Click the Minor Grid check box to toggle the visibility of the thinner grid lines on and off.

7. The minor grid is composed of thinner lines and fills in the major grid by the specified number of subdivisions. Change the number of subdivisions by typing a new number into the Subdivisions text field, and then press Enter. You can also use the Up and Down arrows to the right of the Subdivisions field to adjust the number of subdivisions.

8. To change the color of the minor grid, click on the color block. This automatically opens the Color palette where you can select a color from several different tabs: Wheel, RGB, HSB, Grays, Image, and List. Typically, the first three tabs offer the easiest way to make the color selection you desire.

9. When the Print Grid box is checked, the grid will automatically be printed to paper from the printer. This feature is helpful when you are working with schematic drawings.

10. The Clip Grid to Page Margins setting limits the grid to the extents of the margins. The presentation margins are controlled in the Paper tab.

11. When the Draw Grid on Top box is checked, the grid will appear on top of any viewports and geometry created in LayOut.

TIP You can adjust how tools interact with the grid by right-clicking in the presentation background. From this right-click menu, you can turn the grid and object snap on or off, as well as toggle whether the grid is visible or not.

Paper Tab

The paper properties are where you indicate the overall size of the sheet of paper you will use for your presentation and where you determine the quality of the renderings within your presentation (Figure 10.6).

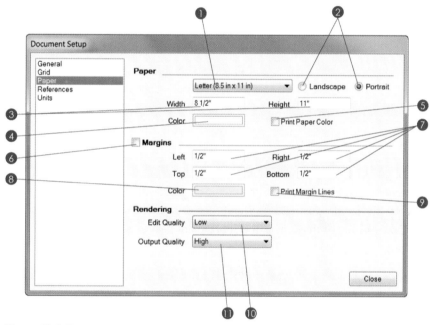

Figure 10.6 The Paper tab

1. Click the Paper drop-down menu to choose from preloaded standard paper sizes.

2. The Portrait and Landscape radio buttons allow you to select the orientation of the sheet, portrait or landscape.

3. You can create a custom paper size by entering the dimensions of the sheet into the Width and Height text fields. Press Enter to lock in the dimension entries.

4. Change the color of the paper, or presentation background, by clicking on the color block. This automatically opens the Colors Inspector (discussed later in this chapter), where you can select a color from several different tabs: Wheel, RGB, HSB, Grays, Image, and List. Typically, the first three tabs provide the easiest way to make the color selection you want.

5. Check the Print Paper Color box only if you are using someone else's printer. This will actually waste expensive ink by reproducing the background color on the paper, which is rarely necessary.

6. Turn on the margins by clicking the Margins check box.

7. Set your margin depths by entering the dimensions in the Left, Right, Top, and Bottom fields.

8. Change the color of the margin lines by clicking on the color block. This automatically opens the Color Inspector where you can select a color from several different tabs: Wheel, RGB, HSB, Grays, Image, and List. Typically, the first three tabs provide the easiest way to make your color selections.

9. Click the Print Margin Lines check box so that the margin lines will appear on the final prints and exports.

10. The Edit Quality setting determines the rendering quality while you're working in a LayOut presentation. In other words, it indicates the quality (or how clear) the SketchUp models and images will appear on the screen while you're working in LayOut.

11. The Output Quality setting determines the final rendering quality when the project is exported or printed. In other words, it determines how clear the SketchUp models and images will appear on the paper that comes out of the printer.

TIP Always use low quality settings when you're editing a document. If you don't, you will waste a lot of time rendering at a high resolution you don't need.

References Tab

A *reference* is an external file that is inserted into your LayOut presentation and connected with a *link* (or path). The References tab allows you to control what files are linked, and it shows whether or not those files are current (Figure 10.7). LayOut can reference text, image, and SketchUp files.

Figure 10.7 The References tab

1. When the Check References When Loading this Document box is checked, LayOut will alert you to any out-of-date references when a file opens. If a reference has been modified, it will appear in red in the References tab and its status will read "Out of Date." This is a good setting to use when you're first learning LayOut; however, as you become more familiar with the program, you will probably update the links manually.

2. The File Name column displays the name and extension of the linked file.

3. The Status column indicates whether the file's reference is current or not—in other words, it tells you if the file needs to be updated. A reference's status is Current, Out of Date, or Embedded. Current files are up-to-date and no action is necessary. Out-of-date files need to have the references updated. An Embedded status means the file is no longer linked to the original source; instead, it is part of the LayOut presentation.

4. The Insertion Date column tells you when the file was added to the LayOut presentation.

5. To update a link, highlight the out-of-date red filename and click the Update button at the bottom of the Document Setup window. A selected viewport will highlight the reference within the References tab, and vice versa.

6. Relink a missing file by highlighting the filename and then clicking Relink. Navigate to the file you want to relink to, or swap, and choose Open. You'll need to do this if you move the original file or want to swap to a different version of the original file.

7. If you click the Unlink button at the bottom of the Document Setup window, the file will be *embedded* (become part of the LayOut presentation).

8. Click the Edit button to automatically open the reference in the associated program. You can assign preferred programs for word documents and images in the Preferences menu (covered later in this chapter).

9. Click the Purge button to delete references that are no longer used in your presentation. Purging will keep the file size small and the presentation running fast.

TIP References are shown similar to the details view in a file explorer. Click on the File Name, Status, and Insertion Date headers to sort the files.

Units Tab

The Units tab is where you indicate the type of measurement units to use, as well as the level of precision or accuracy (Figure 10.8).

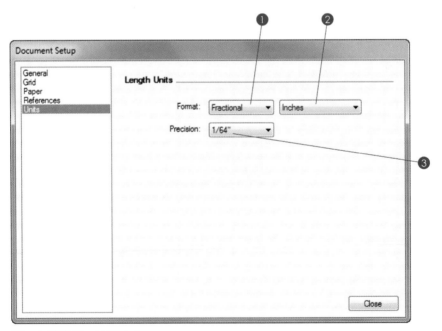

Figure 10.8 The Units tab

1. Click the Format drop-down menu to choose decimal or fractional.

2. Click on the next drop-down menu to set the default units of the current presentation to Inches, Feet, Millimeter, Centimeter, Meter, or Points.

3. Click on the Precision drop-down menu to set the precision of the units used. Fractional units can be displayed at a precision from 1″ to 1/64″. Decimal units can be displayed at precisions up to .01″.

PREFERENCES WINDOW

The Preferences window is where you set up your system preferences for LayOut. It contains the default settings that will be the same every time you open LayOut, regardless of which presentation you open or start new. To adjust the settings, click the Edit (LayOut in Mac) drop-down menu and choose Preferences.

Applications Tab

The Applications tab contains the settings for default programs (Figure 10.9). These programs will launch automatically when you right-click on a reference and choose Edit from the right-click menu or from the References tab in the Document Setup window.

Figure 10.9 The Applications tab

1. Set the Default Image Editor to your favorite image editor, such as Adobe Photoshop.

TIP GIMP is a free and very powerful image editor available at **www.gimp.org**.

2. Set the Default Text Editor to your favorite text editor, such as Microsoft Word.

TIP OpenOffice is a free and very powerful word processor available at **www.openoffice.org**.

Backup Tab

You can use the BackUp settings to keep your work safe by creating additional files and automatically saving your work in case a file crashes or is corrupted (Figure 10.10).

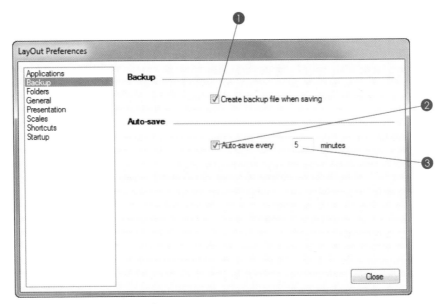

Figure 10.10 The Backup tab

1. The Create Backup File When Saving feature will create a duplicate of the file prefixed with BACKUP_. Even though using this feature requires double the storage space, it provides extra piece of mind in case of a catastrophic crash or a corrupt file.

2. When the Auto-Save Every box is checked, your presentation is saved automatically at a set interval of time.

3. Typically, five minutes is reasonable.

Folders Tab

Add your own Template and Scrapbook collections to be accessed in LayOut (Figure 10.11). By default, the collections folders are already *pathed* (referenced) to the program files provided by LayOut, now add your own folder locations. This will give you easy access to your custom title blocks, templates, and scrapbooks.

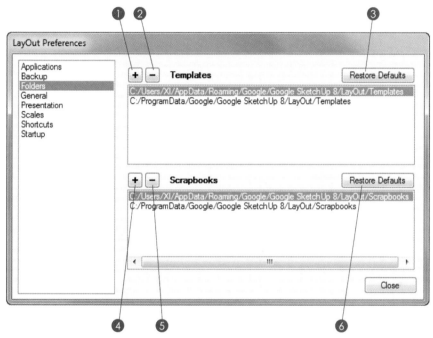

Figure 10.11 The Folders tab

1. Templates are displayed in the Getting Started window on the New tab. They can be title blocks, plain paper, or graph paper. You can add more locations by clicking on the plus sign (+).

2. Click on the minus sign (−) to remove a selected folder from the Templates collection.

3. Click the Restore Defaults button to go back to the LayOut default folders.

4. The Scrapbooks folder contents are displayed in the Scrapbooks Inspector. Scrapbooks are LayOut presentations that contain prebuilt pieces of annotation and palettes for use in other LayOut presentations. Add more locations by clicking on the plus sign (+).

5. Click on the minus sign (–) to remove a folder from the Scrapbooks collection.

6. Click the Restore Defaults button to go back to the LayOut default folders.

General Tab

The General settings are the catch-all settings that just don't fit anywhere else (Figure 10.12).

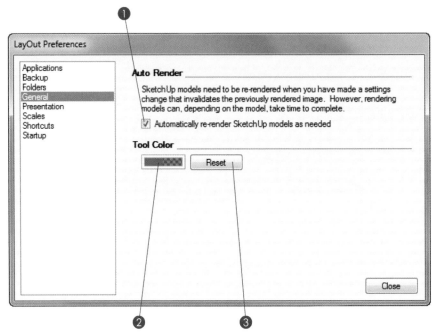

Figure 10.12 The General tab

1. When you update a model or make any settings changes that invalidate the previously rendered image, you will have to re-render your SketchUp model. The Auto Render setting, when turned on, will automatically render all viewports that need to be rendered.

TIP The Auto Render setting is also available in the SketchUp Model Inspector.

2. Change the color of the tools by clicking on the color block. This automatically opens the Color palette where you can select a color from several different tabs: Wheel, RGB, HSB, Grays, Image, and List. Typically, the first three tabs provide the easiest way to make the color selection you want.

3. Click on the Reset button to go back to the default LayOut tool color.

Presentation Tab

When you are using multiple monitors to make a presentation, you can display the presentation on the Same monitor as window, Primary monitor, or the Secondary monitor. You can make this selection in the Presentation tab (Figure 10.13).

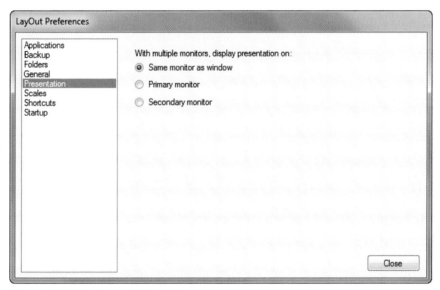

Figure 10.13 The Presentation tab

Scales Tab

Under the Scales tab, you can manage the available scales at which to render your drawings (Figure 10.14).

1. The Available Model Scales section lists all of the scales that are available in LayOut.

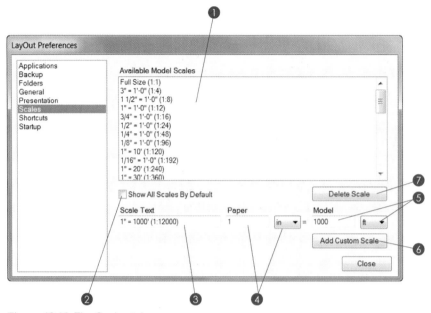

Figure 10.14 The Scales tab

2. Check the Show All Scales by Default check box to list all of the scales in the SketchUp Model dialog box. Uncheck the Show All Scales by Default check box to filter the scales based on the LayOut document's units setting. Documents using metric units will display only metric scales, and documents using imperial units will display only imperial scales.

3. The Scale Text box displays the name of a scale. This box will fill in automatically when you create a new scale; you can decide if you want to rename the scale.

4. To add a new custom scale, such as 1′ = 1000′-0″, click in the Paper text box and enter **1** (the paper distance). Set the units as inches.

5. In the Model text box, define how the paper relates to the model space. Enter **1000** in the Model text box and choose ft as the units.

6. Click the Add Custom Scale button to finish.

7. To delete any scales that you do not need, click on the unwanted scale and then click the Delete Scale button. Hold down the Ctrl key to make multiple selections, or hold down the Shift key to select everything between two selections, then click the Delete Scale button.

Shortcuts Tab

You can add keyboard shortcuts to expedite the drafting process in LayOut (Figure 10.15).

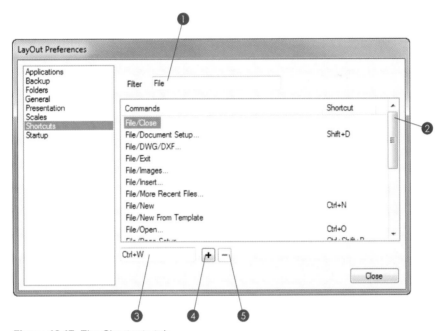

Figure 10.15 The Shortcuts tab

1. To help locate what you are looking for faster, enter a command into the filter.

2. Using the bar on the right side, scroll down to see all of the commands that are eligible for a keyboard shortcut.

3. Enter the desired shortcut key into the text box. Use modifier keys such as Ctrl, Alt, and Shift to make several variations of one key.

4. Click on the plus sign (+) to add the current shortcut.

5. To remove an already assigned shortcut, select a command that already has a shortcut and then click on the minus sign (−).

TIP See Chapter 11, "The Professional's LayOut Environment," for tips on adding custom keyboard shortcuts and optimizing the LayOut interface.

Startup Tab

Upon first opening LayOut, you can tell it what to do to get started (Figure 10.16).

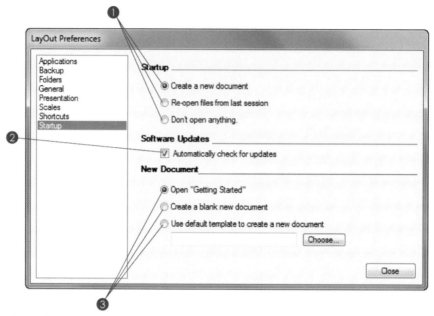

Figure 10.16 The Startup tab

1. Upon opening, you can tell LayOut what to do to get started. Choose Create a New Document, Re-open Files from Last Session, or Don't Do Anything. The settings you choose in the Startup tab are really based on your personal preferences.

2. The self-explanatory Automatically Check for Updates setting is a good one to turn on so your software is always current.

3. Once LayOut is open, you can tell LayOut what to do when you start a New Document. Choose from Open "Getting Started" (opens the window), Create a New Blank Document, and Use Default Template to Create a New Document (selects the default you've indicated).

INSPECTORS

Inspectors give you full control over LayOut's geometry, viewports, and annotations. Take a moment to become familiar with all of the LayOut Inspectors. All Inspectors are accessed from the Window drop-down menu in LayOut.

Colors Inspector

The Colors Inspector does not stand alone; it mainly supports the Text Style and Shape Style Inspectors, along with any dialogs or menus that require a color selection (Figure 10.17). When choosing colors for strokes, fills, and text you will use the Color Selection tools in the Colors Inspector.

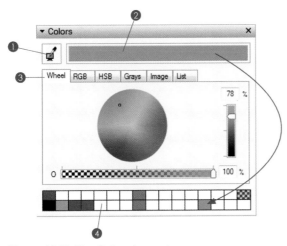

Figure 10.17 The Colors Inspector

1. The sample color from Screen tool allows you to match the active color to any pixel on your screen.

2. The Active Color Selection box displays the results from the Color Pickers.

3. This Inspector box has six tabs that accomplish the same goal of selecting a color: Wheel, RGB, HSB, Grays, Image, and List. Each tab allows you to mix and create using different properties of colors, although typically the first three are the easiest to use.

4. Click and drag your color selection to the white squares at the bottom of the Colors Inspector to create a collection of favorite colors for easy use in any LayOut presentation. These favorites are local to your machine and will be available for every LayOut presentation that you open.

Shape Style Inspector

The Shape Style Inspector is where you change the appearance of shapes and lines (Figure 10.18). If an entity is selected, modifying the shape style will affect the selection. If no entity is selected, modifying the shape style will set the current tool's Shape Style defaults.

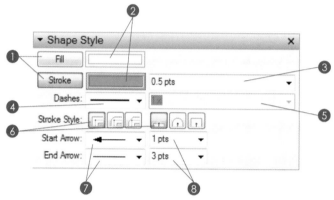

Figure 10.18 The Shape Style Inspector

1. When an entity is selected, you can toggle on the fill and stroke. *Fill* refers to the color within the shape. *Stroke* refers to the line surrounding the shape as well as any single lines (Figure 10.19). In Figure 10.18, the Fill is toggled off and the Stroke is toggled on, indicated by the blue highlight on the button.

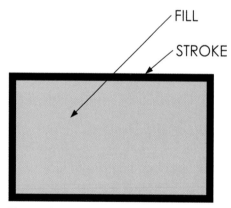

Figure 10.19 Stroke and Fill

2. Click on the Fill or Stroke color to modify it within the Colors Inspector. In Figure 10.18, the Stroke color is active in the Colors Inspector, indicated by the darker box around the color swatch.

3. Change the stroke thickness by clicking on the Stroke Thickness drop-down menu. Select a stroke thickness from the list or type in your own number and press Enter.

4. Assign dashes to a stroke by selecting a dashes pattern from the Dashes drop-down menu. A Dash pattern must be assigned to choose a dash's Scale.

5. Adjust the Dash pattern's length interval with the dash's Scale drop-down menu. Select a dash's Scale from the list, or type in your own number and press Enter.

6. Stroke Style refers to the visual properties of the edges around the shape. Corners can be set to miter, round, or beveled. Ends can be set to flat, round, or square. Miter corners with flat ends will typically give you the most desired effects.

7. You can adjust the Start Arrow and End Arrow lines by clicking on the drop-down menu and selecting from several arrow types.

8. Adjust the size of an arrow by clicking on the Arrow Scale drop-down menu with numbers. Select an Arrow Scale from the list, or type in your own number and press Enter.

SketchUp Model Inspector

The SketchUp Model Inspector provides settings that affect the manner in which SketchUp Models are displayed in LayOut. The SketchUp Model Inspector has two tabs: View and Styles.

View Tab

The View tab contains the settings to adjust what is shown in the selected viewport as well as how it is shown (Figure 10.20). The most effective workflow is to first create scenes in SketchUp that already have all of the camera view, style, and shadow properties assigned. Then in LayOut, select a scene from the View tab within the SketchUp Model Inspector. You must select a viewport in order to use the SketchUp Model Inspector to modify a viewport's properties.

1. Use the Scenes drop-down menu to choose from scenes already created in the SketchUp model. Using Scenes gives you the most control over a viewport and is by far the best method to use for this workflow.

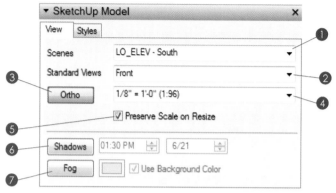

Figure 10.20 The SketchUp Model Inspector's View tab

2. Use the Standard Views drop-down menu to access top, bottom, front, back, left, and right views.

3. With the viewport selected, click on the Ortho button to toggle between perspective and parallel projection views.

4. Click on the Scale drop-down menu to assign an architectural scale to the selected viewport. A viewport must be selected and Ortho must be on in order to assign a scale.

5. The Preserve Scale on Resize button will keep your drawing at the scale regardless of how you modify the viewport. When this check box is unchecked, the drawing will change scale to match the modified viewport.

TIP Scale a viewport about the center by holding down the Alt key (Command on Mac) and clicking and dragging on the perimeter. Scaling about the center overrides the "Preserve Scale on Resize" setting.

6. Click the Shadows button to display shadows in the selected viewport. You can modify the shadows by adjusting the time of day and date.

7. Click the Fog button to display fog in the selected viewport. Click on the color swatch to change the color of the fog, or check the Use Background Color box to set the fog color to be the same as the Style's background.

TIP LayOut has limited Shadow and Fog settings. For the best results, create a scene in SketchUp with the desired view, as well as the desired Shadow and Fog settings, and then assign the scene to a viewport in LayOut.

Styles Tab

The Styles tab gives you access to any style in your model and even in your Styles library (Figure 10.21).

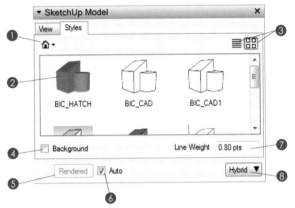

Figure 10.21 The SketchUp Model Inspector's Styles tab

1. Click on the house icon to navigate through the In Model styles. Also, use the drop-down menu to navigate through your entire Styles library.

2. Change the style applied to a viewport by first selecting the viewport and then clicking on a style within the Styles tab.

3. Display the Styles in list view or thumbnail view, depending on your personal preference.

4. Click on the Background check box to fill in the background of a viewport. This means that nothing behind the viewport will be visible through the images in the foreground. This setting comes into play when you are creating a collage of several views and models and do not want the sky or background to show.

5. An exclamation mark on a yellow triangle next to the Render button indicates that a viewport needs to be rendered. To render a viewport, select the viewport and then click on the Render button in the SketchUp Model Inspector. Once the viewport is rendered, the Render button will change to Rendered.

6. Check the Auto check box to automatically render all viewports when they are out of date. This setting is also available in the Preferences dialog on the General tab.

7. Change the overall line weight applied to the selected viewport by entering a new number.

8. To change the rendering settings of a selected viewport, click on the Rendering Settings drop-down menu and choose Raster, Vector, or Hybrid.

Line Weight Theory

The number you enter into the Line Weight field is the thinnest line that will be displayed in the viewport. Any profiles, section cuts, or depth cues will be multiplied by this number to thicken them up (Figure 10.22). For instance, if the section cuts are set to 3, the profiles are set to 2, and the viewport Line Weight is set to .25; the thinnest lines will be .25, the profiles will be .5, and the section cuts will be .75.

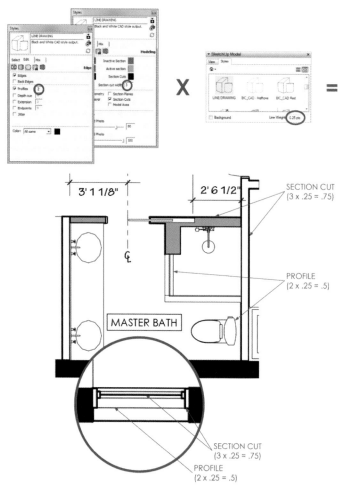

Figure 10.22 A line weight in LayOut is the product of the multipliers assigned to styles in SketchUp, combined with the line weight assigned to the viewport in LayOut.

You will need to adjust this number based on the detail in your drawing as well as the size and scale of your drawing. The topic of line weights and stacking viewports is covered in Chapter 20, "Construction Documents."

Rendering Settings Theory

LayOut provides expanded rendering settings. You should set each viewport to render independently of the next as a vector, raster, or hybrid. Raster is ideal for anything heavy with texture images (Figure 10.23), and Vector is ideal for large, high-resolution prints of fairly simple line drawings (Figure 10.24). A hybrid combines both styles for a composite view with vector linework and raster texture images (Figure 10.25). Keep in mind that hybrid rendering can often take up to twice as long to complete.

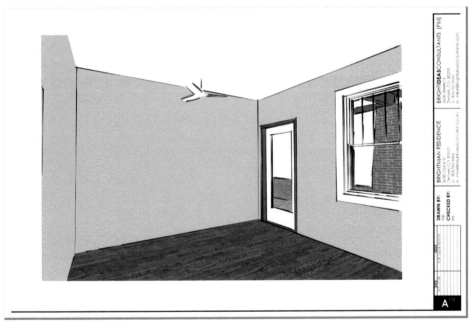

Figure 10.23 The Raster rendering setting is best utilized on viewports with complex styles and texture images.

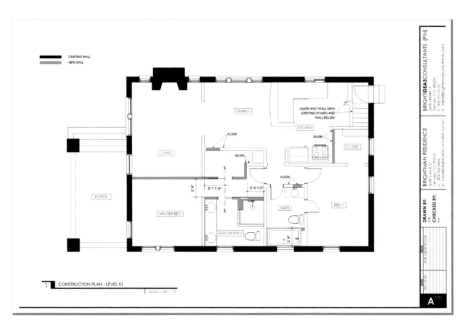

Figure 10.24 The Vector rendering setting is best utilized on viewports representing CAD-style black-and-white output.

Figure 10.25 The Hybrid setting is best utilized on viewports that have fairly simple styles with straight lines, combined with texture images and shadows.

Dimension Style Inspector

The Dimension Style Inspector gives you full control over dimensions (Figure 10.26). Use it to set the default properties for the Dimension tool. Also, you can select a dimension and modify the properties of the selection within the Dimension Style Inspector.

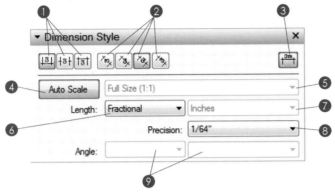

Figure 10.26 The Dimension Style Inspector

1. Adjust the placement of the dimension text as either above, center, or below the dimension line.

2. Set the dimension text orientation to either vertical, horizontal, aligned, or perpendicular. Typically, dimensions are best shown aligned.

3. Toggle whether or not the units are displayed at the end of the dimension text.

4. Auto Scale will automatically set the dimension scale, depending on the scale assigned to the viewport you click on with the Dimension tool.

5. When the Auto Scale feature is turned off, you can set the Dimension Scale manually.

6. Length can be displayed as Decimal, Architectural, Engineering, or Fractional.

7. The unit type can be set to Inches, Feet, Millimeters, Centimeters, Meters, or Points only when the Length value is set to Decimal.

8. The Precision of the dimensions can be set to 1/64″ or .01″, the same precision tolerances used in SketchUp.

9. Angular dimensions can be set to radians or degrees. The precision tolerances can be set up to .01 degrees or .0001 radians. The Angular Dimension tool must be activated to adjust these settings.

TIP The visual properties of dimension lines are set within the Shape Style Inspector. Activate the Dimensions tool, and then set the default stroke thickness, arrow type, arrow scale, and color within the Shape Style Inspector.

Text Style Inspector

The Text Style Inspector has a familiar interface that is used in most word processors and email programs (Figure 10.27). Activate the Text tool and then use the Text Style Inspector to set the default text properties. You can also select a piece of text within a text box and modify the properties of the selection with the Text Style Inspector.

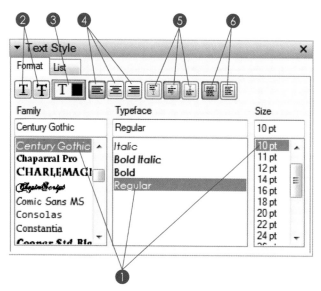

Figure 10.27 The Text Style Inspector

1. In LayOut you can access any font that is loaded in your system fonts. Choose a font family, typeface, and size. Keep in mind that you can select from the Size list or manually enter a font size that is not listed.

2. You can apply an underline and/or a strikethrough to text.

3. Click on the color swatch to modify the text color. This automatically opens the Colors Inspector where you can select a color. The active swatch will have a darker box around it, as shown in Figure 10.27.

4. Justify the text to the left, center, or right of the Text window.

5. Anchor the text to the top, middle, or bottom of the Text window.

6. Text in LayOut can be either bounded or unbounded. *Bounded text* is contained within a window and will drop to the next line as it approaches the boundary of the Text window. *Unbounded text* runs straight across the screen uninterrupted.

Pages Inspector

The Pages Inspector is where you manage the pages in your presentation (Figure 10.28).

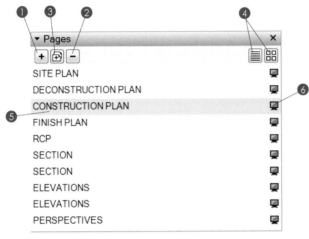

Figure 10.28 The Pages Inspector

1. Click on the plus sign (+) to add a new page.

2. Click on the minus sign (–) to delete the current page.

3. Click on the Duplicate Page button to make a copy of the current page. You'll be using this button frequently to create new pages and at the same time copy annotation pieces of the title block from page to page. Once a page is duplicated, it is easier to just erase what you don't need.

4. Display the pages in list view or thumbnail view. Typically, list view is sleeker and allows you to see more of the pages in your presentation.

5. The current page is highlighted in blue. Double-click on a page name to rename the page. Click and drag a page to reposition it within your presentation.

6. Click on the monitor icon to the right of the page name to toggle whether or not that page is included in the screen presentation.

TIP Right-click on the page to see a context menu. This also allows you to move the page up or down, rename the page, duplicate it, and choose whether or not to include the page in your screen presentation.

Layers Inspector

Layers in LayOut are similar to most page-creation software in that they control what is shown on top by the layer order, as well as what layers are visible. You manage layers in the Layers Inspector (Figure 10.29).

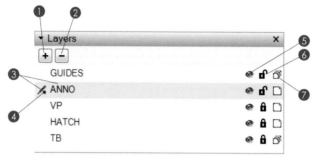

Figure 10.29 The Layers Inspector

1. Click on the plus sign (+) to add a new layer.
2. Click on the minus sign (–) to delete the selected layer. If you delete a layer with entities on it, you will be prompted to delete the entities completely or move them to the active layer.
3. The active layer is highlighted in blue and is also indicated by a pencil icon to the left of the layer name.
4. A selected entity's layer is represented by a small box to the left of the layer name.
5. Click on the eye icon to toggle the layer visibility on and off. The entities on the layer will disappear and reappear. Layer visibility is set on a per-page basis, meaning that if you turn a layer off on one page, it is still visible on other pages.
6. Click on the padlock icon to lock the layer. *Locking* a layer prevents the entities on it from being deleted or modified. Locking a layer applies across all pages.
7. Click on the last icon to toggle whether or not the layer is shared. A shared layer's contents will appear the same on every page. If the contents of a shared layer are modified, they will be modified on every page. Repeating entities, such as title blocks and guides, should be on a shared layer.

TIP To change an entity's layer, first make the layer to which you want to move the entity active. Next, right-click on the entity and choose Move to Current Layer. Be sure to move the active layer back to the desired layer; it is easy to forget this step!

Scrapbooks Inspector

The Scrapbooks Inspector allows you to seamlessly access collections of prebuilt pieces of annotation from preloaded libraries as well as your own (Figure 10.30).

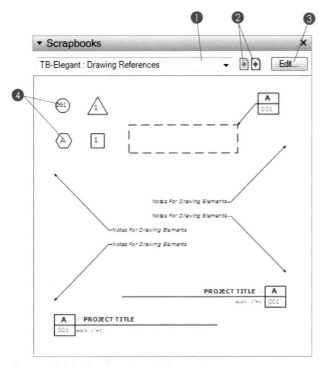

Figure 10.30 The Scrapbooks Inspector

1. Select a scrapbook collection from the drop-down menu. LayOut comes with several scrapbooks that stylistically match the preloaded title blocks.

2. Use the arrows next to the Collections drop-down menu to navigate through the pages of the scrapbook.

3. Click on the Edit button to edit the scrapbook. This automatically opens the LayOut scrapbook file. Add, edit, or delete scrapbook pieces, and then close the

file and save your changes. The updated scrapbook will appear in the Scrapbook Inspector.

4. Add a scrapbook by clicking on a Scrapbook symbol in the Scrapbook area, and then click in your presentation to place it.

TIP Scrapbooks aren't some magical file type buried in LayOut. A *scrapbook* is simply a LayOut file containing lines, shapes, text, and fills grouped together into meaningful symbols. You will create and organize your own custom collection of Scrapbooks in Chapter 13: "LayOut Collections."

Instructor Inspector

The Instructor Inspector will help you explore LayOut and find hidden functions buried in the tools (Figure 10.31). Activate any tool and you'll see the instructions for using that tool, as well as invaluable modifier keys associated with the tool.

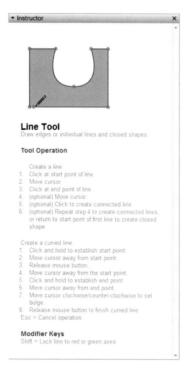

Figure 10.31 The Instructor Inspector

CHAPTER POINTS

☑ The Document Setup dialog box controls the settings that travel with a model.

☑ The Preferences dialog box controls the settings that are local to your machine and are the same every time you open LayOut.

☑ Take the time to become familiar with the settings that each menu and inspector controls, and then use this chapter as a reference.

Chapter 11
The Professional's LayOut Environment

A professional's work environment is streamlined, logical, and organized. LayOut provides a default environment that is great for getting started, but ultimately it is not adequate for a professional. Fortunately, you can customize the LayOut environment in several different ways to make it work best for you. You can customize toolbars, optimize system resources, and remove visual clutter. By adding your own set of shortcuts, you can even access all of your frequently used commands with just a few keystrokes. In this chapter, you will learn how to use all of the settings needed to increase productivity, computer performance, and quality of design.

NEW PRESENTATION

To get started and create a new presentation, follow the steps detailed here (Figure 11.1).

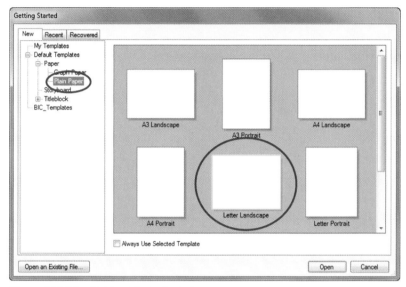

Figure 11.1 The Getting Started window

1. Open LayOut.
2. If you see the Getting Started window, move on to the next step; otherwise, click on the File drop-down menu and choose New.
3. Select Default Templates › Paper › Plain Paper.
4. Select the Letter Landscape template.
5. Click the Open button to begin.

SYSTEM PREFERENCES

System preferences do not travel with a model, but they will be the same for every LayOut presentation you create on your computer. To set your preferences, click on the Edit (LayOut on Mac) drop-down menu and choose Preferences. Take a moment to optimize the System Preferences with the following settings.

Applications

LayOut is powerful by itself, but it can also be complemented by external programs that exclusively work with text and raster graphics. You can assign external applications to handle these text and image files in the Applications tab (Figure 11.2).

1. In the Applications tab, click the Choose button for the Default Image Editor.

2. Navigate to and select the executable (.exe) file for your favorite image editor.

3. Click the Open button to assign the Default Image Editor.

4. Repeat steps 1 through 3 for the Default Text Editor.

Figure 11.2 The Applications tab optimized

TIP When you're navigating to the application shortcut or .exe file, first look on your desktop. If you can't find a shortcut there, you can find it somewhere in the C:/program files folder.

Folders

To access your own custom collections in LayOut, add default folders in the Folders Tab by following the steps listed here (Figure 11.3).

1. Click on the plus sign (+) next to Templates, and then navigate to and select the RESOURCES/TEMPLATES folder.

2. Click the Open button. Now any template added to the TEMPLATES folder can be accessed from the Getting Started window in LayOut.

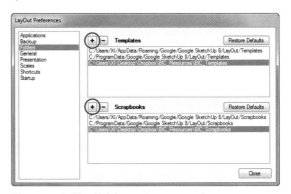

Figure 11.3 The Folders tab optimized

3. Click on the plus sign (+) next to Scrapbooks, and then navigate to and select the RESOURCES/SCRAPBOOKS folder.

4. Click the Open button. Now any scrapbook file added to the Scrapbooks folder can be accessed from the Scrapbooks Inspector.

Auto Render

Rendering is the number one memory hog in LayOut. Depending on the size, complexity, and organization of the model, rendering can take a significant amount of time to complete. It is important to keep in mind that a clean and organized SketchUp model is the best way to shorten rendering times. In addition, it is pertinent to render only at the necessary resolution and only when absolutely necessary.

The Auto Render feature allows LayOut to always render a viewport when it is updated and needs to be rendered. This is a helpful button to have turned on when you are learning to use LayOut; but as your presentations grow and your SketchUp models become more detailed, you will want to turn off this setting and manually control rendering (Figure 11.4). Consider keeping Auto Render off at all times, and render using your keyboard commands, using the SketchUp Model Inspector, or by right-clicking on the presentation background and choosing Render Images on Page.

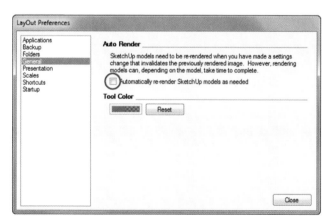

Figure 11.4 Rendering settings optimized

To manually control rendering, follow these steps:

1. Navigate to the General tab.

2. Uncheck the Auto Render check box.

TIP The Auto Render setting is also available in the SketchUp Model Inspector, where it is called Auto. Keep in mind that this setting does not travel with the presentation; it is a global setting that applies to every presentation you open in LayOut.

Shortcuts

Just as in SketchUp, keyboard shortcuts will enable you to work faster. Try to avoid using the icons on your screen, even if it feels slower at first. Once you learn all of the keyboard shortcuts, you will become amazingly faster (Figure 11.5).

Figure 11.5 Use the Shortcuts tab to add keyboard shortcuts to your favorite and most-used commands.

1. Click on the Shortcuts tab.
2. Type **Render** in the Filter text box. As you are typing, the list will get shorter.
3. Click the Render Images in Document command.
4. Click in the Shortcut text box at the bottom-left corner of the dialog. Hold down the Ctrl and Shift keys, and then press the R key. (The modifier keys will appear in the text box.)
5. Click on the plus sign (+) to add the shortcut.

Consider adding the helpful keyboard shortcuts in Figure 11.6.

HELPFUL SHORTCUTS	
KEY	**COMMAND**
Ctrl + R	Other/Render Images on Page
Ctrl + Shift + R	Other/Render Images in Document
Ctrl + Right	Pages/Next
Ctrl + Left	Pages/Previous
Q	Tools/Join
W	Tools/Split
Shift +E	View/Zoom to Fit
Ctrl + D	Window/Hide Tray
Ctrl + G	Edit/Group
Ctrl + Shift + G	Edit/Ungroup
Shift + D	File/Document Setup

Figure 11.6 Suggested keyboard shortcuts

TIP You can add a simple shortcut such as a letter, or you can add combinations of keys by holding down modifier keys such as Alt, Ctrl, and Shift while you press a key. The modifier keys give you almost endless possibilities for adding keyboard shortcuts.

CUSTOM TOOLBARS

The default toolbar is adequate, but a few vital buttons are missing from it. Not every command has a logical keyboard shortcut; to compensate, you can keep a row of tool icons on your screen. You can optimize the LayOut workspace by building your own custom toolbars (Figure 11.7).

1. Click on the View drop-down menu and choose Toolbars › Customize. Click the New button to add a new toolbar.

2. Name the toolbar **DRAWING**.

3. From the drop-down menu, select an initial location for the toolbar. The

Figure 11.7 The Customize Toolbars window

exact location doesn't really matter because you can drag the toolbar and dock and undock freely, but Floating makes it easier for you to work on the new toolbar. Click OK.

4. Click on the Commands tab (Figure 11.8).

5. Sort through the categories to narrow your search, and select the Tools/Lines category.

6. Drag the Line command from the Commands column into your new toolbar.

7. Continue adding the desired commands to the toolbar. Click the Close button when you are finished.

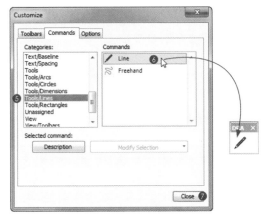

Figure 11.8 The Commands tab

Consider turning off the Main toolbar and adding these custom toolbars to your professional LayOut environment (Figure 11.9):

DRAWING: Line, Rectangle, Circle

ANNOTATION: Text, Leader Text, Dimensions

MODIFICATION: Select, Split, Join, Erase, Style

PRESENTATION: Next Page, Previous Page, Duplicate Page, Delete Page

NAVIGATION: Zoom to fit, Actual Size. .

ALIGN: Top, Bottom, Right, Left, vertically, horizontally.

ARRANGE: Move Backward, Move to Back, Move to Front, Move Forward.

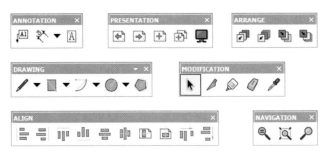

Figure 11.9 Custom toolbars

TIP Right-click on a toolbar and choose Lock the Toolbars. This will hold the toolbars in place and remove the draggable lines for docking and undocking. You can always right-click on a toolbar again to unlock it.

You can personalize some of the toolbar behaviors on the options tab. Be sure to turn off all fades and animations to optimize system performance (Figure 11.10). Activating the Show Screen Tips on Toolbars option will be helpful when you're learning to use a tool. Even more valuable is to turn on the Show Shortcut keys in Screen Tips option to remind you of the shortcut key.

Figure 11.10 The Toolbar Options tab optimized

TRAYS

Trays allow you to organize the LayOut Inspectors in the Windows operating system only. Create custom trays to make specific Inspectors readily available for certain tasks. By grouping Inspectors together by task, you can streamline your workflow. Just follow these steps (Figure 11.11).

Figure 11.11 The PRESENTATION and ANNOTATION custom trays

1. Click on the Window drop-down menu and choose New Tray.

2. Name the new tray **PRESENTATION**. The PRESENTATION tray will contain everything you need to navigate your LayOut presentation.

3. Check the SketchUp Model, Pages, and Layers Inspector check boxes.

4. Click the Add button to finish creating the tray.

5. Click on the Window drop-down menu and choose New Tray.

6. Name the new tray **ANNOTATION**. The ANNOTATION tray will contain everything you need to make annotations in your presentation.

7. Check the Colors, Shape Style, Dimension Style, Text Style, and Scrapbooks Inspector check boxes.

8. Click the Add button to finish creating the tray.

After you've created the tray, click the pushpin icon next to the Close button to set the tray to auto-hide. Now, when the tray is not in use, it will automatically close and give you more working screen space. To access the tray, simply hover on the Tray tab. Click and drag on a tray to make it floating, or dock it at the top, bottom, or sides of the LayOut application. Now that you know all of the methods, you can organize your screen any way you like.

TIP If you click on the View drop-down menu and choose Restore Default Workspace, you will return to the default LayOut environment and all custom trays and toolbars will be deleted.

TIP If you don't prefer the Auto Hide feature, use the Ctrl+D keyboard shortcut to toggle between hiding and unhiding the trays.

BASIC LAYOUT TEMPLATE

Create a basic, blank layout template to use as a starting point for any new presentations or title blocks you make in the future. All of the settings that travel with the file will be optimized to ensure that LayOut is running at full speed.

Rendering Quality

Each model has a paper quality setting (Figure 11.12). Set the Edit Quality to Low, which is acceptable for the screen resolution. Typically, the Low setting will render everything well enough that you can evaluate a model without having to wait for a high-quality render. Set the Output Quality to High for exports and presentations. Rendering at a High setting is worth the wait when you're creating the final output.

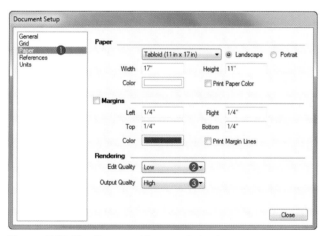

Figure 11.12 The Paper settings optimized

To optimize the Paper settings, follow these steps:

1. Click on the File drop-down menu and choose Document Setup › Paper.
2. Click on the Edit Quality drop-down menu and choose Low.
3. Click on the Output Quality drop-down menu and choose High.

Layers

Layers in LayOut work in the traditional fashion of stacking and visibility. If a layer is turned on, the contents on that layer are visible. If a layer is turned off, the contents on that layer are not visible. The stacking order of the layers will determine which entities are on top. So, if a layer is on the bottom of the stack, any object on the layers above will cover up the bottom layer entities.

There are only three layers that a professional absolutely needs in every presentation; they are ANNOTATIONS, DRAWINGS, and TITLE BLOCK.

At the top of the stack is the ANNOTATIONS layer. This layer contains labels, leaders, dimensions, text, and lines that further explain drawings and images. Also on the ANNOTATIONS layer is anything within the title block that does not repeat, such as page numbers and descriptions. This is typically the most-used layer in LayOut, and it is usually unlocked.

The DRAWINGS layer contains any entity that is inserted into LayOut. This includes SketchUp models, images, maps, and photos. Basically, anything that you are going to annotate belongs on the DRAWINGS layer. Typically, you will insert several entities onto the DRAWINGS layer, and then lock the layer as you annotate.

The TITLE BLOCK layer is a shared layer that contains the presentation graphics (Figure 11.13). This layer appears on every page of your presentation. Repeating graphics, watermarks, project information, logos, and page dividing lines belong on the TITLE BLOCK layer. Entities on this layer might be modified at the beginning of a project, but the layer typically remains locked most of the time.

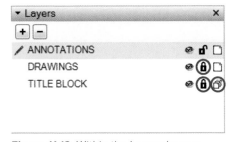

Figure 11.13 Within the Layers Inspector, add the suggested default layers in LayOut.

To create the new layers, follow these steps:

1. Click on the plus sign (+) to add another new layer. Name the new layer **TITLE BLOCK**.

2. Click on the Share Layer toggle to share the layer.

3. To lock the layer, click on the padlock next to the layer name.

4. Click on the plus sign (+) again to add another new layer. Name the new layer **DRAWINGS**.

5. To lock the layer, click on the padlock next to the layer name.

6. Within the Layers Inspector, click on the plus sign (+) to add a new layer. Name the new layer **ANNOTATIONS**.

Now that you have optimized the presentation, save it at this clean, blank state to use for creating new presentations and title blocks in the future (Figure 11.14).

Just follow these steps:

1. Click on the File drop-down menu and choose Save as Template. Name the presentation **BIC_8.5 x 11 – Landscape**.

3. Select the RESOURCES/TEMPLATES folder.

4. Click the OK button. Now this template will be available every time you start a new presentation in LayOut.

Figure 11.14 The Save As Template dialog.

CHAPTER POINTS

☑ Keeping your LayOut workspace clean and organized will help increase your speed and efficiency.

☑ Every professional's workspace evolves based on personal preference. It is important to know all of the ways you can optimize your workspace, but you don't need to use all of them.

☑ There are also features you can turn off within your operating system. Personalize your Windows experience and turn off Transparencies in Windows. When you're working on a laptop, be sure that you are using the High Performance setting, rather than Balanced or Power Saver.

☑ Spend a small amount of time optimizing your work environment, and you will save an enormous amount of time on every project.

☑ The basic BIC_8.5x11 - Landscape template can be used to start any new document or title block in the future, with the settings and layers already optimized.

Chapter 12

LayOut Tools

Layout has a simple, sleek toolset, but don't let the simplicity fool you! With the toolset, you can accurately create any shape you would ever need. It is deceptively simple. Every tool is described in detail in this chapter. Take a few minutes to read the description for each one, open a blank presentation, and then perform the steps following the description to practice using the tool.

NAVIGATING LAYOUT

LayOut is essentially a hybrid 2D page-creation and drafting software package. The best way to navigate the 2D LayOut environment is to use a three-button scroll-wheel mouse (Figure 12.1). Push down on the scroll-wheel to pan up, down, left, and right. Roll the scroll-wheel toward the screen to zoom in, and roll away from the screen to zoom out. Just as in SketchUp, the focal point of your navigation is your cursor.

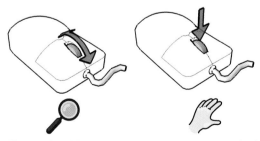

Figure 12.1 When you use a three-button scroll-wheel mouse, the Navigation tools in LayOut are always at your fingertips.

DRAWING TOOLS

Use the Drawing tools to add geometry, symbols, annotations, title blocks, and decorations to your LayOut presentation. Each of the Drawing tools has additional features and options buried within it. Pay special attention to the modifier keys and specific processes required to effectively use all of the functions of the tools in LayOut.

Default Settings

When you activate any of the Drawing tools, the Drawing tool's default settings are displayed in the Shape Style Inspector. By adjusting the properties in the Shape Style Inspector, you can change the default settings for any tool that draws lines and fills. Test the new default properties of the Drawing tools by switching to the Text tool, and then go back to any Drawing tool. You will see the settings switch back when you change tools.

All of the Drawing tools share the same default settings. For instance, if you change the default fill for the Rectangle tool, this fill will also apply to circles, lines, and polygons.

Use the Pick Style tool to set the default settings for any tool. Just follow these steps:

1. Activate any Drawing tool.

2. Hover on a scrapbook and click to match the current tool's default settings to the selected scrapbook's settings. (See Chapter 13, "LayOut Collections," for more information on using scrapbooks as time-saving palettes.)

3. To match an entity in the presentation area, press the S key, which is the default shortcut for the Pick Style tool.

4. Click on an entity to match the current tool's Inspector settings to the entity that you sampled. The entity can be in the presentation space or in a scrapbook.

TIP A tool's default settings are some of those "buried" features in LayOut. It may not be quite clear how to use the default settings when you first attempt to use them. Patiently studying and practicing so you can fully understand how the default settings operate will save you a tremendous amount of time in the future.

Lines

Use the Line tools to create straight lines, curved lines, and freehand lines. Generating lines is a key component of drawing, and there is no exception in LayOut. The Line tools will help you create annotations, title blocks, schedule grids, tables, ground lines, details, and many other entities. Take a moment to explore all of the methods for drawing different types of lines.

Straight Lines

The simplest type of line to create is a straight line (Figure 12.2).

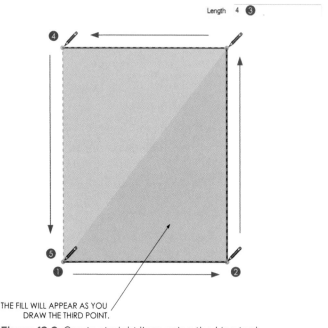

Length 4 ③

THE FILL WILL APPEAR AS YOU
DRAW THE THIRD POINT.

Figure 12.2 Create straight lines using the Line tool.

1. Activate the Line tool and set the stroke width to 1. Turn on the Fill and set the color to Gray. Click once in the presentation area to start.

2. Move your cursor to the right along the red axis, and click again to finish the segment.

3. Move your cursor up on the green axis. Note that the Line tool has Fill properties. This time, let go of the mouse and type a precise dimension, such as **4**, then press Enter.

4. Move your cursor back to the left along the red axis. Note that there is an inference engine. To finish the line segment, click where the inference line meets the active line.

5. Move your cursor back down on the green axis, and click on the starting point to finish.

TIP Press the Esc key at any time to cancel the current line segment. This will also cancel just about any command in LayOut.

Once a segment is finished, you can click on an endpoint with the Line tool to continue the segment. You will see the previous line segments light up blue, indicating that you are continuing that segment. Follow the previous steps to continue the straight line segment.

TIP The *inference engine* in LayOut allows you to snap to and encourage inferences from endpoints, midpoints, and edges. It is very similar to the inference engine in SketchUp.

Curved Line

You aren't limited to straight lines. Using the Line tool, you can also create curves (Figure 12.3).

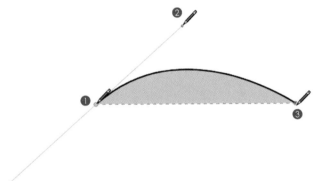

Figure 12.3 Create a curved line using the Line tool.

1. Click and drag away from the starting point to define the tangent line.
2. Release the cursor to set the curve's tangent line relative to the starting point.
3. Double-click to finish the line segment.

Instead of double-clicking to finish the line, click and drag again to continue the curved line segment.

Click and drag on an endpoint of a completed line to continue a curved line segment. The existing line segment will light up blue, indicating that you are continuing that segment.

TIP To add a straight line segment to a curved line, single-click to finish the curved line segment, then continue to single click to add straight lines. To add a curved line segment to a straight line, you can click and drag to finish the straight line segment and add a curved line segment.

Freehand Tool

Use the Freehand tool to create sketchy, loose, and organic forms (Figure 12.4). This tool is ideal for complementing drawings, tracing topography, creating sketchy annotations, and creating unique geometry.

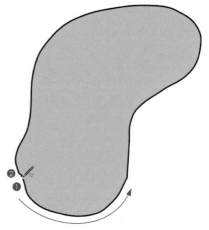

1. Activate the Freehand tool. Click and drag to draw a loose and sketchy line.

2. Release the click to finish the line.

Click and drag on an endpoint to continue the freehand line segment. The previous line segments will light up blue, indicating that you are continuing that segment.

Figure 12.4 The Freehand tool

Rectangles

LayOut's Rectangle tools enable you to draw rectangles and squares that are always on axis and in line with the paper (Figure 12.5). In addition to a traditional rectangle, LayOut has several types of rectangles: lozenged, bulged, and rounded. Each type has its own tool icon and each operates as described here.

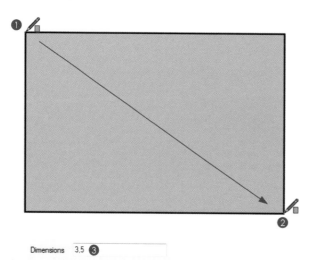

Figure 12.5 The Rectangle tool

To draw a rectangle, follow these steps:

1. Activate the Rectangle tool. Click once in the presentation area to start the rectangle.

2. Move your cursor away from the starting point to suggest a direction. Click once to loosely define the dimensions of the rectangle.

3. At this point, you can enter a precise dimension, such as **3,5**, then press Enter.

The other types of rectangles function exactly the same way (Figure 12.6).

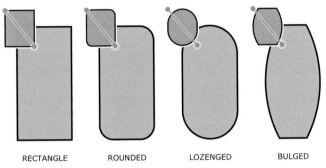

RECTANGLE   ROUNDED   LOZENGED   BULGED

Figure 12.6 Other types of Rectangle tools

A *rounded rectangle* has radiused corners. Activate the Rounded Rectangle tool, or the Rectangle tool, and then press the Up and Down arrow keys to change the radius. To enter a precise radius, type in the desired radius followed with an "r,"—for example, type **1/2r**, then press Enter. This will set the corners to be 1/2″ radius.

A *lozenged* rectangle has half circles at the long ends of the rectangle, so a square would actually appear as a circle. Ultimately, the Lozenged Rectangle tool creates a pill shape.

A *bulged rectangle* has arcs at the left and right side of the rectangle. Use the Up and Down arrow keys to adjust the bulge of the arcs. After you adjust the bulge, you can enter precise dimensions by typing a value and then pressing the Enter key.

There are also several modifier keys that apply to all types of rectangles. Hold down the Shift key to constrain any rectangle to a square. Hold down the Ctrl key (Option on Mac) to create the rectangle about the center point. Use the Up and Down arrow keys to adjust the rounded corners, or lozenged and bulged sides.

TIP LayOut's Measurements box is just like SketchUp's. The Measurements box is always waiting for your input and constantly switches the value, depending on which tool is active and the input LayOut needs to operate effectively.

Arcs

There are several methods for drawing an arc in LayOut. The one you use will depend on your personal preference and previous experience with other drafting programs. The most familiar method probably will be the 2-Point Arc tool because it is the one most similar to the Arc tool in SketchUp. Take a moment to explore all of the tools for drawing arcs.

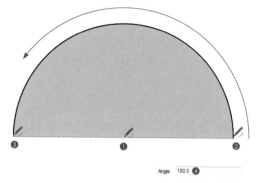

Figure 12.7 The Arc tool

Arc Tool

Using the Arc tool, you can create the outside of a pie chart with ease (Figure 12.7).
To do that, follow these steps:

1. Activate the Arc tool. Click once in the presentation area to define the center point.

2. Move your cursor to the right along the red axis to suggest a direction. Click again to define the start point of the arc.

3. Move your cursor away from the start point and click once more to loosely define the endpoint of the arc.

4. At this point, you can let go of the mouse and type a precise angle, such as **180**, then press Enter.

2-Point Arc Tool

The most familiar arc tool is strikingly similar to the Arc tool in SketchUp (Figure 12.8).

To create an arc with the 2-Point Arc tool, follow these steps:

1. Activate the 2-Point Arc tool. Click once in the presentation area to define the start point. Move your cursor away from the center point to suggest a direction.

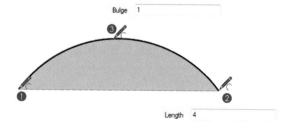

Figure 12.8 The 2-Point Arc tool

2. Click again to define the endpoint of the arc, or enter a precise distance and press Enter.

3. Move your cursor away from the endpoint and click once more to loosely define the bulge of the arc, or type a precise length, such as **3**, then press Enter.

3-Point Arc Tool

Using the 3-Point Arc tool, you can draw arcs about a pivot point (Figure 12.9).
To do that, follow these steps:

1. Activate the 3-Point Arc tool. Click once in the presentation area to define the start point.

2. Move your cursor away from the start point to suggest a direction and click again to define the pivot point of the arc.

3. Move your cursor away from the pivot point and click once more to define the length of the arc.

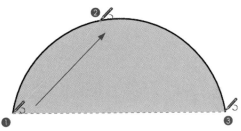

Figure 12.9 The 3-Point Arc tool

Pie Tool

With the Pie tool, you can fill in pie charts and recreate iconic video game characters with ease (Figure 12.10).

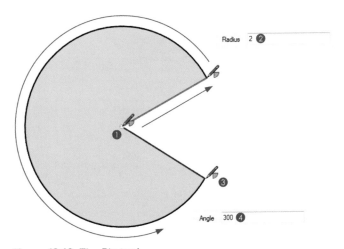

Figure 12.10 The Pie tool

Just follow these steps:

1. Activate the Pie tool. Click once in the presentation area to define the center point of the arc.

2. Move your cursor away from the center point, let go of the mouse, and type a precise radius such as **2**, then press Enter.

3. Move your cursor away from the start point; you can move in either direction, clockwise or counterclockwise.

4. Either click once more to loosely define the endpoint of the arc, or let go of the mouse and type a precise angle such as **300**, then press Enter.

Circles

Circles, ellipses, and polygons are all created the same way. Unlike SketchUp, there are true vector circles in LayOut, so there is no need to enter the number of sides.

Circle Tool

Use the Circle tool to draw circles (Figure 12.11).

Just follow these steps:

1. Activate the Circle tool. Click once to define the center point of the circle.

2. Move your cursor away from the center point to define the radius and click to loosely define the radius of the circle.

3. At this point, you can type a precise radius, such as **2**, then press Enter.

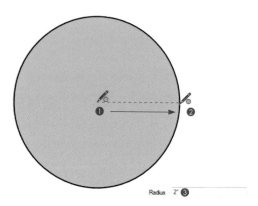

Figure 12.11 The Circle tool

Ellipse Tool

The Ellipse tool is a variation of the Circle tool that creates ellipses (Figure 12.12). This tool operates very much like the Rectangle tool. You can also create ellipses by drawing a circle, and then using the Select tool and Scale grips to distort it.

To create an ellipse, follow these steps:

1. Activate the Ellipse tool. Click once to define the start point of the ellipse.

2. Move your cursor away from the start point and click to loosely define the dimensions of the ellipse.

3. At this point you can type the precise dimensions, such as **3,2**, then press Enter.

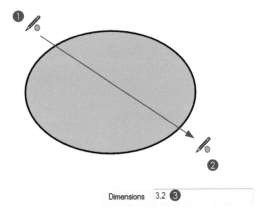

Figure 12.12 The Ellipse tool

The Ellipse tool also has modifier keys. Hold down the Shift key while creating an ellipse to constrain it to a circle. Hold down the Ctrl key (Option on Mac) to create the ellipse about a center point.

Polygon Tool

The Polygon tool creates geometric shapes with a defined number of sides (Figure 12.13).

1. Activate the Polygon tool. Upon activating the Polygon tool, immediately enter the desired number of sides and press Enter—for example, type **5s**, then press Enter.

2. Click once to define the center point of the polygon.

3. Move your cursor away from the center point and click to loosely define the radius of the polygon.

4. At this point, you can type a precise radius, such as **2**, then press Enter.

The Polygon tool also has modifier keys. Hold down the Shift key to lock the sides of the polygon to an axis. Hold down the Ctrl key (Option on Mac) to create a distorted polygon, similar to what you would create with the Ellipse tool.

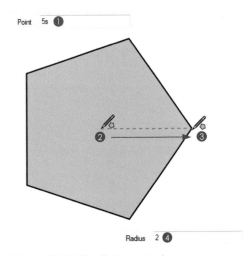

Figure 12.13 The Polygon tool

ANNOTATION TOOLS

Annotation tools give you the ability to explain the graphics in your 2D presentation. Add captions, leader text, and dimensions to provide another level of information.

Default Settings

When you activate any of the Annotation tools, the default settings will appear in the corresponding Inspectors. The Text tool, Label tool, and Dimension tool have default settings in the Text Style Inspector and the Shape Style Inspector. In addition to these Inspectors, the Dimension tool has default settings in the Dimension Style Inspector. You can change the default settings manually by going through each setting in the Text Style, Shape Style, and Dimension Style Inspectors while the corresponding tools are active.

Unlike the Drawing tools, each of the Annotation tools has its own independent default settings. For example, if you change the default font for the Text tool, the text displayed when you create labels or dimensions will not be affected.

Use the Pick Style tool to set the default settings for any tool. Just follow these steps:

1. Activate any Annotation tool.

2. To match the current tool's default settings to a specific scrapbook, hover over the scrapbook and click it. (See Chapter 13 for more information about how scrapbooks can be used as time-saving palettes.)

3. To match an entity in the presentation area, tap the S key. This is the default shortcut for the Pick Style tool.

4. Click on an entity to match the current tool's Inspector settings to the entity that you sampled. The entity can be in the presentation space or in a scrapbook.

Text Tool

LayOut has two types of text: bounded and unbounded (Figure 12.14). *Bounded text* is a constrained text window. As the text reaches the border, it will automatically drop the text to the next line if a word will not fit. *Unbounded text* will just keep going across the page indefinitely as you type, with no boundary or end.

UNBOUNDED TEXT   BOUNDED TEXT

Figure 12.14 The same text shown as unbounded and bounded

Typically, unbounded text is used for drawing titles, page numbers, and short bursts of text. Bounded text is better suited for larger amounts of text, such as project descriptions and notes.

To create unbounded text, follow these steps:

1. Activate the Text tool. Click once to create an unbounded Text window.

2. Enter the desired text in the text box. It will continue across the page with no boundaries.

3. To finish, click outside the text box or press the Esc key.

4. Using the Select tool, double-click on the text to edit it.

TIP When a bounded text box is resized, the bounded text is changed to unbounded. Any text can be changed back and forth from bounded to unbounded. Right-click on the text and choose Make Unbounded or Make Bounded, depending on the setting you need.

To create bounded text, follow these steps:

1. Using the Text tool, click and drag to start the Text window (Figure 12.15).

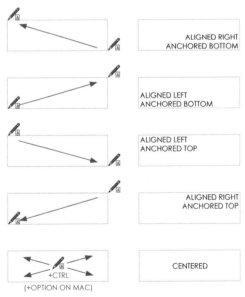

Figure 12.15 When you use the Text tool, the direction in which you click and drag assigns the justification and anchoring of the Text window.

2. Move your cursor away from the start point and release it to define the boundaries of the Text window.

3. Enter the desired text. As the words you type reach the boundary, they will drop to the next line.

4. To finish, click outside the text box or press the Esc key.

5. Using the Select tool, double-click on text to edit it.

TIP You will see a red arrow on the text box when it is not big enough. You can manually resize the text box or right-click on the text and choose Size to Fit to automatically enlarge the text box to fit the text.

Text Properties

The Format tab within the Text Style Inspector is where you can change text properties. While a text box is selected, you can adjust the font family, typeface, type size, and color. You can justify the text to the left, right, or center. You can also anchor the text to the top, bottom, or center of the Text window.

All types of text can take on any property assigned in the Shape Style Inspector (Figure 12.16). You can further modify the selected text's appearance by assigning a fill and stroke in the Shape Style Inspector.

Label Tool

The Label tool adds a leader line and attaches text to it (Figure 12.17). Keep in mind that even though this tool creates a "label," there is no entity defined as a label in LayOut. The Label tool creates two

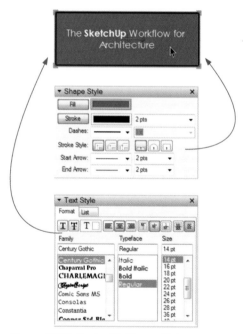

Figure 12.16 Text with Shape Style properties

simple entities at the same time, a piece of unbounded text and a line—each with its own Shape Style properties.

To create a leader line with text, follow these steps:

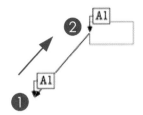

1. Activate the Label tool. Click once to place the arrow for the leader text.

2. Move your cursor away from the arrow and click again to place the text.

3. Enter the desired text.

4. To finish, click outside the text box or press the Esc key.

Figure 12.17 The Label tool

TIP The Label tool creates straight leader lines, but those lines can be modified into curved leaders, too. Using the Select tool, double-click on a line to edit the line's points. Holding the Ctrl key (Option on Mac), click and drag on an endpoint to curve the line. See the "Select Tool" section, later in this chapter, for more information about editing lines.

Dimension Tools

Add dimensions to call out lengths and angles and further explain a design. Keep in mind that the default settings for dimensions are in several Inspectors; Shape Style, Dimensions Style, and Text Style. In LayOut you can create two types of dimensions: Linear (Figure 12.18) and Angular (Figure 12.19).

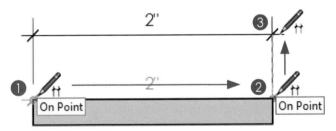

Figure 12.18 Linear dimension

To add linear dimensions to a presentation, follow these steps:

1. Activate the Linear Dimension tool. Click once to define the start point of the dimension.

2. Move your cursor to another point and click again to define the endpoint of the dimension.

3. Move your cursor away from the start and endpoints of the dimension line. Click to place the dimension.

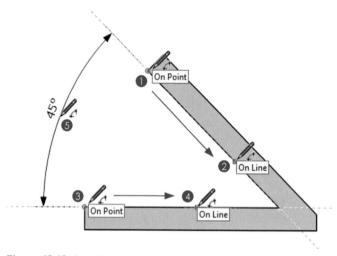

Figure 12.19 Angular dimension

To add angular dimensions to a presentation, follow these steps:

1. Activate the Angular Dimension tool. To define the first point of the first leg of the angle, click on the first line that you want to dimension.

2. Click again on the same line to finish defining the first leg.

3. To define the first point of the second leg of the angle, click on the second line that you want to dimension.

4. Click again on the same line to finish defining the second leg.

5. Move your cursor to adjust the arrows, and then click to position the angular dimension text.

Dimension Properties

Dimensions in LayOut utilize settings from several Inspectors: Shape Style, Text Style, and Dimensions (Figure 12.20). Select a dimension to see all of its properties in the Inspectors.

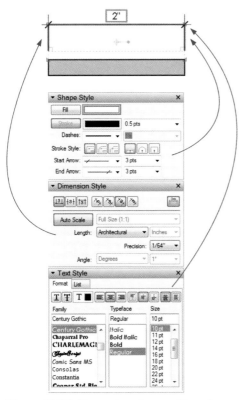

Figure 12.20 Dimensions have settings in the Shape Style, Text Style, and Dimensions Inspectors.

Editing Dimensions

Once a dimension has been created, it can be modified. Using the Select tool, double-click on a dimension to edit the dimension (Figure 12.21).

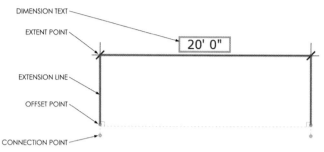

Figure 12.21 Dimension edit mode.

Once in dimension edit mode, follow these steps:

1. Click and drag on the text to reposition.
2. Triple-click on the text to change the shown dimension. Although it is discouraged, you can change the text displayed to force a dimension. To revert back to the automatically measured text, erase all of the forced text and press the Escape key.
3. Click and drag on the extent points to change the distance between the object being measured and the dimension line. This is called the offset.
4. To change the length of an extension line, click and drag on an offset point.
5. Click and drag on a connection point to change the points being measured, and in turn length of the dimension.

TIP Angular dimensions have a very similar edit mode.

MODIFICATION TOOLS

The Modification tools are used to change geometry that is already created. You can use them to move, rotate, copy, split, or join existing geometry to create new complex shapes.

Select Tool

Because it is the most frequently used tool, a safe and helpful habit is to always default to the Select tool. The default keyboard shortcut for the Select tool is the spacebar. The Select tool does much more than just select entities; it allows you to move, rotate, copy, and edit geometry.

Selecting

The Select tool is used to set up many other operations within LayOut. Because it is so important, take the time to become proficient at using it to select entities. Practice these steps:

☑ Single-click on any entity in LayOut to select it. The selected entity's properties will be displayed in the relevant Inspectors.

☑ Hold down the Shift key to add to, subtract from, or inverse a selection.

☑ Click and drag to select entities with a Selection window (Figure 12.22).

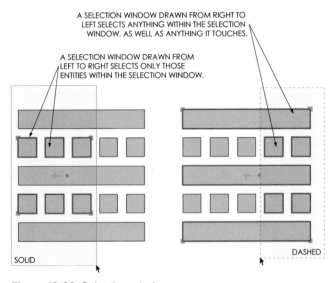

A SELECTION WINDOW DRAWN FROM RIGHT TO LEFT SELECTS ANYTHING WITHIN THE SELECTION WINDOW, AS WELL AS ANYTHING IT TOUCHES.

A SELECTION WINDOW DRAWN FROM LEFT TO RIGHT SELECTS ONLY THOSE ENTITIES WITHIN THE SELECTION WINDOW.

SOLID

DASHED

Figure 12.22 Selection windows

Moving/Copying

Use the Select tool to move and copy entities within LayOut. To do that, follow these steps:

1. Select an entity or select multiple entities.

2. Click and drag on the selection to move the entities all at once.

3. Release the mouse button to finish the move.

4. Immediately type a precise distance, such as **5**, then press Enter.

The Move feature of the Select tool also has modifier keys. Use them as follows:

☑ Click and drag while holding down the Shift key to lock an axis.

☑ Click and drag while holding down the Ctrl key (Option on Mac) to make a copy.

☑ To encourage inferences and create meaningful relationships between LayOut entities, hover endpoints, midpoints, and lines of the entity you are moving on other endpoints, midpoints, and lines of entities in your presentation.

TIP Use the arrow keys on your keyboard to nudge a selected entity 1/64″ in the desired direction. Hold down the **Shift** key while nudging to move an entity 1/4″ in the desired direction.

Precise Moving/Copying

The Precise Move grip allows you to move entities in LayOut with complete control. Use a precise move to align drawings, annotations, title blocks, and geometry to make more accurate and visually appealing presentations (Figure 12.23).

Just follow these steps:

1. Select an entity and notice that the precise move grip appears in the middle of the selection.

2. Click and drag on the left side of the Precise Move grip to pick it up. You can encourage inferences from the Precise Move grip before placing it.

3. Release on a meaningful point to put it down.

4. Click and drag anywhere on the selection to move it.

5. Allow the Precise Move grip to snap to an inference on another entity. You can also encourage inferences from the Precise Move grip.

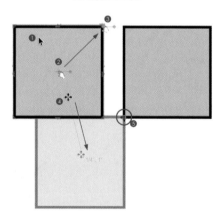

Figure 12.23 A precise move is when you move an entity from one specific point to another specific point.

TIP Hold the Ctrl key (Option on Mac) and Shift key down while performing a precise move to create a copy along an axis.

Rotating/Copying

LayOut doesn't have a dedicated Rotate tool. However, you can accomplish any rotation you'll need with the Precise Move grip, which is the center of any rotation (Figure 12.24).

Follow these steps:

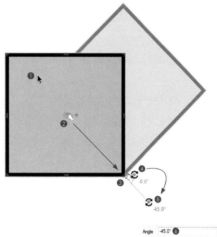

1. Select an entity and notice that the precise move grip appears in the middle of the selection.

2. Click and drag on the left side of the Precise Move grip to pick it up. You can encourage inferences from the Precise Move grip before placing it.

3. Release on a meaningful center point of rotation to put it down.

4. Click and drag on the right side of the Precise Move grip to start the rotation.

5. Release the mouse button to finish.

Figure 12.24 Rotate

6. Now you can enter a precise degree of rotation, type **-45**, then press Enter.

TIP Hold the Ctrl key (Option on Mac) down while rotating any entity to create a copy.

Scaling

Use the Select tool to scale and distort entities in LayOut (Figure 12.25).

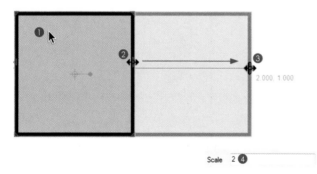

Scale 2

Figure 12.25 Scaling an entity in LayOut

1. Select an entity or multiple entities.

2. Click and drag on the Perimeter grips to distort or scale the selection.

3. Move your cursor away from the Scale grip and release it to loosely set the new scale.

4. Now you can enter a precise scale value, type **2**, then press Enter.

TIP There's not much space for your cursor between the Move and Scale features. Be sure to watch the cursor icon closely to determine which feature you are using.

TIP Hold the control key (Option on Mac) down while scaling any entity to create a copy.

When you are scaling in LayOut, keeps these points in mind:

☑ Hold down the Ctrl key (Option on Mac) to make a copy while scaling.

☑ Hold down the Shift key to constrain the selection's proportions while scaling.

☑ To mirror a selection, scale to −1, or right-click on an entity or selection and choose Flip › Top to Bottom or Flip › Left to Right.

Line Editing

Use the Select tool to edit lines and shapes in LayOut. The methods discussed here apply to all the geometry in LayOut, including lines, rectangles, circles, arcs, polygons, etc. There are several methods for modifying geometry using the Select tool. Double-click on the line or entity and then:

☑ Click and drag on a point to reposition it, ultimately modifying the geometry.

☑ Hold the Ctrl key (Option on Mac) and click along the line to add control points.

☑ Drag a control point onto another control point to delete it.

☑ Hold the Ctrl key (Option on Mac) and click and drag control points to curve the line. A curve can be created from any point along a line.

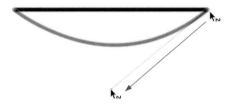

☑ Click and drag the tangent control points of a curve back to the control point to remove the curve, ultimately making the line straight.

Eraser Tool

Use the Eraser tool to delete entities from a presentation (Figure 12.26).

Follow these steps:

1. Click once on an entity to erase it.

2. Alternatively, hold down the mouse button and drag the cursor over the entities. All entities will be erased when the mouse button is released.

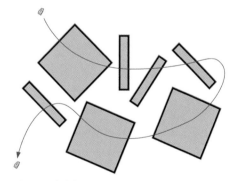

Figure 12.26 The Eraser tool

Style Tool

The Style tool is very similar to a "match properties" tool in other programs

(Figure 12.27). To use it, sample all of the properties from one entity and in one click apply them to another entity. The style tool can sample from and apply to any combination of shapes, edges, viewports, images, text, etc.

Follow these steps:

1. Activate the Style tool. To sample an entity's style, click on it in a scrapbook or in the document presentation area.

2. Click on the entities to which you want to apply the sampled properties.

TIP Tap the Escape key to start over, or hold down the Ctrl key (Option on Mac) to sample another entity.

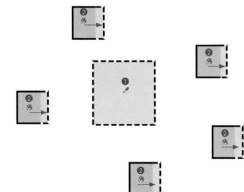

Figure 12.27 The Style tool

Split Tool

The Split tool divides line segments and also creates breaks between overlapping shapes (Figure 12.28).

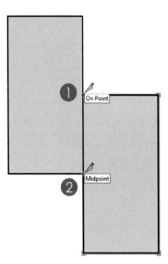

Figure 12.28 The Split tool

To use the Split tool to break LayOut geometry down into simpler forms, follow these steps:

1. Activate the Split tool. Click on an intersection between the two shapes.

2. Click on another intersection between the two shapes. Use the Select tool to examine the results.

Join Tool

The Join tool glues together lines that share a vertex (Figure 12.29). It is used to combine shapes to create more complex geometry.

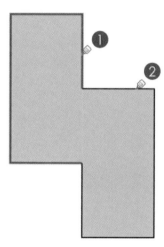

Figure 12.29 The Join tool

To use it, follow these steps:

1. Activate the Join tool. Click on the first entity that you would like to join.

2. Click on the next entity that you would like to join. Use the Select tool to examine the results.

CHAPTER POINTS

☑ Each group of tools has a specific function. Before you perform an operation, make a plan and think it through. Ask yourself, what is the fastest way to complete the task?

☑ Using a combination of the Drawing and Modification tools, you can create any shape, precise or sketchy, in LayOut.

☑ Instead of sorting through several dialogs, use the Pick Style tool to set the defaults for your tools.

☑ When you execute a command, most of the LayOut tools allow you to enter precise dimensions during the command. Some of the LayOut tools allow you to also modify the precise dimensions after you execute the command, until another command is started.

☑ Unlike SketchUp, LayOut is mostly a click-and-drag program.

Chapter 13
LayOut Collections

LayOut has two series of collections: title blocks and scrapbooks. Customizing, organizing, and using each of these types of collections will help you create LayOut presentations more easily and more efficiently. By effectively using LayOut collections, you will be able to open your own title block and already have your company's address and logo inserted, so you won't have to keep changing it; Your office's graphic standards will be available at the click of a button, and shared on a network drive where everyone can add and contribute. All of this and more is possible with LayOut collections.

TEMPLATES

Templates can be quite useful for a number of things. They can be very hard-lined traditional architectural title blocks, or they can even be optimized for screen presentations. In this section, you will create your own customized, architectural title block.

TIP Once you've started making a LayOut presentation with a specific template, you won't be able to switch to a different template. You can, however, modify the new presentation to look however you like.

Creating a Title Block Template

Before you can use a title block template, you'll need to create it. You have already reviewed all of the skills and tools you need to do just that.

Getting Started

Follow these step-by-step instructions to create your own architectural title block.

1. Open LayOut and start a new presentation using the BIC_8.5x11 – Landscape template.

2. Click on the File drop-down menu and choose Document Setup > Grid.

3. On the Grid tab (Figure 13.1), turn on the grid and grid snaps. Also adjust the grid to 1″ with four divisions.

4. On the Paper tab (Figure 13.2), change the paper size to Tabloid and adjust the margins to 1/2″.

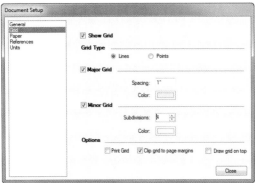

Figure 13.1 The Document Setup dialog, Grid tab

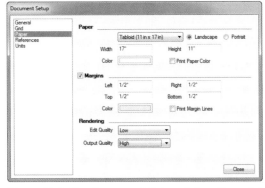

Figure 13.2 The Document Setup dialog, Paper tab

Adding Lines

To develop a unique graphic style, you'll need to add lines, as indicated here.

1. Activate the Line tool, set the stroke width to 3, and turn off the Fill. Click once to start the line at the top-right corner of the margin (Figure 13.3).

Figure 13.3 Use the Shape Style settings to create the margin lines.

2. Draw a line along the margins as shown and then double-click on the bottom-left corner of the margin to finish the line (Figure 13.4).

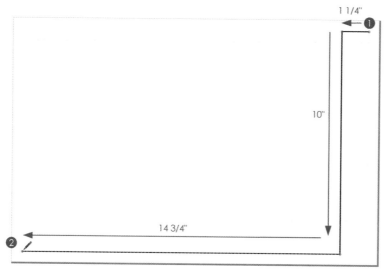

Figure 13.4 The main title-block line drawn along the margins

Adding Text

Use the Text tool to add several informational text boxes to your title block (Figure 13.5). Once a text box is created, use the Select tool to rotate and place the text.

Figure 13.5 Place text boxes in your title block.

Follow these steps:

1. Add a text box for your office name and contact information. Rotate and position the text on the title block as shown.

2. Add a generic text box for the client's name and contact information. Rotate and position the text on the title block as shown.

3. Add a generic text box for the project title and information. Rotate and position the text on the title block as shown.

4. Add a generic text box for the Sheet Description. Rotate and position the text on the title block as shown.

5. Add a generic text box for Sheet Information. Position on the title block as shown.

6. Add a generic text box for the sheet number. The sheet number text is white with a black fill. Position on the title block as shown.

TIP You can assign different properties to the text in a text box. Double-click in the text box and select the top line of text. Within the Text Style Inspector, change the selection to bold, independent of the rest of the text in the Text window (Figure 13.6).

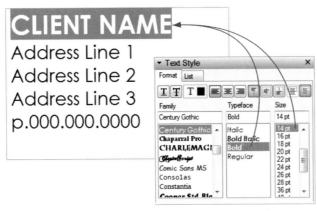

Figure 13.6 Text in a text box doesn't have to have the same properties as other text in the text box.

Adding Images

By following these steps, you can add images to your title block.

1. Click on the File drop-down menu and choose Insert.

2. Navigate to the TSWFA files and choose the `logo.jpg`.

3. Using the Select tool, rotate, resize, and position the logo image on the title block (Figure 13.7).

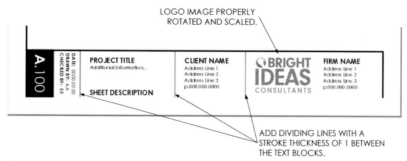

Figure 13.7 The final title block (image rotated for effect)

Assigning Layers

Add all of the title block entities to the TITLE BLOCK layer. These entities will be the same, or repeated, on every page of the presentation (Figure 13.8).

1. Set the active layer to TITLE BLOCK.

2. Select the entities that will appear on every page of the presentation; title block lines, logo, and text boxes.

3. Right-click on the selection and choose Move to Current Layer.

4. In the Layers Inspector, lock the TITLE BLOCK layer.

Add unique entities of the title block to the ANNOTATIONS layer. These text boxes will need to be different on every page of the presentation (Figure 13.8).

1. Set the active layer to ANNOTATIONS.

2. Select the entities that will be unique on every page of the presentation; Drawing Number text box and Sheet Description text box.

3. Right-click on the selection and choose Move to Current Layer.

Figure 13.8 Assign red entities to the ANNOTATIONS layer. Assign gray entities to the TITLE BLOCK layer.

Saving as a Template

Now that you have created your own title block, you can optimize the settings and save it to your collection.

1. Click on the File drop-down menu and choose Document Setup.

2. On the Grid tab, turn off the grid.

3. On the Paper tab, turn off the margins.

4. Click on the File drop-down menu and choose Save as Template.

5. Select the RESOURCES/BIC_Templates folder and save it with the name **BIC_11x17 Landscape – Linear**.

Now, every time you open LayOut or start a new presentation, this title block will be available in the Getting Started window.

SCRAPBOOKS

Scrapbooks are prebuilt pieces of annotation, composed of layout geometry and entities. Scrapbooks are not a special file format; they are simply layout presentations containing layout entities grouped in useful ways. While Scrapbooks serve a functional purpose of further explaining a design, they also contribute to the overall graphic style of the drawings. Lines, shapes, fills, and fonts all contribute to your own personal graphic standards.

Creating a Scrapbook

You have already reviewed all of the skills and tools that you need to create your own scrapbook. Follow these step-by-step instructions to create your own custom scrapbook collection to complement the BIC_11x17 Landscape – Linear template.

Getting Started

To get started, simply follow these steps:

1. Click on the File drop-down menu and choose New. Select the BIC_8.5x11 – Landscape template and choose Open.

2. Click on the File drop-down menu and choose Document Setup. In the Paper tab, change the paper size to $5'' \times 5''$.

3. In the Pages Inspector, double-click on the only page and rename it **SYMBOLS**. Click on the plus sign (+) to add two more pages. Name the pages **CALLOUTS** and **PALETTES** (Figure 13.9).

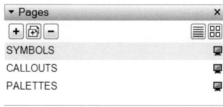

Figure 13.9 Typical scrapbook presentation pages

4. In the Layers Inspector, delete the TITLE BLOCK layer because you don't need it in a scrapbook collection. Rename the DRAWINGS layer to **BACKGROUND**. Rename the ANNO-TATIONS layer to **SCRAPBOOKS** and leave it as the current layer (Figure 13.10).

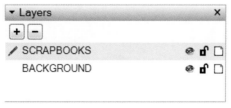

Figure 13.10 Typical scrapbook presentation layers

TIP When you insert a scrapbook, all of its entities are assigned to the active layer in the current presentation. This is why it is pointless to have several different layers in a scrapbook.

Symbols

Symbols are used to add graphic and text information to a drawing. They can be used to count doors and windows, as well as define north and the graphic scale of a drawing. In this section, you will create several commonly used symbols for creating a set of construction documents.

Door Tag

Door tags are used to count new doors, and reference them to the additional information provided in the door schedule. Follow these steps to create a simple door tag:

1. Activate the Circle tool, set the stroke width to .5, and turn off the Fill. Click once to define the center point of the circle (Figure 13.11).

2. Move your cursor away from the center point and click to loosely define the radius.

3. Immediately type a precise radius of **1/8**, then press Enter.

4. Activate the Text tool. While you hold down the Ctrl key (Option on Mac), click and hold on the center point of the circle (Figure 13.12).

5. Move your cursor away from the center point to create the text box, and release the mouse button to finish. Add generic text to the text box, such as "01", and press Esc to finish.

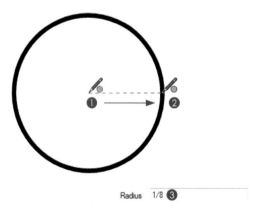

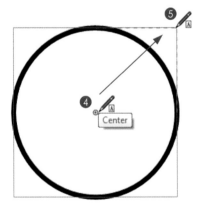

Figure 13.11 Create a precise circle for the door tag.

Figure 13.12 Add text to the door tag.

6. Activate the Select tool, click and drag from right to left to select both the circle and the text entities as shown in Figure 13.13.

7. Right-click on the selection and choose Group.

TIP If a piece of annotation in a scrapbook contains more than one entity, those entities must be grouped for the entire symbol to come in as one.

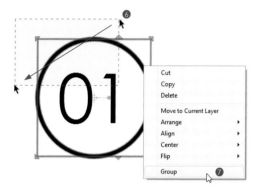

Figure 13.13 Group the door tag so that it functions properly as a scrapbook.

Window Tag

Window tags are used to count new windows, and reference them to the additional information provided in the window schedule. Follow these steps to create a simple window tag:

1. Activate the Polygon tool, set the stroke width to .5, and turn off the Fill. Assign the number of sides by entering **6s**, then press Enter (Figure 13.14).

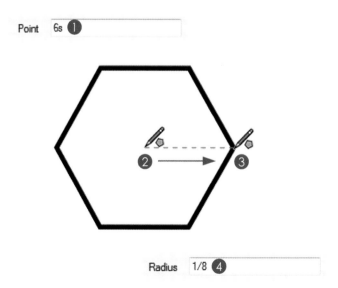

Figure 13.14 Create a precise polygon for the window tag.

2. Click once to define the center point of the hexagon.

3. Move your cursor away from the center point and click to loosely define the radius.

4. Type a precise radius of **1/8**, then press Enter.

5. Activate the Text tool. Hover on the top and side center points to encourage an inference. While holding the Ctrl key (Option on Mac), click and hold on the inferenced center point of the hexagon (Figure 13.15).

6. Move your cursor away from the center point to create the text box. Release the mouse button to finish. Add generic text to the text box , such as "A", and press Esc to finish.

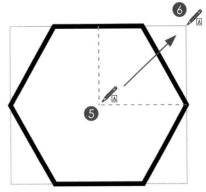

Figure 13.15 Add text to the window tag.

7. Activate the Select tool. Click and drag from right to left to select both the circle and the text entities.

8. Right-click on the selection and choose Group so it functions properly as a scrapbook (Figure 13.16).

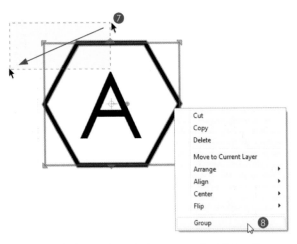

Figure 13.16 Group the window tag so that it functions properly as a scrapbook.

North Arrow

A north arrow graphic shows the viewer an accurate north direction on the drawings. Follow these steps to create a simple north arrow:

1. Activate the Circle tool, and set the stroke width to 1 and the Fill color as white. Click once to define the center point of the circle (Figure 13.17).

2. Move your cursor away from the center point and click to loosely define the radius.

3. Immediately type a precise radius of **1/4**, then press Enter.

4. Activate the Line tool and set the stroke width to 3. Click once on the center point of the circle to start the line (Figure 13.18).

5. Move your cursor away from the start point of the line and double-click on the top point of the circle to finish.

6. Select both entities, and then right-click and choose Group so that it functions properly as a scrapbook.

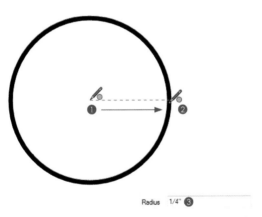

Figure 13.17 Add a precise circle as the base of the north arrow.

Figure 13.18 Add a line to define the north direction.

Graphic Scale

A graphic scale gives the viewer of the drawing a visual reference for the architectural scale applied to the drawing. Follow these steps to create a simple graphic scale:

1. Activate the Rectangle tool, set the Fill to black, and turn off the Stroke. Click once to start the rectangle (Figure 13.19).

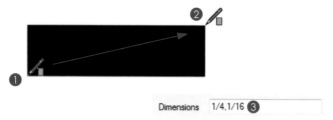

Dimensions   1/4,1/16 **③**

Figure 13.19 Draw a precise rectangle to start the graphic scale.

2. Move your cursor away from the start point and click again to loosely define the dimensions of the rectangle.

3. Type the precise dimensions for the rectangle as **1/4, 1/16**, then press Enter.

4. While holding down the Ctrl key (Option on Mac), click and drag on the rectangle to make a copy (Figure 13.20).

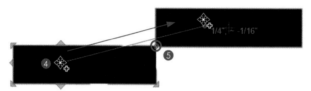

Figure 13.20 Copy the rectangle.

5. Snap the bottom-left corner of the copy to the top-right corner of the original.

6. While holding down the Ctrl key (Option on Mac), click and drag on the second rectangle to make another copy.

7. Snap the top-left corner of the copy to the bottom-right corner of the original.

8. While the rectangle is still selected, click and drag the right Scale grip to the right of your screen (Figure 13.21).

Scale   2.000, 1.000 **⑨**

Figure 13.21 Scale the rectangle.

9. Release the grip to finish loosely scaling, and immediately type a precise scale factor of **2**, then press Enter.

10. Repeat the copying and scaling steps to produce the image shown in Figure 13.22.

Figure 13.22 All rectangles are copied and scaled.

11. Add generic text to each division of the scale as shown in Figure 13.23. This text will need to be edited depending on the scale of the drawing it represents.

0 2' 4'   8'   16'   32'

Figure 13.23 Add text to the graphic scale.

12. Select all graphic scale entities, right-click on the selection, and choose Group so that it functions properly as a scrapbook.

Drawing Title

A drawing title calls out what a drawing is, and also provides a number for coordinating drawings. Follow these steps to create a simple Drawing Title:

Figure 13.24 Draw the main line for the drawing title.

1. Activate the Line tool, set the stroke width to 1, and turn off the Fill. Click once to start the line (Figure 13.24).

2. Draw a line 1/2″ to the right, 1/4″ down, and then 3 1/2″ to the right.

3. Change the stroke width to .5. Click on the existing line to start another line (Figure 13.25).

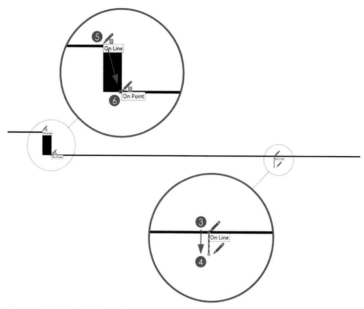

Figure 13.25 Add the detail.

4. Move your cursor down and double-click to loosely finish the line. At this point, type a precise dimension of **1/8**, then press Enter.

5. Activate the Rectangle tool, set the stroke width to 1, and turn on the Fill and color it black. Click once to start the rectangle.

6. Move your cursor away from the start point and click again to finish.

7. Add text to the drawing's title as shown in Figure 13.26.

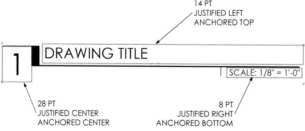

Figure 13.26 Add and arrange text on the drawing's title.

8. Select the entire drawing title, right-click on the selection, and choose Make Group so that it functions properly as a scrapbook.

Callouts

Callouts are used to link and coordinate drawings. A callout is text that references another drawing on another page. Use the Pages Inspector to advance to the Callouts page of your scrapbook presentation. Separating the scrapbooks into pages keeps them organized and makes them easier to use.

Interior Elevation

An interior elevation callout points at an interior wall and references the actual interior elevation with a drawing and sheet number.

1. Activate the Text tool. Set the stroke width to 1, the Fill to white, and the font size to 10.

2. While holding the Ctrl key, click and drag to create a text box.

3. Add the text **0/A.000** and press Esc to finish.

4. Right-click on the text and choose Size to Fit to optimize the vertical size of the text box. Resize the text box horizontally as needed.

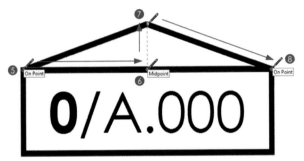

Figure 13.27 Use the Line tool to draw the arrow indicating elevation direction. (Fill is turned off for effect.)

5. Activate the Line tool, and set the Fill color to black. Click on the top-left corner of the text box to start the line (Figure 13.27).

6. Hover on the text box's midpoint to encourage an inference.

7. Move your cursor up and click to end the line segment.

8. Double-click on the top-right corner of the text box to finish.

9. Select the entire elevation callout, right-click on the selection, and choose Make Group so that it functions properly as a scrapbook.

Section

A building section callout defines where a building section is cut through the plan and references the actual building section drawing with a drawing and sheet number.

1. Activate the Line tool, set the stroke width to 1, and turn off Fill. Click once to start the line.

2. Draw a line as shown in Figure 13.28. Double-click on the last inferred point to finish the line.

Figure 13.28 The baseline of the section callout

3. Activate the Split tool and click on the two endpoints as shown (Figure 13.29).

Figure 13.29 The Split tool breaks lines into separate segments, which can have different Shape Style properties.

4. Select the two ends and assign a stroke width of 2.

5. Select the middle line and assign a dash pattern to represent the section cut line.

6. Activate the Text tool and add a text box on the long end of the section callout baseline. Enter the generic text **0/0.00**. Reposition and resize the text box as needed (Figure 13.30).

Figure 13.30 Add text to the section callout.

7. Select the entire section callout, right-click on the selection, and choose Make Group so that it functions properly as a scrapbook.

Detail

A detail callout defines the portion of a building condition to be further explained and enlarged, and references the actual detail drawing with a drawing and sheet number.

1. Activate the Rectangle tool, set the stroke width to 1, and turn off the Fill. Press the Up arrow key to switch to a rounded-corner rectangle and immediately type a precise radius of **.25**, then press Enter (Figure 13.31).

2. Click once to define the start point of the rectangle.

3. Move your cursor away from the start point and click to loosely define the dimensions.

4. Immediately type the precise dimensions **1,1**, then press Enter.

5. Use the Line tool to draw a leader line as shown in Figure 13.32.

6. Use the Split tool to break the leader line as shown in Figure 13.33.

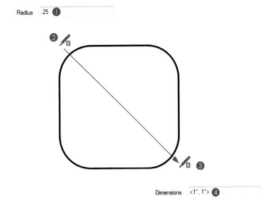

Figure 13.31 Draw a rectangle with rounded corners to start the detail callout.

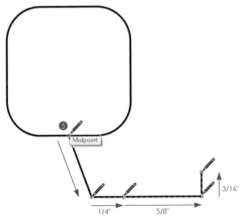

Figure 13.32 Draw the leader line.

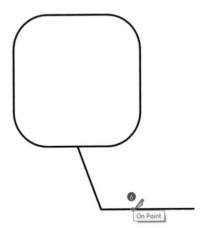

Figure 13.33 Use the Split tool to break the leader line into two segments.

7. Select the rectangle and assign a dash pattern. Adjust the Pattern Scale as needed. Keep in mind that any entity can be modified after it is created.

8. Select the leader line and assign a stroke width of .5.

9. Select the end of the leader line and assign a stroke width of 2.

10. Activate the Text tool and add a text box on the long end of the leader line. Enter the generic text **0/0.00**. Reposition and resize the text box as needed (Figure 13.34).

11. Select the entire detail callout, right-click on the selection, and choose Make Group so that it functions properly as a scrapbook.

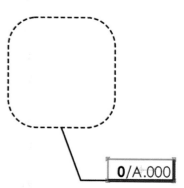

Figure 13.34 Add text to the Detail callout.

Palette

You can use a palette scrapbook as a quick way to assign default settings. With most tools, you can hover in the Scrapbooks Inspector and match the default properties of the active tool to a specific scrapbook. Add these entities to your palette so you can draw much more efficiently in LayOut.

TIP Entities that will never be sampled or inserted into a drawing can be placed on a locked layer. For example, the text that describes the scrapbook won't be imported; assign it to the BACKGROUND layer , then lock the BACKGROUND layer.

To create a palette scrapbook, follow these steps:

1. Draw a line approximately 2″ long.

2. Using the Select tool, hold down the Ctrl key to make a copy, and then hold down the Shift key to lock the axis. Click and drag the line down by 1/16″. Copy the line 10 times as shown in Figure 13.35.

3. Select all of the lines, right-click on the selection, and choose Group.

4. Add a text box to the right of the group and enter the generic text **Description** on the first line and **0.00 pt** on the second line (Figure 13.36).

Figure 13.35 If you place several lines close together instead of placing just one, clicking on a line will be easy even when the palette is condensed into the smaller Scrapbooks Inspector.

DESCRIPTION
0.00 pts

Figure 13.36 The beginning of a palette

5. Copy the group and the generic description down the page seven times. Use the Precise Move tool to space the copies at equal intervals.

6. Select the first group of lines and assign a stroke width of .18.

7. Select the top group of lines and change the stroke width to 0.18 pts in the Shape Style Inspector. Also, change the text description to **Fine** on the first line and **0.18 pts** on the second line.

8. Change all stroke widths and corresponding descriptions as shown in Figure 13.37.

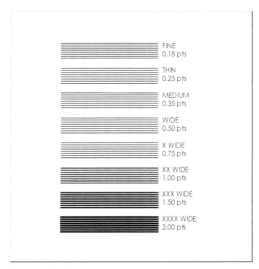

FINE
0.18 pts

THIN
0.25 pts

MEDIUM
0.35 pts

WIDE
0.50 pts

X WIDE
0.75 pts

XX WIDE
1.00 pts

XXX WIDE
1.50 pts

XXXX WIDE
2.00 pts

Figure 13.37 The final palette

9. Make the BACKGROUND layer the current layer. Select all of the descriptions, right-click on the selection, and choose Move to Current Layer.

10. Lock the BACKGROUND layer. Entities on a locked layer cannot be sampled or inserted as a scrapbook.

Saving Scrapbooks

Now that you have created a custom scrapbook, add it to your collections. Just follow these steps:

1. Click on the File drop-down menu and choose Save as Scrapbook.

2. Select the RESOURCES/SCRAPBOOKS folder and save it as **BIC_Linear**.

Now this scrapbook will always be available in the Scrapbooks Inspector collections drop-down.

USING COLLECTIONS

Take a few minutes to experiment with your new creations.

1. Click on the File drop-down menu and choose New.

2. Select the BIC_11x17 Landscape – Linear template that you just created and click on Open.

3. In the Scrapbooks Inspector, click on the Collections drop-down menu and choose the BIC_Linear scrapbook.

Practice adding scrapbooks to your presentation and using scrapbooks as palettes. While you're practicing, keep the following tips in mind:

☑ Activate a tool, then hover over a scrapbook and click to absorb the scrapbook's properties as the tool's default settings.

☑ Tools can pull default settings from any scrapbook entity. For example, the Text tool can absorb default settings from lines, and the Line tool can absorb default settings from a piece of text within a scrapbook.

☑ With the Select tool active, click on a scrapbook in the Scrapbooks Inspector and then click in your presentation to place it.

☑ Scrapbooks are simply grouped layout entities. Use the Select tool to double-click into a scrapbook and modify it once it is inserted into your presentation. This operation is similar to navigating containers in SketchUp.

CHAPTER POINTS

☑ You can share your scrapbooks and download other people's scrapbooks at **www.suexch.com**.

☑ Multiple entities must be grouped together to function as a single scrapbook.

☑ Be creative and develop your own scrapbooks and drawing style. There are no rules and the possibilities are endless!

☑ A scrapbook can be one entity or a mixture of any entities available in LayOut, including images, SketchUp models, text, dimensions, and geometry.

☑ Anything that you use over and over should be made readily available as a scrapbook. Consider creating a Detail Library scrapbook full of 3D SketchUp details.

☑ Use the Linear graphic style to add additional symbols, callouts, and palettes to expand your Linear Style scrapbook.

Chapter 14

Inserting Content

To move a 3D design into a 2D LayOut presentation, you simply insert the SketchUp model into LayOut. You can insert all sorts of content, including SketchUp models, images, and text, to describe your design. Any inserted content can be lightly edited in LayOut, or seamlessly sent to a program more suited for editing the specific file, while maintaining the dynamic link. In this chapter, you will insert and edit all of LayOut's insertable entities.

WORKING WITH SKETCHUP MODELS

Hands down, the most important file you'll insert into LayOut is the SketchUp file (.skp). The dynamic link between a SketchUp file and a LayOut presentation allows more than one person to work on a project. For example, someone could work on the text while someone else works on the presentation. By presenting your 3D model as 2D drawings and diagrams, you will be able to accurately and efficiently describe your designs and ideas.

New LayOut Presentation

To begin your new LayOut presentation, follow these steps:

1. Open LayOut and start a new presentation. Select the BIC_11x17 Landscape - Linear title block that you created in the last chapter, or you can choose any title block you want.

2. Within the Layers Inspector, unlock and set the current layer to DRAWINGS. Anything that you insert into SketchUp will typically be assigned to this layer.

Inserting the File

To insert the SketchUp file, follow these steps:

1. Click on the File drop-down menu and select Insert. This launches the Open dialog box.

2. Navigate to the Class Files folder for this chapter and select the `BIC_Denver Row House.skp` file.

3. Click on the Open button at the bottom-right corner of the dialog box. The SketchUp model will be inserted into a viewport in your LayOut presentation (Figure 14.1).

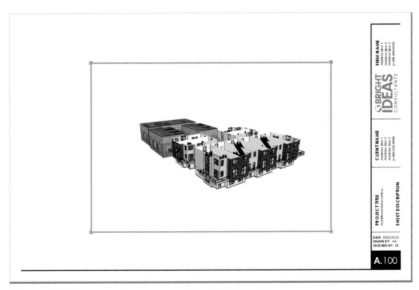

Figure 14.1 The new viewport created within LayOut

Assigning a Scene

The new viewport will be set to Last Saved View. This is the camera view that was shown when your model was last saved. Every time you save your SketchUp model, the Last Saved

View will change. It is always best to assign a static view, or scene, to the viewport. To assign a scene in the SketchUp Model dialog, follow these steps:

1. Using the Select tool, select the viewport.

2. In the SketchUp Model Inspector, set the Viewport Scene to LO_Perspective 01 and the Rendering setting to Hybrid.

3. Using the Select tool, expand the viewport so that it encompasses most of the presentation area on the page (Figure 14.2).

4. If Auto-Render is off, render the models manually by right-clicking on the presentation background and choosing Render Models on Page.

Figure 14.2 Expand the viewport.

Clipping Mask

A *clipping mask* lets you control what part of an object you see. This is helpful when you're cropping viewports and images in LayOut. Clipping masks work with images and SketchUp model viewports. Just follow these steps:

1. Activate the Rectangle tool and encourage inferences from the top-right and bottom-left corners of the title block. Click once to start the rectangle where the inference lines converge.

2. Move your cursor away from the start point to draw a shape covering the portion of the viewport you want to see (Figure 14.3).

Figure 14.3 Encourage inferences while you draw the clipping mask.

3. Using the Select tool, select both the viewport and the clipping mask shape.

4. Right-click on the selection and choose Create Clipping Mask (Figure 14.4).

Figure 14.4 Use the clipping mask to cover the part of the object you want to be seen. The part that is covered will be the part that is visible when the clipping mask is applied.

To edit a clipping mask, double-click on the masked viewport/image with the Select tool. Use the Select tool to move and scale the clipping mask shape. Sometimes it is easier to just right-click on the clipped object, choose Release Clipping Mask, and then edit the shape and re-create the clipping mask.

TIP Use any of the Drawing tools to create a shape for clipping. The final clipping mask shape must be one complete shape, not a group or collection of shapes. Use the Split and Join tools to finalize a complex clipping mask shape.

Editing the Model

A SketchUp model can be opened directly from LayOut, which will create a seamless link between SketchUp and LayOut. To enhance your design and see the results within your presentation immediately, follow these steps:

1. Right-click on the viewport and choose Edit in SketchUp.

2. Make your changes to the SketchUp model.

3. Close the model and save it.

4. All of the viewports linked to that model will be updated when the file is saved. If Auto-Render is off, you will need to render the viewports manually.

WORKING WITH IMAGES

Images provide another level of information and complement the style of visual information. You can insert all sorts of images, including locator maps from Google Earth or Google Maps, project photographs, watermarks, and other diagrams.

Inserting Images

LayOut offers the option to insert images as .jpg or .png files. A .png file contains an alpha or transparency layer. This transparency gives you the ability to create watermarks without having to create elaborate clipping masks in LayOut. To insert an image, just follow these steps:

1. Click on the File drop-down menu and choose Insert.

2. Navigate to the Class Files folder and select the `BIC_01 - Site Context.jpg` file. Click the Open button at the bottom-right corner of the dialog.

3. Using the Select tool, scale and reposition the image on the presentation area as shown in Figure 14.5. When scaling, be sure to use a corner grip and hold the Shift key to lock the aspect ratio.

ALIGN ENTITIES USING OBJECT
SNAPS AND INFERENCES.

Figure 14.5 The context photograph inserted, scaled, and properly positioned in the presentation

Editing Images

The Edit Image command allows you to work seamlessly between LayOut and your favorite image editor. Use an image editor to touch up photos, and crop, scale, and resize images. Just follow these steps:

1. Right-click on an image and choose Open with Photoshop, or whatever image editor you assigned in Chapter 6, "The Professional's SketchUp Environment."

2. Modify the image within your image editor.

3. Close and save the file.

4. The image automatically updates in LayOut. If it does not update immediately, right-click on the image and choose Update Reference.

WORKING WITH TEXT

Insert text into a presentation to explain the graphics and include details such as schedules, notes, and drawing lists. The dynamic link enables the text to be edited in a word processor, which will have additional helpful features such as spellcheck.

Inserting Text

You can insert text as a `.txt` file or an `.rtf` file. You can't save visual text properties (such as colors, fonts, and formatting) in a `.txt` file, which limits its usefulness as an import. An `.rtf` file can store all of the visual properties you apply to text. Once you have created your text in a word processor, you can save the file as an `.rtf` file and insert into LayOut. Just follow these steps:

1. Click on the File drop-down menu and choose Insert.

2. Navigate to the Class Files folder for this chapter and select the `Denver Rowhouse Description.rtf` file.

3. Click on Open.

4. Reposition and scale the text as desired. See Figure 14.6.

Figure 14.6 Inserted text and the final presentation

TIP You can export spreadsheets to .txt files and then import them into LayOut, although your formatting options will be limited in LayOut. Typically, the best solution is to build spreadsheet-type graphics in LayOut. See the "Schedules" section in Chapter 20, "Construction Documents."

Editing Text

The text is now part of your presentation, but you can still edit it with your favorite word processing program. To edit text outside of LayOut, follow these steps:

1. Right-click on the text and choose Edit Text.

2. Modify the text in the default text editor.

3. Close the file and save your changes. You will see the text update within LayOut.

TIP When you double-click on text and edit in LayOut, you will break the dynamic link between the inserted file and the LayOut text. There is no way to relink edited text without reinserting the original file.

CHAPTER POINTS

☑ Right-click on any linked content to open with the external editor set in Chapter 6 "The Professional's SketchUp Environment."

☑ Editing text within LayOut breaks the dynamic link. Typically, editing the bulk of your text in a word processor and then inserting that text into LayOut works best. Once it's inserted, make all of your final text edits in LayOut.

☑ You can manage all of your inserted content, or references, within the Document Setup › References dialog. From there, you can relink, unlink, and edit in an assigned external program.

Part IV

The Architectural Design Process

Relating to *The SketchUp Workflow for Architecture*, the architectural design process has been whittled down into four main phases: Site Analysis (SA), Schematic Design (SD), Design Development (DD), Construction Documents (CD). In this section you will first learn to gather a wealth of 2D and 3D information about the site in a very short amount of time, including site plans, site sections, topography lines, and building context. You will then leverage the Google Geo features and the tools available in SketchUp Pro and LayOut to expedite measuring and drafting as-built drawings. Next, you will respond to the site data existing conditions with thoughtful designs represented in efficient and organized 3D study models. The study models will seamlessly evolve into a detailed proposed conditions model optimized for any type of presentation, animation, or photorealistic rendering. Ultimately, the organization methods you learn in this section will allow you to share .dwg backgrounds with consultants, move to other CAD programs, and easily create construction documents using LayOut. You will soon realize how the entire architectural design process can be expedited, and how your designs can be more intelligent, by implementing *The SketchUp Workflow for Architecture*.

Chapter 15

Site Analysis: Digital Site Survey

The first step of responsible design is to understand not only the client's needs, but also the constraints and potential of the building site. *Site analysis* involves obtaining geographical information, maps, aerial photos, topographic data, building context information, as-built drawings, preliminary code information, and anything you'll need to make informed design decisions. This preliminary information will enable you to make realistic decisions about what can actually be built.

Obtaining all of this data can be a huge task. SketchUp Pro allows you to grab preliminary 3D data, everything you need to get started sketching, estimating, and designing while you wait for the hard data to show up. In this section, you will learn techniques to gather accurate 2D and 3D site data in a short amount of time. This data will allow you, as a designer, to make informed decisions, saving time and headaches later when real data arrives.

A *digital site survey* is the process used to create a 2D site plan, 2D/3D contour map, and site sections from Google 3D data without leaving your desk. By converting 3D data into 2D drawings, or sketch backgrounds, you can get started on a project immediately and make informed design decisions. The ability to generate a two-dimensional site plan of just about any building or site allows you to immediately assess project scope and make more accurate estimates of time and work. This process can fit into any designer's workflow and style, whether it is sketching by hand or diving right into 3D modeling. The techniques illustrated in this section allow you to gather a wealth of 2D and 3D information digitally without ever visiting the site (Figure 15.1).

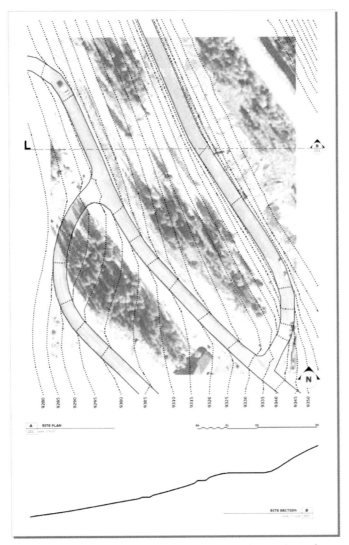

Figure 15.1 2D/3D Site Plans and Sections are the product of a digital site survey.

GEO-LOCATION

The first step of a digital site survey is to geo-locate the site in SketchUp. *Geo-location* is the process of identifying a precise real-world geographic location and assigning it to a SketchUp model. During the geo-location process you will import 2D aerial imagery, 3D terrain, precise latitude and longitude coordinates, and the exact Solar North direction. With this data attached to your model, you will be able to make informed decisions about existing conditions, topography, and sun angles.

By accurately geo-locating a model, you also open the door to a multitude of possibilities for integrating with other data-rich Google "geo" services. This connection to Google is one of the unique features that sets SketchUp apart from other 3D software packages. As you will see, SketchUp is seamlessly integrated with popular Google products such as Maps, Street View, Earth, and Building Maker. These additional Google products allow you to easily pick a location, generate context building models, find optimized building facade textures, and view your designs in a real-world context.

Adding a Location

For this exercise, you should have the Google toolbar open. Click on the View drop-down menu and choose Toolbars › Google. To geo-locate a model using the Add Location feature, follow the steps discussed here (Figure 15.2).

1. Start a new SketchUp model by either opening SketchUp, or by clicking on the File drop-down menu and choosing New.

2. Click the Add Location button on the Google toolbar (Figure 15.3). This automatically launches a Google Maps interface where you can search for and find any location on planet Earth.

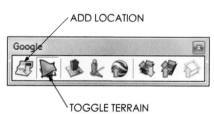

Figure 15.2 The Google toolbar

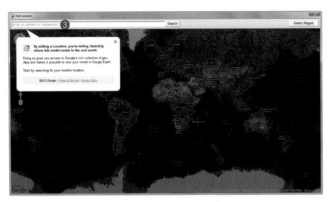

Figure 15.3 The Add Location window

3. The search bar at the top of the Add Location window will accept an address, zip code, intersection, city name, or popular landmark. For this example, enter **507 Summit Pl, Winter Park, Co**. Click the Search button (or press Enter) to start the search; the map will zoom into the specified location.

TIP Navigate the Add Location window the same as you would Google Maps. Click and drag to pan the map up, down, and side to side. Double-click on the map to zoom in. Double-right-click on the map to zoom out. You can also use the Screen Navigation tools in the top-left corner of the map.

4. Zoom out two to three clicks so you can see more of the site as shown in Figure 15.4.

Figure 15.4 Extents of the example site

5. Click the Select Region button at the top-right corner of the Add Location window. This adds a selection rectangle to the map with pins on the four corners.

6. Select the site by repositioning the pins as shown in Figure 15.5. Typically, you will select the desired site plus any surrounding context that will be visible and potentially influence your design. Not to worry, you can easily add more terrain if you decide that you want more of the site in the future.

7. Once the selection rectangle surrounds the desired site, click the Grab button at the top-right corner of the Add Location window. This closes the Add Location window and returns your active screen to SketchUp. Now there is a full-scale aerial snapshot of the selected site in your SketchUp model.

8. In addition to the flat aerial imagery, you have also imported the 3D terrain of the site (Figure 15.6). Click the Toggle Terrain button on the Google toolbar to toggle between the flat aerial imagery and the 3D terrain. The 2D aerial imagery and 3D terrain are simply locked groups of geometry that are automatically added to the Google Earth Snapshot layer and the Google Earth Terrain layer. The Toggle Terrain button simply switches these layers on and off.

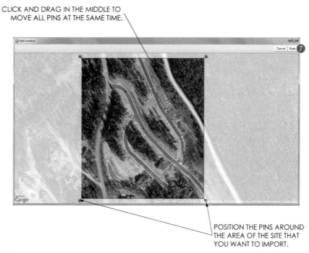

CLICK AND DRAG IN THE MIDDLE TO MOVE ALL PINS AT THE SAME TIME.

POSITION THE PINS AROUND THE AREA OF THE SITE THAT YOU WANT TO IMPORT.

Figure 15.5 Choose a precise site by adjusting pins within the Add Location window.

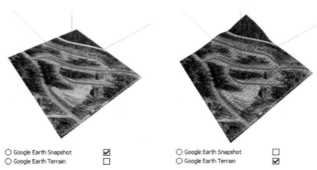

Figure 15.6 Aerial imagery (left) and 3D terrain (right) and their corresponding layers

Verifying Model Location

The Add Location feature attached a precise Earth location to your SketchUp model. You can verify the actual location by clicking on the Window drop-down menu and choosing Model Info, then click on the Geo-location tab (Figure 15.7). This tab displays the latitude and longitude, and it allows you to clear the location, add more imagery, and set the location manually (which is rarely necessary).

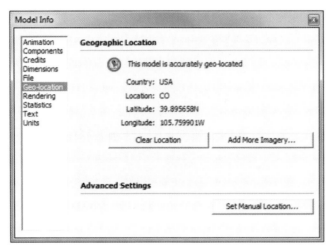

Figure 15.7 Model Info a Geo-location

Verifying Solar North

By adding a precise location to your model, you also added an accurate Solar North direction. *Solar North* establishes the path of the sun relative to your SketchUp model to create extremely accurate shadows. To access the Solar North tools, click on the View drop-down menu and choose Toolbars › Solar North (Figure 15.8). The first button on the Solar North toolbar toggles the North arrow on and off. The green axis is north by default, and Solar North is often very closely aligned with the green axis.

It is possible to change the Solar North direction of a model, but doing so is not recommended. The remaining two buttons on the Solar North toolbar, Set North tool and Enter North Angle tool, allow you to modify the Solar North direction with precision. If you do

Figure 15.8 The Solar North toolbar

change the Solar North direction, the shadows will no longer be real. For best results, leave Solar North alone after you add a location to a SketchUp model.

SITE PLAN

After you add a location to your SketchUp model, generating a detailed site plan is simple. Use the SketchUp Drawing tools to trace the flat 2D aerial imagery and create vector linework that can be set to an architectural scale in LayOut or can be exported to other drafting programs. This makes a great starting point for any designer who wants to understand site constraints and the general scope of a project.

2D Plan

There are endless ways to approach the task of tracing a site. Once you are comfortable in SketchUp, you will find a few favorite tools that you will tend to lean on.

Trace Roads

Use the Drawing tools to trace the 2D aerial imagery and create a 2D site plan. Here are a few tips for tracing:

- ☑ Confirm that the Toggle Terrain button is off so that only the 2D aerial imagery is showing.
- ☑ Set the length snapping to a round dimension, such as 1′ or 1″ to keep your dimensions clean. In the Model Info dialog's Units tab, check the Enable Length Snapping check box and enter the desired tolerance.
- ☑ Use the Materials browser's Edit tab to desaturate and lighten the aerial imagery. This will make the lines stand out against the imagery and make it easier to see what you are working on.
- ☑ After tracing the road, close off the ends to create a surface. Then make them a group.
- ☑ Draw one side of the road, and then use the Offset tool to create the other side.
- ☑ Advanced tools, such as the `bezier.rb` script, will help you accurately trace curved roads.
- ☑ It is okay to be loose and sketchy when you're tracing insignificant details.
- ☑ Use the Axes tool to align the axes with the buildings that you are tracing. Remember, it is a three-click process. First, click to set the origin; second, click to set the red axis; third, click to set the blue axis.

☑ Use the Rectangle tool instead of the Line tool to trace buildings. The Rectangle tool draws all lines on axis and generates significantly more geometry per click. Quickly clean up extra geometry by clicking and dragging over extra lines with the Eraser tool.

☑ Trace the house footprints and extrude them into 3D. Make each house a group (Figure 15.9).

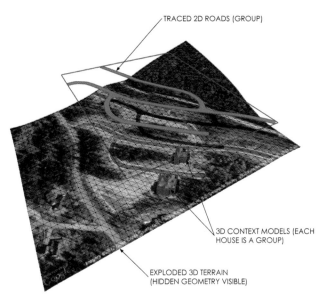

TRACED 2D ROADS (GROUP)

3D CONTEXT MODELS (EACH HOUSE IS A GROUP)

EXPLODED 3D TERRAIN (HIDDEN GEOMETRY VISIBLE)

Figure 15.9 The final traced plan floating above the terrain

Converting to 3D Roads

Now that you have created a 2D site plan, drape it onto the 3D terrain to create the 3D roads. This step uses, but does not require, the Instant Road plugin from **www.valiarchitects.com**. If you use this script, the roads will have accurate topography lines. If you don't use it, they won't. They aren't critical, but accurate topography lines make more realistic graphics, and using Instant Road is easy!

1. Toggle the 3D Terrain on.

2. Right-click on the terrain and choose Unlock.

3. Right-click on the terrain again and choose "Explode."

4. Using the Select tool, select the terrain mesh and the grouped 2D roads (Figure 15.10).

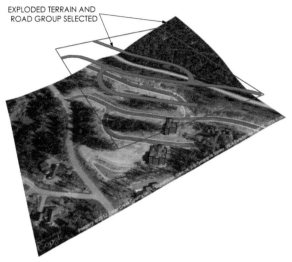

EXPLODED TERRAIN AND
ROAD GROUP SELECTED

Figure 15.10 Select the Terrain and Road group for the
Instant Road plugin.

5. Click on the Plugin drop-down menu and choose Instant Road › Create Road from Face(s). Assign the appropriate settings. The free version limits the road shoulder to 3′. If you're using the Pro version, set the Shoulder Width to 10′, set Make Curb to No, and set Edit Additional Properties to yes. Click OK to run the operation (Figure 15.11).

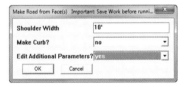

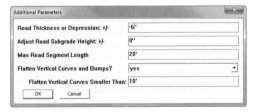

Figure 15.11 Instant Road plugin settings

6. Select the new roads and the extra group of lines, then right-click on the selection and choose "Explode."

7. Activate the Paint Bucket tool. Hold down the Alt key (Command on Mac) and click on the terrain to sample the GE Snapshot material.

8. While holding down the Ctrl key (Option on Mac), click on the new road to apply the GE Snapshot material with the "clicked on" material to all of the connected faces (Figure 15.12).

Figure 15.12 Apply the GE Snapshot material to the new roads and shoulder.

9. Using the Select tool, triple-click on the terrain; assign Layer0 to all of the terrain edges and surfaces.

10. Right-click on the selection and choose Make Group.

11. Assign the Google Earth Terrain layer to the new 3D Terrain group.

12. Right-click on the new group and choose Lock to lock the group.

TIP Instead of performing step 5, you could use the Drape tool to simply drape the 2D roads onto the 3D site. However, this won't set the contour lines to accurately represent the roads later.

Always save before you perform any sandbox or instant road operations. You should do this not because the Sandbox tools are buggy, but because if you click on the wrong object, you could find yourself waiting a long time. The Sandbox tools have the potential to process and/or generate a huge amount of geometry with one click.

3D Topographic Survey

Imagine getting your paws on a complete topographic survey of a proposed site within five minutes of receiving a new project, without leaving your desk—and for free! Although a full survey can take weeks to schedule and days to complete, with SketchUp you can generate a schematic topographic survey based on the 3D terrain data from Google Earth.

How accurate is the imported terrain data? Old terrain is 90-meter resolution, better terrain is 30-meter resolution, and excellent terrain is 10-meter resolution. All 3D terrain can be used for preliminary schematic design, but it's not a replacement for a survey. In other words, don't build off of the imported terrain data! The Grand Canyon at 10-meter resolution is spectacular, as you can see in Figure 15.13.

THE GRAND CANYON (10 METER RESOLUTION)

A FIELD IN KANSAS (90 METER RESOLUTION)

Figure 15.13 The Grand Canyon at 10-meter resolution (top); a field in Kansas at 90-meter resolution (bottom)

Slicing the Terrain

A topographic survey represents the earth sliced horizontally at regular intervals. Google provides the 3D terrain so you just need to slice it. Use simple rectangles and the Intersect menu to create topography lines, as discussed here:

1. Use the Toggle Terrain button on the Google toolbar to turn on the 3D terrain.

2. Using the Eraser tool, hold down the Shift key and click and drag over the houses to hide them if you have created them.

3. Draw a rectangle that is larger than the site. Double-click the rectangle using the Select tool to select the surface as well as the bounding edges. Right-click on the selection and choose Make Group (Figure 15.14).

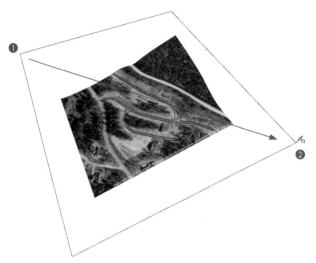

Figure 15.14 Draw the large rectangle.

4. Move the rectangle down on the blue axis until it is obviously underneath the site geometry (Figure 15.15).

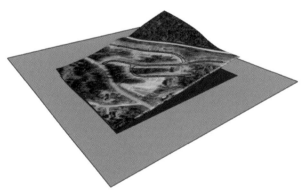

Figure 15.15 The rectangle is just below the terrain; shadows are turned on for effect.

5. Copy the rectangle up along the blue axis 5′ (or whatever interval you want your topographic map to read; for example, 1′, 10′, 25′). Immediately after you make a copy, type **150x**, then press Enter, to make 150 additional copies of the original rectangle, each at the same interval. The goal is to make sure that the entire 3D terrain is covered with the rectangle slices (Figure 15.16).

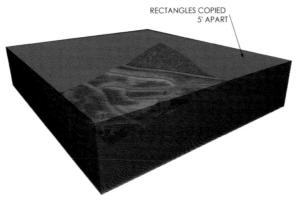

Figure 15.16 Rectangles slices are copied up on the blue axis at 5′ intervals to completely cover the terrain; X-ray mode is turned on for effect.

6. Select all of the rectangle slices and terrain. Right-click on the selection and choose Intersect Faces › With Selection (Figure 15.17). This draws all of the slices the rectangles make when they penetrate the 3D terrain, thereby creating topography lines.

7. Delete all of the rectangle slices. You no longer need them after the topography lines are created (Figure 15.18).

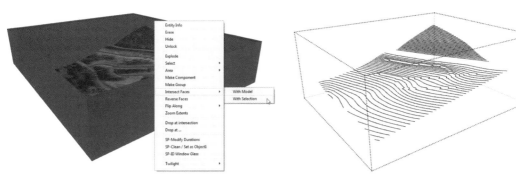

Figure 15.17 Selected rectangles

Figure 15.18 The topography lines are isolated; the Hide Rest of Model option is on for effect.

8. Click on the Edit drop-down menu and choose Select All. Right-click on the selection and choose Make Group. Because the 3D terrain is locked, only the topography lines will be included in the group.

TIP At this point, you could export the model to a 3D .dwg file so you can use it in your favorite CAD program. Click on the File drop-down menu and choose Export › 3D Model. Set the export type to .dwg and save to the appropriate folder.

Site Plan Scenes

You have created all of the geometry you need for the site plan and section. Now you need to create scenes to display the geometry in a meaningful way in LayOut. It is best to first create all of the geometry and scenes in SketchUp, and then move them to LayOut to create a presentation.

To create the scene representing the topographic lines, follow these steps:

1. Click on the Camera drop-down menu and choose Standard Views › Top.

2. Click on the Camera drop-down menu and check on Parallel Projection.

3. Click on the Camera drop-down menu and choose Zoom Extents.

4. Open the Layers dialog box by clicking on the Window drop-down menu and choosing Layers. Turn off both the Google Earth Terrain and Google Earth Snapshot layers. The site topography lines will remain.

5. Verify that the context houses are hidden.

6. Open the Scenes dialog by clicking on the Window drop-down menu and choosing Scenes. Click on the Add Scene button (+) in the top-left corner of the Scene dialog. Rename the scene **LO_5′ TOPOGRAPHY**. Place checks beside all of the properties to save.

7. Slide the new scene to the end of the line by clicking on the Move Scene Down button near the top-right corner of the Scenes dialog (Figure 15.19).

TIP Before starting the next scene, click on the LO_5′ TOPOGRAPHY scene and be careful not to move the camera. To properly align in LayOut, two scenes need to have the same camera view.

To create the scene that represents the site plan, follow these steps:

1. Click the Add Scene button (+) in the top-left corner of the Scene dialog. Rename the scene **LO_SITE PLAN**. Place checks beside all of the Properties to Save.

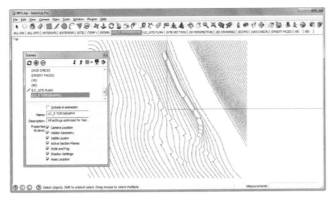

Figure 15.19 The completed LO_5′ TOPOGRAPHY scene in SketchUp

2. Click on the Edit drop-down menu and choose Unhide All. You should be able to see the context houses again.

3. Hide the topography lines by holding down the Shift key and scrubbing over them with the Eraser tool. The entire group will be hidden with one swipe.

4. Toggle on the 3D terrain by using the Toggle Terrain button on the Google toolbar.

5. Turn on the shadows (Figure 15.20).

6. Right-click on the LO_SITE PLAN scene tab at the top of the screen and choose Update (Figure 15.21).

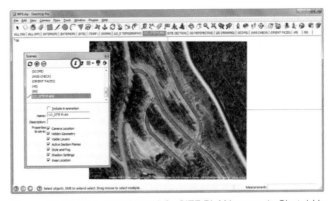

Figure 15.20 The Shadow settings   Figure 15.21 The completed LO_SITE PLAN scene in SketchUp

The 5′ TOPOGRAHY and SITE PLAN scenes are complete, but you won't need them until later in this section when you create the final presentation in LayOut.

SITE SECTION

Site sections clearly describe level changes throughout a site. Using the Section tool in SketchUp to cut through the 3D site topography will allow you to generate unlimited site sections.

Section Plane

Use a section plane to slice the site and clearly describe the elevation changes present at the site. Just follow these steps:

1. Orbit into a 3D view and zoom out to take in the entire 3D terrain on one screen.

2. Activate the Section Plane tool from the Google toolbar. Find the proper orientation for the section plane, hold Shift to lock the orientation, and then click to place the section plane (Figure 15.22).

3. Use the Move tool to adjust the location of the section plane as shown in Figure 15.23.

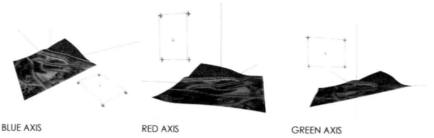

BLUE AXIS   RED AXIS   GREEN AXIS

Figure 15.22 Find the proper section plane orientation on an axis before you place the plane. Hovering on the invisible plane present at each axis will help you find the correct orientation

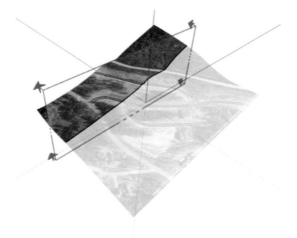

Figure 15.23 The section plane properly located

Site Section Scene

Now that you have added a section through the site, you will need to add a scene to create the Site Section drawing in LayOut. Just follow these steps:

1. Click on the 2D DRAWING utility scene tab at the top of your screen.

2. To open the Scenes dialog, click on the Window drop-down menu and choose Scenes.

3. Click on the plus sign (+) to add a scene. Check on all of the properties to save. Name the scene **LO_SITE SECTION**.

4. Right-click on the section plane and select Align View to set the camera angle perpendicular to the section plane.

5. Click on the Camera drop-down menu and verify that the camera is set to Parallel Projection.

6. Click on Zoom Extents to maximize the geometry on your screen.

7. Right-click on the LO_SITE SECTION scene tab at the top of the screen and choose Update.

8. Click the Move Page button to slide the new scene to the end of the line (Figure 15.24).

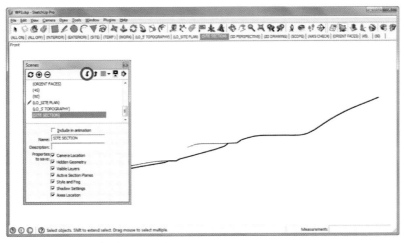

Figure 15.24 The final site section scene

At this point, you must save your model to the appropriate project folder or TEMP folder. You will need the saved file to create the final LayOut presentation. Name this file BIC_Winter Park Site.skp.

FINAL DRAWINGS

Now that you have created all of the scenes you need for the digital site survey, you are ready to present them in LayOut. In this section, you will arrange the scenes and use advanced LayOut operations to create background drawings you can use for your sketches during the design process. After some practice, you should be able to generate this type of digital-site survey graphic in just a few minutes. These graphics are also great to use when you are sitting down with a client to discuss a new project.

Site Plan

Create a site plan to think through site logistics and explain site improvements. Just follow these steps:

1. Open LayOut. Select the BIC_8.5 x 11_Landscape template (Figure 15.25).

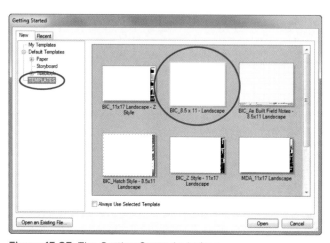

Figure 15.25 The Getting Started window

2. Click on the File drop-down menu and choose Document Setup › Paper. Adjust the paper settings to tabloid size with a portrait orientation (Figure 15.26).

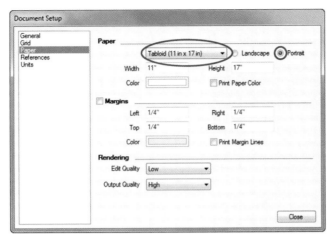

Figure 15.26 Adjust the paper size and orientation.

3. Click on the File drop-down menu and choose Insert. Navigate to the folder containing the `BIC_Winter Park Site.skp` file, select the file, and choose Open.

4. The `BIC_Winter Park Site.skp` file in the new viewport will be set to Last Saved View. With the viewport selected, assign the SITE PLAN scene in the SketchUp Model Inspector. Set the viewport to render as Hybrid so both the raster imagery and the vector linework will show. Set the viewport scale to 1″ = 50′ (Figure 15.27).

5. Use the Select tool to resize and move the viewport to fit the page as shown in Figure 15.28.

6. On the Style tab of the SketchUp Model Inspector, set the line weight to 2. If Auto-Render is unchecked, you should render the models on the page at this time (Figure 15.29).

Figure 15.27 The SketchUp Model settings indicate the scene, scale, and render settings.

7. With the viewport selected, click on the Edit drop-down menu and choose Duplicate. This will make a copy of the viewport exactly 1″ down and 1″ to the right.

8. In the SketchUp Model Inspector, on the View tab, assign the LO_5′ TOPOGRAPHY scene to the viewport. Set the viewport to render as Vector (Figure 15.30).

Figure 15.28 The site plan extents

Figure 15.29 The SketchUp Model settings' Style tab

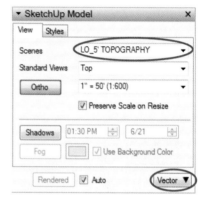

Figure 15.30 The SketchUp Model settings

9. While holding down the Shift key, tap the Left arrow key four times and then tap the Up arrow four times. When the Shift key is held down, each nudge is 1/4″.

10. Click on the Edit drop-down menu and choose Explode. The contents of the viewport become LayOut geometry and are no longer linked to the SketchUp model.

11. In the Shape Style Inspector, set the line weight to 2, the dash pattern to dots, and the dashes scale to .25 (Figure 15.31).

12. Right-click on the LO_SITE PLAN viewport and choose Explode. The raster contents of the viewport are now represented as an image in LayOut, and the vector contents of the viewport are now represented as LayOut geometry.

13. Both the raster and vector contents are contained in a group. Right-click again on the group and choose Ungroup.

14. Using the Rectangle tool, draw a mask shape around the site as shown in Figure 15.32. Draw the shape to cover up what you want to see.

15. Using the Select tool, select both the mask shape and the image, right-click on the selection, and choose Create Clipping Mask. You can modify the mask shape by double-clicking on the masked image and then double-clicking on the masking shape. Press the Esc key to finish the edit (Figure 15.33). See Chapter 14 "Inserting Content" for more information on editing clipping masks.

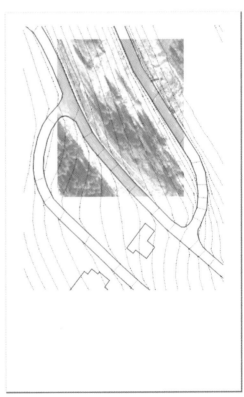

Figure 15.31 The Shape Style settings

Figure 15.32 Draw a clipping mask.

Figure 15.33 The final masked drawing

Site Section

Create a site section to think through site grading and level changes. Just follow these steps:

1. Click on the File drop-down menu and choose Insert. Once again, navigate to the folder containing the `Winter Park Site.skp` file, select the file, and choose Open.

2. Within the SketchUp Model Inspector, assign the SITE SECTION scene to the new viewport. Set the viewport to render as Vector. Set the scale to 1″ = 50′ (Figure 15.34).

3. Resize and move the viewport to fit the page and include the site section drawing as shown.

4. Right-click on the viewport and choose Explode.

5. Right-click on the new group and choose Ungroup.

6. Delete the unwanted geometry as shown in Figure 15.35.

Figure 15.34 The SketchUp Model Inspector settings

Figure 15.35 Delete the unnecessary lines.

7. Select the Site section line. In the Shape Style Inspector, set the stroke width to 3 (Figure 15.36).

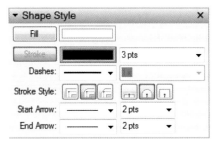

Figure 15.36 The Shape Style settings

Annotation

1. Open the Scrapbooks Inspector and navigate to the TB - Elegant collection.
2. Add drawing titles to the presentation. Using the Select tool, double-click in the scrapbooks to change the drawing title, drawing number, and scale (Figure 15.37).

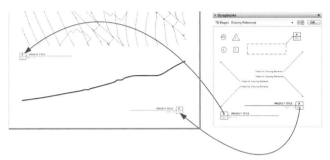

Figure 15.37 Add drawing titles.

3. Using the Next Page button in the Scrapbooks Inspector, navigate to the Sections and Elevations page of the TB-Elegant scrapbook. Add a section cut line where the section plane was added in SketchUp (Figure 15.38).

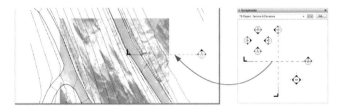

Figure 15.38 Insert a section cut callout.

4. Modify the section tag and drawing titles using the Select tool. Double-click on text to edit and correctly coordinate the drawings and tags.
5. Using the Next Page button in the Scrapbooks Inspector, navigate to the Site Graphics page of the TB-Elegant scrapbook.
6. Add a graphic scale and North arrow from the collection (Figure 15.39).

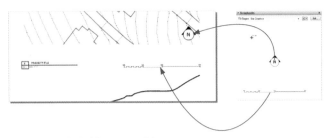

Figure 15.39 Add site graphics.

7. Use the Text tool to assign elevations to the topography lines. Find accurate elevations by hovering your cursor over points in Google Earth. You can quickly access the site in Google Earth by clicking on the File drop-down menu in SketchUp and choosing Preview in Google Earth (Figure 15.40, Figure 15.41).

ELEVATION AT
CURSOR LOCATION

Figure 15.40 Use Google Earth to find topographic elevations.

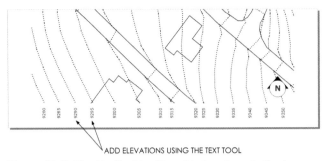

ADD ELEVATIONS USING THE TEXT TOOL

Figure 15.41 Use the Text tool to add elevations to the topography lines.

Exporting PDF

Now that the presentation is complete, it is time to print and start designing. Click on the File drop-down menu and choose Export › PDF to create a `.pdf` file you can print or email. Navigate to an appropriate project folder, or your TEMP folder, and select Save (Figure 15.42).

Uncheck Create PDF Layers from LayOut Layers. Typically, you won't need to have these layers available in the `.pdf`, and they can sometimes cause problems at the print shop.

Set the Output Quality to High. Final output should always be at the highest resolution and quality possible (Figure 15.43).

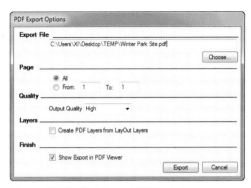

Figure 15.42 The Export PDF window

CHAPTER POINTS

☑ You can explode viewports in LayOut for existing conditions because the existing conditions do not change.

☑ Many of the operations completed in this chapter can be accessed from several different places; an Inspector, a keyboard shortcut, a custom toolbar, a right-click menu, or from the drop-down menus at the top of the screen. Use whichever method feels best to you.

☑ You should export LayOut presentations to a `.pdf` file and print from there because a `.pdf` file gives you the most printing options. Avoid using the Print command in LayOut.

☑ After you practice making the digital site survey exercise five times, you should be able to do the whole thing in less than fifteen minutes.

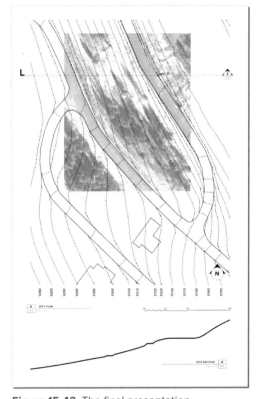

Figure 15.43 The final presentation

☑ You can unlock and modify the terrain, but don't move it. If you move the terrain, the geo-location settings and shadows will no longer be accurate.

Chapter 16

Site Analysis: Building Context

The built environment surrounding your site can influence design, provide interesting reactions, or be totally insignificant and better off ignored. Regardless of how you view the surrounding environment, you should always consider building context when you are making a site analysis. With a geo-located model, you can find and generate the buildings surrounding a site in several ways, regardless of how little or how much information you have to start.

THE PROJECT SITE

Imagine for a moment that you have been asked to design a structure on a lot near the very visible Golden Triangle Museum District in Denver. As a responsible designer, you want to address the context, but how do you address the critically famous and complex context at this site, which includes Michael Grave's Geometric Central Library; the brand-new, sleek, minimalist Clyfford Still Museum; and Daniel Libeskind's abstract extension to the art museum? How in the world would you even build something like the art museum extension in SketchUp? In this chapter, you will collect and build the context near the Golden Triangle Museum District in Denver (Figure 16.1).

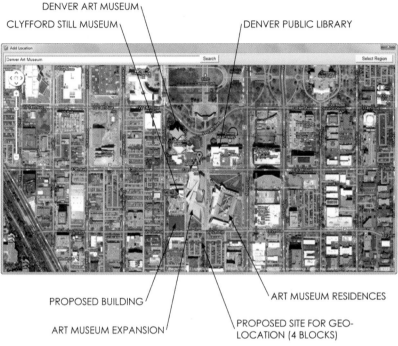

Figure 16.1 The proposed context zone and building site

To define the site, follow these steps:

1. Start a new model by opening SketchUp, or click on the File drop-down menu and select New.

2. Click the Add Location button on the Google toolbar to geo-locate the model.

3. Enter **Denver Art Museum** in the search bar and zoom out several clicks to locate the site, as shown in Figure 16.1.

4. Click the Select Region button.

5. Position the pins around the four city blocks that compose the site, as shown in Figure 16.2.

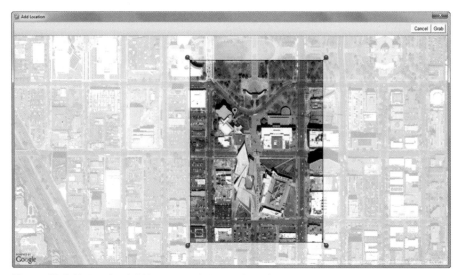

Figure 16.2 Using the Add Location dialog, select the site with pins.

6. Click the Grab button to import the selected site.

7. Toggle the Google Earth Terrain off and add a proposed building mass on the southwest corner of the site, as shown in Figure 16.3.

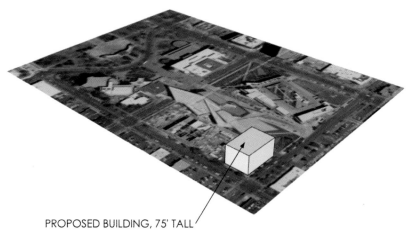

PROPOSED BUILDING, 75' TALL

Figure 16.3 The proposed building at the southwest corner of the site

FINDING NEARBY BUILDINGS

Instead of spending hours trying to measure and build your own context models, find someone else's. Geo-located models uploaded to 3D Warehouse, as well as some buildings from Google Earth, are searchable and available for download through the Components browser. Once a location is attached to your model, you will be able to find other buildings that are close to your site in the Nearby Buildings collection. To do that, follow these steps:

1. To open the Components browser, click on the Window drop-down menu and choose Components.

2. In the Components browser, click on the Collections drop-down menu and choose Nearby Buildings (Figure 16.4). Remember, this collection is available only after a model has been geo-located.

3. Click on the thumbnail icon to immediately download a model directly into the current SketchUp model. Find and import the models indicated with red dots in Figure 16.5.

4. Double-click on each of the context building models, click on the Edit drop-down menu, and choose Unhide > All. The lines you need to create a complete building-elevation line drawing will appear.

5. Unlock and delete the 3D terrain and aerial imagery in all of the imported context models. The most current and accurate terrain is already imported into your model (Figure 16.6).

TIP The Nearby Buildings collection is very helpful for working with heavily populated areas. Useful models are readily available for most downtown areas, while models for the suburbs are typically not.

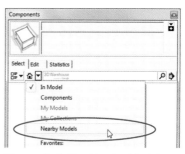

Figure 16.4 The Nearby Models collection is available in the Collections drop-down menu.

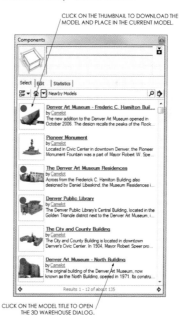

CLICK ON THE THUMBNAIL TO DOWNLOAD THE MODEL AND PLACE IN THE CURRENT MODEL.

CLICK ON THE MODEL TITLE TO OPEN THE 3D WAREHOUSE DIALOG.

Figure 16.5 Import four models from the Nearby Models collection.

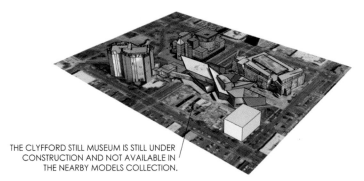

THE CLYFFORD STILL MUSEUM IS STILL UNDER
CONSTRUCTION AND NOT AVAILABLE IN
THE NEARBY MODELS COLLECTION.

Figure 16.6 The final site with context models

GEO-MODELING

If you don't find everything you need in the Nearby Models collection, you can always build models yourself.

Match Photo is a SketchUp feature that allows you to reverse engineer the perspective of a photograph to trace a 2D image and ultimately produce a 3D model. You may have completed a studio project in college where you enlarged a photograph on a copy machine, taped it to your desk, and then used a T-square to project the vanishing points onto your neighbor's desk. Then, you used those points to trace the rest of the photograph and generate new designs with the same perspective. SketchUp allows you to do the same thing in a much more efficient digital interface.

The photograph is taped to your digital desk in SketchUp as an image file import. The T-square to trace the photograph and project the vanishing points is replaced with the axes bars in the Match Photo interface. Your pencil is replaced with SketchUp's Drawing and Modification tools.

Once Match Photo is set up, the process can be as easy as tracing a 2D photograph with the Drawing tools to create a 3D model. In the following exercise, you will leverage Match Photo by combining a properly scaled building footprint imported from Google Earth with a perspective photograph to create an accurate and detailed 3D SketchUp model.

Photographing a Building

When you're taking photographs to use in Match Photo, keep the following tips in mind:

☑ Do not use any special lenses on your camera. A typical, inexpensive camera or even a phone camera will work just fine.

☑ Walk around the entire site and photograph the entire building from every angle possible.

☑ Photograph the building's details up close—for example, signs, materials, entries, windows, and doors.

☑ Too many pictures are better than too few. When you're working at 2:00 A.M., you don't want to need more than you shot.

☑ Do not crop or resize the images before you import them into SketchUp.

Creating a Mass Model

To create a building mass model, follow these steps:

1. For now, hide the four context models and the proposed building mass. To do this, select all of them, right-click on the selection, and choose Hide.

2. Click on the File drop-down menu and select the Geo-Location menu. Uncheck the Show Terrain option so that only the flat 2D aerial imagery is showing.

3. Activate the Rectangle tool and click once on the top-left corner of the building footprint.

4. Move your cursor away from the start point and click again on the bottom-right corner of the building footprint to finish the rectangle (Figure 16.7). There is no need for precise dimensions on this geo-model.

5. Use the Push/Pull tool to extrude the rectangle up to an exaggerated height as shown in Figure 16.8.

6. Set the origin at an appropriate starting point for sketching. For this model, and most others, set the axes at the front-bottom corner of

Figure 16.7 Use the Rectangle tool to trace the building footprint.

the model when viewing the model from a vantage point similar to the Match Photo photograph.

7. Within SketchUp, position yourself in a view similar to the photograph you are using for Match Photo (Figure 16.9).

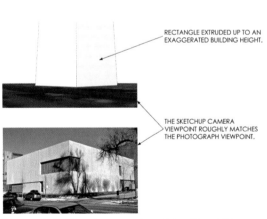

RECTANGLE EXTRUDED UP TO AN EXAGGERATED BUILDING HEIGHT.

THE SKETCHUP CAMERA VIEWPOINT ROUGHLY MATCHES THE PHOTOGRAPH VIEWPOINT.

Figure 16.8 The photograph and the SketchUp model shown in similar views

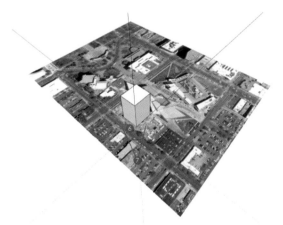

Figure 16.9 Set the origin at the front-bottom corner of the building based on the photograph you are using for Match Photo.

Using Match New Photo

To use the Match Photo interface, follow these steps:

1. Click on the Camera drop-down menu and choose Match New Photo.

2. Navigate to your Project Files folder and select the Match Photo image BIC_01 - Clyfford Still Museum.jpg. Click on Open to return to SketchUp; an admittedly intimidating grid will appear over the photograph. Take a moment to study the image in Figure 16.10.

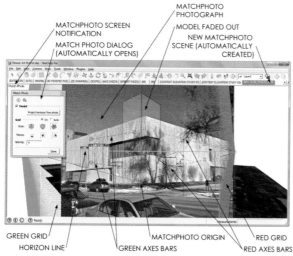

Figure 16.10 The Match Photo interface

3. Navigate the Match Photo interface using familiar mouse navigation techniques. Push down and hold the scroll-wheel button to pan the screen up, down, left, and right. Roll the scroll-wheel toward the screen to zoom in, and away from the screen to zoom out. Click outside of the Match Photo photograph to exit Match Photo mode.

TIP To get back to Match Photo mode, right-click on the automatically created Match Photo Scene tab and choose Edit Matched Photo.

4. In the Match Photo dialog box, uncheck the Model check box to turn off the model and clarify the Match Photo screen, which will make working with the Match Photo interface much easier.

5. Align the axis bars with parallel elements on the building, such as window headers and mullions, ledges, and roof lines. The green axis bars should be aligned with parallel elements on the west side of the building, and the red axis bars should be aligned with parallel elements on the south side of the building (Figure 16.11).

TIP Avoid using the ground plane as a parallel element because it will never be perfectly parallel with the building.

6. Position the Match Photo origin at an appropriate starting point for sketching (Figure 16.12). This will be at the same front-bottom corner you positioned the axes at in the beginning of the exercise.

7. In the Match Photo dialog, turn on the model.

8. Zoom the Match Photo photograph to match the model by clicking and dragging on an axis until the vertical walls of the SketchUp model match the walls of the Match Photo photograph (Figure 16.13). The footprint is correct now; that is why you align the vertical walls. The building height is not yet correct and should be ignored for now because it was drawn at an exaggerated height.

9. In the Match Photo dialog, click the Done button.

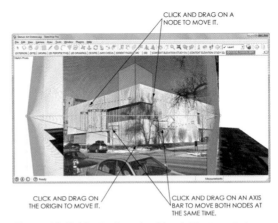

Figure 16.11 Manipulate the Match Photo axis bars and origin.

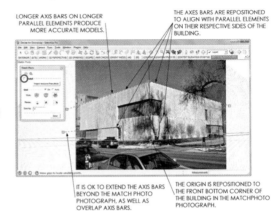

Figure 16.12 The Match Photo axis bars and origin aligned with the Match Photo photograph

Figure 16.13 Click and drag on any axis to zoom the photo.

Setting Building Height

To accurately set the height of the building, follow these steps:

1. Orbit to a bird's eye view. Activate the Push/Pull tool and click once on the top of the building (Figure 16.14).

2. Click on the Match Photo Scene tab to get back to Match Photo mode.

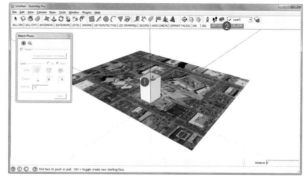

3. Move your cursor down until the top of the 3D building mass is aligned with the top of the building in the photograph (Figure 16.15). Click to finish the Push/Pull command.

Figure 16.14 Use the Push/Pull tool to adjust the building's height.

4. Take a moment to orbit around and inspect the 3D mass model.

The building width and height are now accurately set. You know this because the building length and width are derived from the building footprint imported from Google Earth. The height of the building is accurately determined by reverse engineering a perspective photograph and aligning it with the known building footprint.

Figure 16.15 Align the top of the model with the top of the building in the photograph.

Adding 3D Detail

To add detail to your model, follow these steps:

1. Once again, click on the Match Photo scene tab at the top of your screen.

2. In the Match Photo dialog, click on Project Textures to apply the Match Photo photograph to the 3D surfaces. This is what makes a geo-model so "light." The detail is held in a photograph rather than represented by 3D geometry.

3. Orbit to a 3D view, and then trace over the applied texture images using the SketchUp Drawing tools to create the major breaks in the facades.

4. Use the Modification tools to turn those breaks in the surfaces into further developed 3D details. Go back to the Match Photo scene to use the photograph as a guide for modeling. Draw from other photographs and your own experience when modeling.

5. Using the Paint Bucket tool, hold the Alt key (Command on Mac) to sample the Google Earth Snapshot, then apply the Google Earth Snapshot to the roof (Figure 16.16).

Figure 16.16 Context model with added detail

TIP You can gather additional texture images by using Google Street View in SketchUp. The imagery pulled from Street View is not nearly as high-resolution as an imported image or Match Photo, but it is often all you need to generate detail on a context building that you can't photograph in person. Right-click on a surface and choose Add Photo Texture to launch the Street View imagery dialog.

Importing 2D Detail

Match Photo is best used to create the broad strokes of a model, or the massing in general. Once a building mass is complete, you can use imported images to add high-resolution texture images where they are needed. Use the import image as material technique to replace low-resolution match photo materials with your high-resolution close-up photographs.

1. Zoom in on the entry of the building (Figure 16.17).

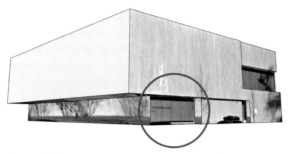

Figure 16.17 Zoom into the entry of the building for a strategic view.

2. Click on the File drop-down menu and choose Import.

3. Verify that the Files of Type drop-down menu is set to All Supported Image Types , and the "Use as Texture" radio button is on. Navigate to the class files folder for this chapter and select *BIC_02 - Clyfford Still Museum Entry*.jpg. Click the Open button.

4. Click once directly on the surface to place the image (Figure 16.18).

Figure 16.18 Click directly on the surface. Avoid using edges and points when you initially place an image as a texture.

5. Move your cursor away from the start point to loosely scale the image; click again to finish the import. The image will repeat, or tile, across the surface.

Tweaking a Texture

You can use the Texture Tweaker pins to fine-tune your texture images. Just follow these steps:

1. Right-click on the surface with the new image, and select Texture › Position to modify the imported texture image.

2. Each of the Texture Tweaker fixed pins has a specific job for modifying the texture image. Click once on a pin to pick it up, and click again to put it down. Reposition the four pins on the four corners of the entry wall in the photograph shown in Figure 16.19.

3. Click and drag the red pin to the bottom-left corner of the entry wall in the model. This will move the entire texture image (Figure 16.20).

4. Click and drag the green pin to the bottom-right corner of the entry wall in the model. This will properly scale and rotate the image to align with the model (Figure 16.20).

5. Click and drag the blue pin to the top left corner of the entry wall in the model. This will properly scale and shear the image to further align with the model (Figure 16.20).

6. Click and drag the yellow pin to the top-right corner of the entry wall in the model. This will properly distort the image so that it fits the entry wall perfectly (Figure 16.20).

7. Press the Enter key to finish the Texture Tweak and apply the changes (Figure 16.21).

Figure 16.19 Click on the pins to reposition them as shown.

Figure 16.20 Click and drag the pins as shown to tweak the texture image.

Figure 16.21 The final, tweaked texture image is clearer than the original Match Photo image.

TIP Another way to remove unwanted objects from a texture image is to use an external image editor. Right-click on a surface with a texture applied to it and select Texture › Edit Texture Image. This will open the texture image in the assigned image editor.

Making Unique Materials

The Make Unique Material feature allows you to find a good chunk of one material and make another unique material from that. You can apply the new, optimized material to the rest of the model, eliminating trees, shadows, and low-resolution texture images (Figure 16.22).

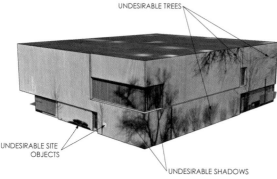

Figure16.22 Use the Make Unique Material function to clean up unwanted objects in the texture image.

1. Draw a rectangle around a piece of the scored concrete that is free of trees, shadows, and objects. A projected texture image's quality will be best toward the foreground of the Match Photo image (Figure 16.23).

2. Right-click in the rectangle and select Make Unique Texture. This will create a new material cropped to the extents of the rectangle.

3. Activate the Paint Bucket tool. Hold down the Alt key (Command on Mac) and click on the new unique material to sample it, making it the current material.

4. To apply the new, optimized material, click on surfaces that have a lower-resolution texture image (Figure 16.24).

Another benefit to making a material unique is that you eliminate pieces of images that are not being used, resulting in smaller file sizes.

1. Right-click on the front-entry wall-texture image and select Make Unique Material. You won't see a difference in your model, but everything in the image that is not shown on the surface will be deleted.

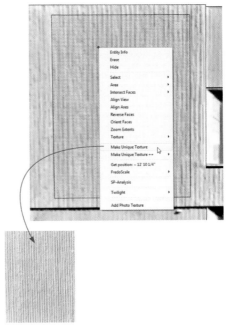

Figure 16.23 The "best" portion of the scored concrete material is captured in a rectangle.

Figure 16.24 The Clyfford Still Museum context model with optimized texture images applied

TIP View your designs in the context of the real world in Google Earth. Google Earth lets you view all context in the entire city as well as 3D terrain that extends as far as the eye can see. Click on the File drop-down menu and choose Preview in Google Earth.

Continue to use the import texture image and make unique texture strategies to further develop and add detail to the Clyfford Still Museum context model.

Creating Scenes

Now that the proposed building and context are in a model, you can closely study the interaction between a proposed design and existing site conditions. One way to do this is through a shadow study. Create scenes to illustrate the effects of shadows on your neighbors. Just follow these steps:

1. Orbit to a 3D perspective view, click on the Edit drop-down menu, and choose Unhide › All.

2. To switch to a line-drawing style and turn on the shadows, click on the 2D DRAWING Scene tab at the top of your SketchUp template.

3. Adjust the shadow settings time to 9:00 A.M.

4. In the Scenes browser, click on the plus sign (+) to add a scene.

5. Rename the scene **LO_ Shadow Study - 900AM** and check on all of the Properties to Save . Move the scene to the bottom of the list using the "Move Scene Down" button in the Scenes dialog (Figure 16.25).

6. Repeat steps 3 through 5 for the following scenes: 1100AM, 100PM, 300PM, 500PM, and 700PM. Adjust the shadow time to the respective scene name.

7. Save the model to your TEMP folder or a logical project folder. Name the file BIC_Golden Triangle Museum District.skp.

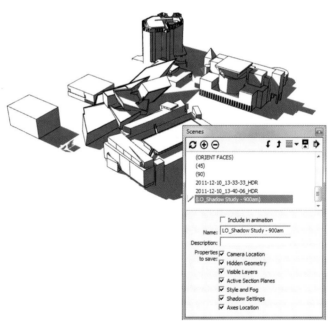

Figure 16.25 The LO_Shadow Study scene in SketchUp and the Scene properties to be saved

TIP Purge your models to completely remove unused entities. Click on the Window drop-down menu and choose Model Info. In the Statistics tab, click on Purge Unused to remove all unused layers, materials, styles, and components. Purging before saving often drastically reduces the size of the file.

Now that you have the context models, you might want to send them over to your favorite 2D or 3D CAD program. To do that, follow these steps:

1. Right-click on the surface of an elevation and select Align View.
2. Click on the View drop-down menu and choose Zoom Extents.
3. Click on the File drop-down menu and select Export › 2D Graphic.
4. Set the Export Type to `.dwg`/`.dxf` and click the Export Options button to select a `.dwg` format.
5. Click the Export button to finish.

LAYOUT DIAGRAMS

To create and annotate a shadow study, send the SketchUp model to LayOut. Just follow these steps:

1. Within SketchUp, click on the File drop-down menu and choose Send to LayOut.
2. Within LayOut, select the BIC_8.5x11 – Landscape template (or your favorite template or title block).
3. Move and scale the viewport so that it takes up the top-left one-sixth of the page.
4. Select the viewport; in the SketchUp Model Inspector, assign the LO_Shadow Study - 900AM scene.
5. Shadows must render as rasters, and lines look best when rendered as vectors. Therefore, set the viewport to render as Hybrid.
6. While holding down the Ctrl key, click and drag on the viewport to make a copy.
7. In the SketchUp Model Inspector, change the scene to LO_Shadow Study - 1100AM.
8. Repeat steps 6 and 7 for each additional shadow study scene.
9. Below each image, add text that indicates the time of day (Figure 16.26).

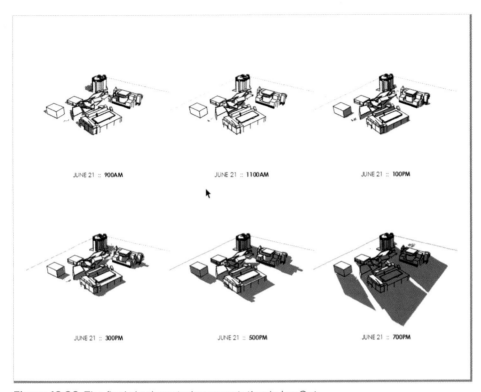

Figure 16.26 The final shadow study presentation in LayOut

TIP It is possible to modify a viewport's style and shadow settings in the SketchUp Model Inspector, although it is almost always better to assign these properties to a scene in SketchUp and then assign each scene to a viewport in LayOut.

CHAPTER POINTS

☑ For those really tricky buildings that you just can't see on Street View and can't take any worthwhile pictures of, try using Building Maker. Building Maker uses multiple aerial shots combined with simple Shape tools to create photo-textured models. Click on the File drop-down menu and choose Building Maker › Add New Building.

☑ Market your firm with an online portfolio of geo-models representing completed projects. Submit your designs to be included in Google Earth through the 3D Warehouse upload. Click on the File drop-down menu and choose 3D Warehouse > Share Model.

☑ There are other, more advanced techniques for using Match Photo. View a tutorial that explains how to use multiple Match Photos to further advance the Clyfford Still Museum model at **www.suexch.com/TSWFA.**

☑ Match Photo is best for creating the building mass. Use a combination of projected photos and higher-resolution imported photos to get the best results. Use the texture-tweaking tools to optimize higher-resolution photo-textures.

☑ Geo-modeling is not an exact science. Don't hesitate to sketch in minor details to make the model more complete.

Chapter 17

Site Analysis: Documenting an Existing Building

Creating accurate as-built drawings is a critical early step in the design process. When you're making decisions about new construction, it is important to be well informed about existing conditions. The techniques in this section will give you an organized plan of attack for measuring and documenting any building.

THE PROJECT

For this exercise, you will prepare for a site visit to a house where the client would like to remodel the main floor and add a new kitchen, bathroom configuration, and master bedroom suite. You will record and document the existing conditions using SketchUp and LayOut to expedite the process.

Preparing for a Site Visit

Often when visiting a site, you'll spend hours pacing off the building, sketching the footprint, and trying to record everything on one landscape page—or even trickier, you might try to break things up on multiple pages. This is a difficult task! Fortunately, there is a way to create your initial field sketch in 5 minutes—before you even leave the office. Follow the steps in this section to trace the building footprint in SketchUp and print at an ideal scale from LayOut onto custom grid paper.

Adding the Location

To add the location, follow these steps:

1. Open SketchUp and start a new model.

2. Click on the File drop-down menu and select Geo-Location › Add Location. In the search bar, type **3458 Steele St, Denver, Co**, then press Enter (Figure 17.1).

3. Once you track down the correct residence, click the Select Region button.

4. Use the pins to position the selection area over the entire property (Figure 17.2).

5. Click the Grab button to import the selected Google Earth Snapshot and Terrain.

Figure 17.1 The Add Location dialog

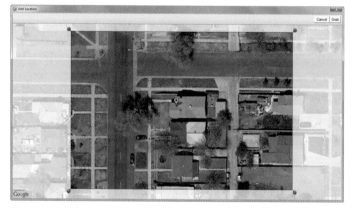

Figure 17.2 Grab plenty of context around the site—just in case!

Creating the Building Footprint

To create the building footprint, follow these steps:

1. Click the File drop-down menu and choose Geo-Location, and uncheck the Show Terrain option. To do this, you could also use the Toggle Terrain button on the Google toolbar.

2. Trace the roof outline using the Rectangle tool. For this task, it is faster to use the Rectangle tool to trace over each portion of the roof rather than using the line tool (Figure 17.3).

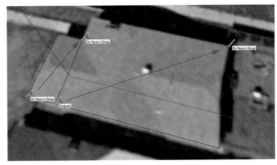

Figure 17.3 Use the Rectangle tool to trace the roof outline.

TIP Enable Length Snapping to make what seem to be loose sketches much cleaner with precise round measurements. Typically, when you're tracing a site, a 1″ tolerance for Length Snapping is ideal. Click on the Window drop-down menu and choose Model Info. Then click on the Units tab to adjust the length snapping features.

3. Using the Offset tool, offset the roof outline by 18″ to create the exterior wall line (Figure 17.4).

4. Offset the exterior wall line by 12″ to create the interior wall line (Figure 17.4).

5. Use the Eraser tool to delete any extra unwanted edges.

6. Save the model to your TEMP folder or appropriate project folder as **BIC_3458 Steele St – Existing Conditions.skp**.

7. Using the Select tool, triple-click on the sketch of the building footprint to select all the connected geometry.

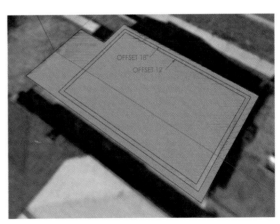

Figure 17.4 Offset the outer lines to create an estimated building footprint.

8. Click on the Edit drop-down menu and choose Make Group.

9. Click on the Edit drop-down menu and choose Copy.

Pasting into LayOut

Typically, graph paper lines are spaced apart at 1/10", 1/8" or 1/4", which can make field sketching difficult if the drawing size is not suited to one of these scales. LayOut allows you to create a custom grid that matches any architectural scale, even a custom or irregular scale. Just follow these steps:

1. Start a new LayOut presentation using the BIC_8.5x11 – Landscape template.

2. Click on the Edit drop-down menu and choose Paste. The SketchUp geometry will be inserted into LayOut as a generic SketchUp model linked to the LayOut presentation, displayed in a viewport (Figure 17.5).

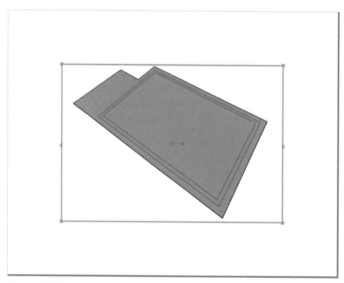

Figure 17.5 The pasted viewport in LayOut

3. Expand the viewport to cover the entire page.

4. Select the new generic viewport and adjust the properties in the SketchUp Model Inspector, as shown in Figure 17.6.

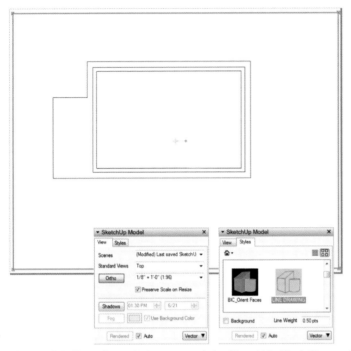

Figure 17.6 The adjusted viewport and the SketchUp Model Inspector

Creating an Optimized Scale

The as-built sketch does not fit perfectly on the page at 1/8″ = 1′-0″; it is too small. At 1/4″ = 1′-0″, the drawing is too big. What you really need is an irregular scale that falls somewhere between these scales. In this section, you will create a custom scale in LayOut so that your as-built drawing is maximized on the page, giving you the most space to work with in the field.

1. Experiment with different standard scales in the SketchUp Model Inspector. You'll see that a standard scale does not work well for this drawing.

2. At the bottom of the Scale drop-down menu, click the Add Custom Scale button.

3. This automatically launches the LayOut Preferences dialogue box. Technically, 1/4″ scale is equivalent to 1″ = 4′-0″, so try to work one level up; 1″ = 5′-0″ fits perfectly (Figure 17.7).

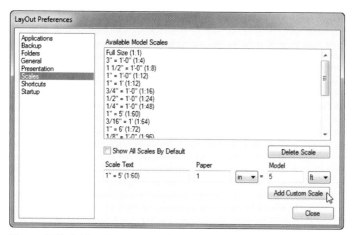

Figure 17.7 Add an irregular scale in the Preferences dialog.

4. Assign the 1″ = 5′-0″ scale to the viewport, and then resize and reposition the viewport on the page as needed (Figure 17.8).

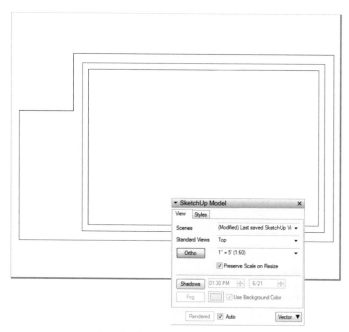

Figure 17.8 The 1″ = 5′-0″ scale maximizes the drawing on the sheet.

Matching the Grid to Scale

Now that you have created an irregular scale to maximize your drawing size, you will want to match your grid to the irregular scale of $1'' = 5'-0''$ (Figure 17.9). This will make the task of field sketching faster, easier, and much more accurate. Follow these steps:

1. Click on the File drop-down menu and choose Document Setup. Click on the Grid tab in the left column.

2. Click the Show Grid check box to toggle on the grid visibility.

3. Set the Major Grid spacing to $1''$.

4. Set the number of divisions to 5.

5. While you have this tab open, check on the Print Grid feature.

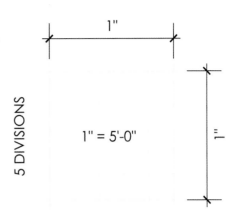

Figure 17.9 A $1''$ grid with five divisions perfectly matches the scale, $1'' = 5'-0''$.

Aligning the Drawing with the Grid

Now that the scale is set, you'll want to align the drawing with the grid (Figure 17.10). Just follow these steps:

1. Right-click in the LayOut work area and check on the Grid Snap feature. This will allow you to perfectly align the drawing with the grid.

2. Using the Select tool, select the viewport. Click and drag on the Precise Move grip to pick it up, and then release to place it on the inside corner of the wall in your drawing.

3. Click and drag on the drawing within the viewport, and allow the Precise Move grip to snap to the grid.

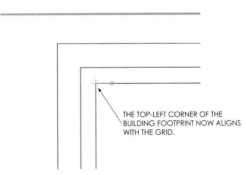

Figure 17.10 Align the top-left inside corner with the grid.

TIP At this point you could explode the building outline plan and apply a more complex graphic style using the Shape Style Inspector in LayOut. For instance, you could make the roof outline dashed and adjust line weights.

Exporting the PDF

Now that your building outline is ready for the field, you'll need to export to PDF, print, and head to the site.

1. Click on the File drop-down menu and select Export › PDF.

2. Save this file in your TEMP folder, or in the EXPORTS folder in the appropriate project folder.

3. The PDF options dialog opens automatically. Adjust the settings as shown in Figure 17.11.

4. When the export finishes and the .pdf opens, click on the File drop-down menu and choose Print. Print a copy of the drawing for each floor that you intend to document, and make some extra copies just in case.

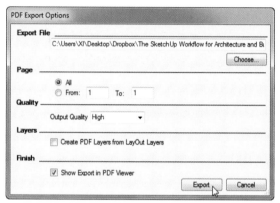

Figure 17.11 The Export Option settings

RECORDING FIELD NOTES

Recording dimensions in the field can be a tricky task. The following tips will help you stay organized when you're taking notes in the field and ultimately prepare your field notes for importing and efficient 3D modeling.

☑ Record the measurements only in inches, rather than feet and inches (Figure 17.12). This will ultimately make modeling in SketchUp easier. For instance, write **88.75**, rather than 7'-4-3/4". This will save you room on the page and keystrokes in SketchUp.

Figure 17.12 Record your measurements in decimal inches.

☑ Note the inside wall-to-wall dimensions instead of trying to draw wall thicknesses at a small scale. If there are several different wall types/thicknesses, use a highlighter to call out the wall thicknesses from a wall type key. Alternatively, you can make a general note—for example, "all walls are 5″ unless otherwise noted"—rather than dimensioning every wall's thickness (Figure 17.13).

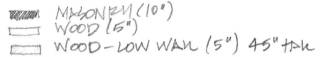

Figure 17.13 A wall key saves room on the drawings by eliminating dimensions.

☑ Give yourself plenty of room by always working at the largest scale possible. If the building is very large, it could make more sense to use a tabloid-size sheet or multiple letter-size sheets.

☑ Use general notes to minimize repetitive notes on the field notes drawing (Figure 17.14). Call out general ceiling heights, door heights, finishes, etc.

Figure 17.14 Use general notes to eliminate repetitive and ambiguous notes.

☑ Add the overall room dimensions in the center of the room in a drawing (Figure 17.15). Use the same X-distance/Y-distance format every time.

☑ Record the sill heights and window heights on the outer perimeter of the plan, with the text oriented to be read from the outside of the page (Figure 17.16). Use the format: Sill height/Head height.

☑ Avoid using dimension lines. Record wall, window, and door dimensions within the building drawing oriented in line with the dimensions they define (Figure 17.17).

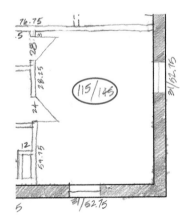

Figure 17.15 Overall room dimensions provide a reality check to insure that all measurements add up correctly.

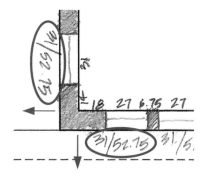

Figure 17.16 Sill heights and window heights should be oriented to be read from the outside of the plan.

Figure 17.17 Dimensions running along the walls

☑ Record the wall locations only on the main plan. Bring letter-sized tracing paper to document additional layers, such as equipment (Figure 17.18), reflected ceiling plans, framing, etc. This will help you keep your drawing clean and organized. Be sure to mark where each drawing sits by tracing the corners of your plan (Figure 17.19).

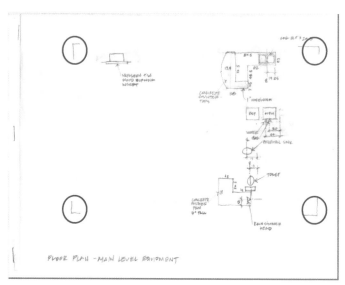

Figure 17.18 The Equipment information and dimensions are recorded on a separate piece of trace paper.

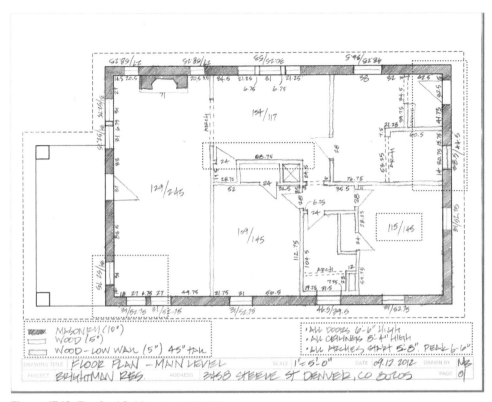

Figure 17.19 The final field measurements

THE AS-BUILT 3D MODEL

Creating the as-built 3D model is possibly the most important step in the design process for a renovation project. All design decisions will be made from this model, so it must be extremely accurate. Any mistakes made here will carry through every model and drawing you create, and ultimately these mistakes will drastically affect the actual construction!

Importing the Field Notes

To import your field notes, follow these steps:

1. Scan all the pages of your field notes and save them in the IMAGES folder for the project. To maintain your organization, create a subfolder in the IMAGES folder and name it **YYMMDD_Field Measurements**, using today's date. To complete this exercise you will use the scanned field notes from the class files folder.

2. In SketchUp, open the `BIC_3458 Steele St - Existing Conditions.skp` file.

3. In the Layers dialog, turn off the Google Earth Snapshot and Google Earth Terrain layers.

4. Click on the File drop-down menu and select Import. Set the Files of Type setting to All Supported Image Types. If you don't, you won't be able to see your scanned image files. Make sure the Use as Image radio button is activated for the import type (Figure 17.20).

5. Navigate to the TSWFA folder and select the `BIC_3458 Steele St - Main Level Floor Plan.jpg` scan and click the Open button.

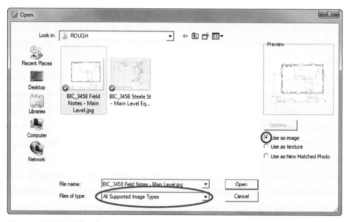

Figure 17.20 The Import settings

6. Click once to place the image, and then move your cursor away to scale the image. You don't need to be exact right now because you will scale precisely in the next step (Figure 17.21). Click again to finish placing the image.

7. Right-click on the image and select Explode. Exploding an image converts it to a surface with a material applied to it. The material's texture image is the imported image.

8. Double-click the surface, and then right-click and choose Make Group.

9. Select the new group containing the field notes; in the Entity Info dialog, assign the CONC – Background layer.

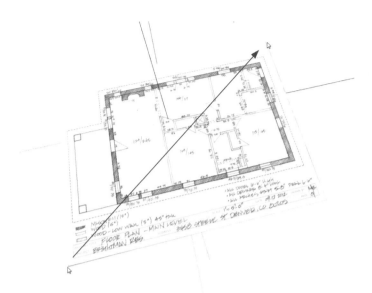

Figure 17.21 You don't need to be precise when you insert the image.

Scaling the Field Notes

After you insert the field notes, you'll need to scale them.

1. Activate the Tape Measure tool. Find a known dimension. Measure the overall distance of the building and remember that distance (Figure 17.22).

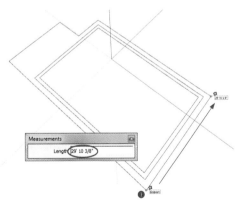

Figure 17.22 Measure the overall length of the building outline.

2. Using the Select tool, double-click into the Field Notes group.

3. Using the Tape Measure tool, measure that same overall distance on the field notes (Figure 17.23).

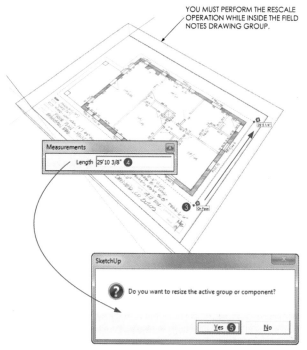

Figure 17.23 Measure the same overall length of the field notes image.

4. Immediately after the second click, enter what the actual distance should be, then press Enter. This is the distance that you remembered from step 1, in this example 29' 10 3/8", although on your model this distance might be slightly different.

5. SketchUp asks if you would like to "resize the active group or component." Choose Yes. This sets the measurement to be the same as what you just typed in.

6. Close the Field Notes Drawing group.

7. Perform a precise move to align the field notes drawing with the original building footprint sketch (Figure 17.24).

8. Right-click on the Field Notes group and select Lock.

9. Delete the original building footprint sketch. You no longer need it.

10. Click on the File drop-down menu and choose Save.

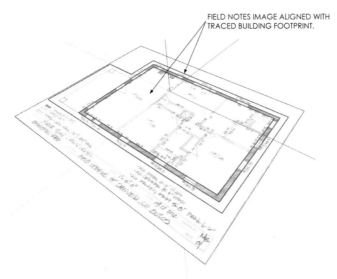

Figure 17.24 Align the properly scaled field notes drawing with the traced building outline.

Modeling from the Field Notes

Now you are ready to draft the existing conditions. The beauty of this technique is that there is no need to look back and forth between your field notes and the computer because your field notes are already in the model.

1. Draw a square at 12″ × 12″ in the corner of the plan (Figure 17.25).

2. Push/pull the square up to the recorded ceiling height of 8′4″ (Figure 17.26).

3. Using the Push/Pull tool, extrude the plan horizontally (Figure 17.27, Figure 17.28). As you are push/pulling, tap the Ctrl key (Option key on Mac) to toggle the Create New Starting Face command. This leaves a copy of the starting face and edges behind

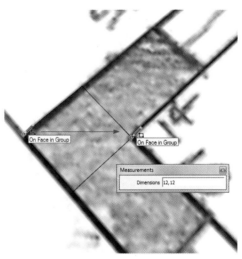

Figure 17.25 Square drawn in the southwest corner of the plan

and allows you to mark horizontal breaks and openings. Leave a starting face at every major opening, such as walls, doors, and windows.

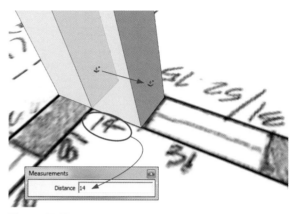

Figure 17.27 Extrude the plan horizontally using the Push/Pull tool. Read the dimensions of each section off of the field notes drawing.

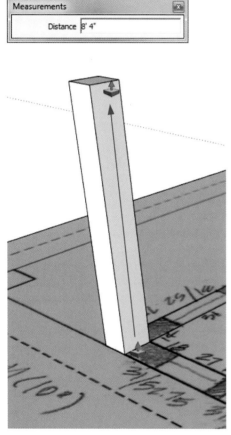

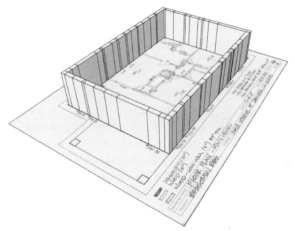

Figure 17.26 Pull the square up to the recorded ceiling height to begin to form the exterior walls.

Figure 17.28 Continue extruding the plan horizontally around the entire house and complete all the exterior walls.

4. Navigate to the outside of the model. Use the Move tool to copy the bottom lines of the door and window openings up to the noted sill heights, and then again for the head heights (Figure 17.29, Figure 17.30, Figure 17.31).

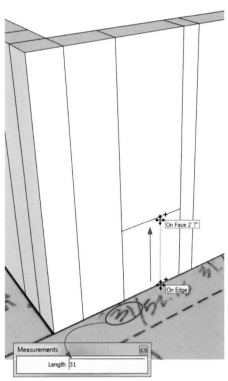

Figure 17.29 Use the Move tool to copy edges up to the sill heights noted on the field notes drawing. (Southwest corner of the plan is shown.)

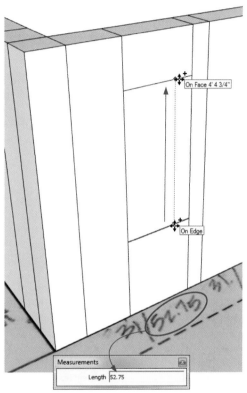

Figure 17.30 Use the Move tool to copy edges up to the head heights noted on the field notes drawing. (Southwest corner of the plan is shown.)

TIP You can create the openings using several different methods. You could use the Tape Measure tool to create guides, and then use the Rectangle or Line tool to create the rest of the opening. Use the tools and methods that you find the most efficient.

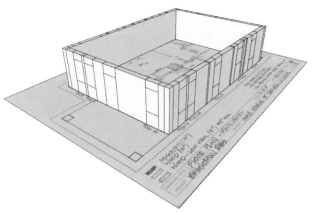

Figure 17.31 The exterior walls extruded with starting faces that define major openings

5. Using the Eraser tool, delete all of the extra edges on the inside walls of the model, as well as any unwanted geometry on the outside walls. Leave behind all of the lines that define the openings.

6. Use the Push/Pull tool to create all major openings as shown in Figure 17.32. Push from the outside of the house in. After creating the first opening, you can double-click on the other openings and use the memory of the Push/Pull tool.

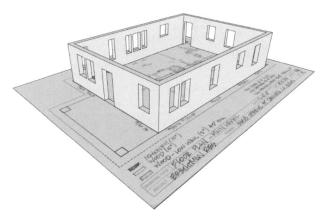

Figure 17.32 The final exterior walls

7. Select all of the new walls, right-click on the selection, and choose Make Group.

8. Draw the interior walls using the same techniques. Leave a starting face at all major openings for the doors and arches, and to turn the corners. When you are finished, select all interior walls and make them a group as well.

Layering and Organizing

You need to organize your model from the moment you begin creating it and continue that organization throughout the process. To start organizing the model, follow these steps:

1. Select both groups of walls: interior and exterior.

2. Right-click on the selection and choose Make Group.

3. Right-click on the group and choose Entity Info.

4. In the Entity Info dialog, assign the ARCH – Walls layer to the group containing the walls (Figure 17.33).

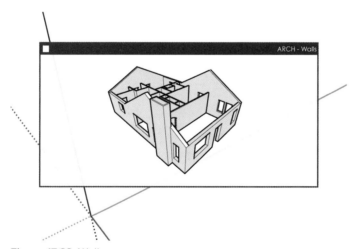

Figure 17.33 Walls

5. Using the Select tool, double-click into the new group of walls. In the Entity Info dialog, assign the Exterior Walls group to the CONC – Exterior layer and assign the Interior Walls group to the CONC – Interior layer (Figure 17.34).

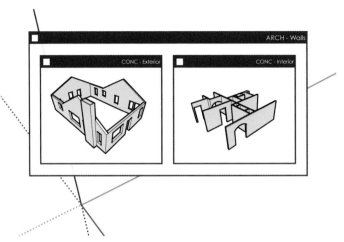

Figure 17.34 Walls with interior and exterior "switches"

6. Double-click into the Exterior walls. Select all of the exterior walls, right-click on the selection and choose Make Group. Assign the group to the CONC – Existing layer, as shown in Figure 17.35.

7. Double-click into the interior walls. Select all of the interior walls, right-click on the selection, and choose Make Group. Assign the group to the CONC – Existing layer, as shown in Figure 17.35.

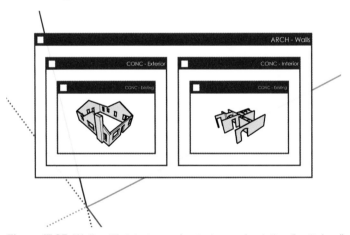

Figure 17.35 Walls with interior and exterior, and existing "switches"

TIP In the Entity Info dialog (Figure 17.36), name groups by the layer on which they reside. This way the Outliner will show an easy-to-navigate model structure.

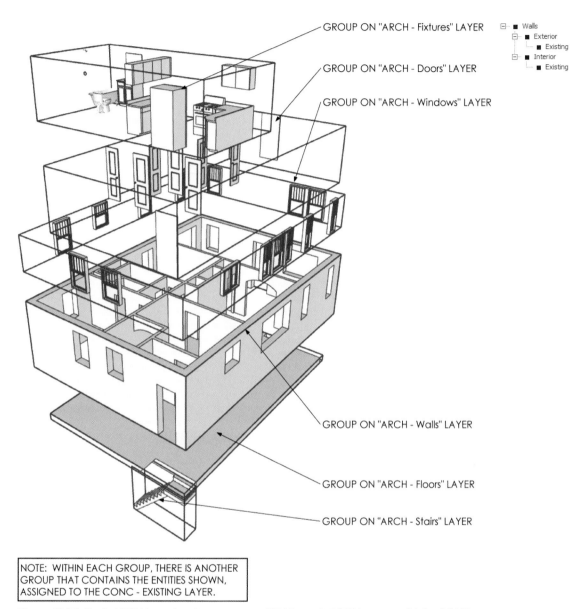

GROUP ON "ARCH - Fixtures" LAYER

GROUP ON "ARCH - Doors" LAYER

GROUP ON "ARCH - Windows" LAYER

GROUP ON "ARCH - Walls" LAYER

GROUP ON "ARCH - Floors" LAYER

GROUP ON "ARCH - Stairs" LAYER

Walls
  Exterior
    Existing
  Interior
    Existing

NOTE: WITHIN EACH GROUP, THERE IS ANOTHER GROUP THAT CONTAINS THE ENTITIES SHOWN, ASSIGNED TO THE CONC - EXISTING LAYER.

Figure 17.36 Each ARCH layer has its own group. Within each ARCH group, add the CONC switches for Interior/Exterior and Existing. (Exploded view is shown.)

Adding Detail

Now you are ready to add the doors, windows, fixtures, floors, and stairs using the same organization techniques, as shown in Figure 17.37. The components shown are available in the chapter files you downloaded earlier from **www.suexch.com/TSWFA**. To complete your existing conditions model, follow these steps:

1. Click on the File drop-down and choose Import. Make sure that the Files of Type drop-down is set to SketchUp Models (*.skp).

2. Navigate to your class files folder for this chapter and select the Fixtures.skp component. Click on the Open button to finish the import.

3. Assign the ARCH - Fixtures layer to the Fixtures.skp component.

4. Continue to insert components and apply the model organization and layering strategies shown in Figure 17.36.

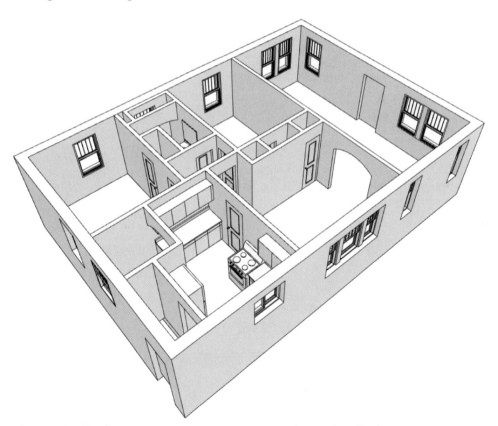

Figure 17.37 The final model with detail added (ceilings hidden for effect)

TIP Completely finish the as-built 3D model before you move on to the design phases. To move forward immediately, you could use the completed model from your chapter files.

WORKING WITH EXISTING CAD DRAWINGS

If you already have DWGs, you might not need to go out and take field notes at the site. You can simply import the .dwg files and trace over them using the same techniques and model organization you would use to trace an image of your field notes. The only difference would be that you have points to snap to rather than handwritten dimensions. Here are a few tips that will help you when you're working with someone else's CAD drawings:

- ☑ Don't always trust someone else's CAD work. Use the CAD cleanup scripts (available at www.smustard.com) in SketchUp, or better yet open the DWGs in your CAD program and run Flatten, Overkill, and Purge commands.

- ☑ In SketchUp, extrude the plan horizontally rather than trying to fill in the plan and extrude vertically.

- ☑ When you use the File › Import dialog, be sure to set Files of Type to .dwg.

- ☑ Group the CAD drawing, add to the CONC – Background layer, and lock just as you did with the field notes.

CHAPTER POINTS

- ☑ When you're recording dimensions, develop a system and stick to it.

- ☑ It is absolutely critical that you complete the accurate and organized as-built 3D model before you move on to the design phases.

- ☑ Download the `BIC_Field Note - Letter Landscape.layout` template at **www.suexch.com** and save to your RESOURCES/TEMPLATES folder. This template is set up with spaces for the critical information that you will typically record when you are completing as-built drawings.

Chapter 18

Schematic Design

During the schematic design (SD) phase, you interpret the site analysis (SA) data and develop the initial draft presentation of your design ideas. In this section, you will learn how to efficiently organize your model for rendering, sharing with consultants, exporting to other CAD programs, and preparing for construction documents.

REMODEL DESIGN

Now that you've collected all the data during the SA phase, it's time to utilize it. In this section, you'll further develop the 3D as-built model and transform it into a design model. Working with existing conditions lends itself to precise modeling. If you are working from an accurate as-built, there is no need to convolute it with new inaccurate "sketchy" geometry. Stick with the plan and continue to treat this model as a pristine, accurate, and organized model.

Proposed Conditions Model

The *proposed conditions model* is where you will demolish select existing conditions and add your new design. At this point, having a complete *existing conditions model* is imperative. In the future, any changes you make to the existing conditions model will need to be duplicated in your new proposed conditions model. So make sure you take the time to accurately finish the as-built model. When you are ready to transition your existing conditions model to a proposed conditions model, just follow these steps:

1. In SketchUp, open the `BIC_3458 Steele St - Existing Conditions.skp` model from Chapter 17, "Site Analysis: Documenting an Existing Building."

2. Click on the File drop-down menu and select Save As.

3. Name the file **BIC_3458 Steele St – Proposed Conditions.skp**.

4. Navigate to your TEMP folder or the appropriate project folder and click the Save button.

Demolition

Often, you will need to demolish portions of an existing building in order to complete your renovation. Within the model, simply remove the walls you want to demolish and delete any entities you do not want as part of your design.

If at some point you need to restore a demolished entity, you can copy it from the existing conditions model and paste it in place in the proposed conditions model. For walls, it is fairly intuitive to just redraw them in the existing container.

There is no need to save anything that is being demolished in the proposed conditions model. You will see in Chapter 20 "Construction Documents" that the the demolition plan is a product of the existing conditions model combined with the proposed conditions model.

New Construction

To complete the design, you'll need to add new walls and entities to your model. To do that, all you need to do is add one more layer *"switch"*, or level of organization to the model. Within each of the ARCH groups, at the same level as the CONC – Existing container, add a container assigned to the CONC – New layer. This is where you will add new entities based on the container on which you are working (Figure 18.1). Add a CONC – New container to each of the ARCHITECTURAL layers as you are adding the new entities.

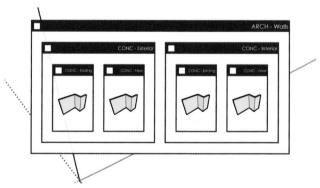

Figure 18.1 A remodeling project will utilize the CONC – New and CONC – Existing layers.

Scope Diagram

When you're working on a remodel design, you can view the model as a Scope Diagram to see which entities are new and which are existing (Figure 18.2). This will help you make informed design decisions visually, without always having to check the layering of the model.

Open the completed `BIC_3458 Steele St - Proposed Conditions.skp` model from the chapter files. Click on the scope diagram's Scene tab and explore the model's organization strategies and layering.

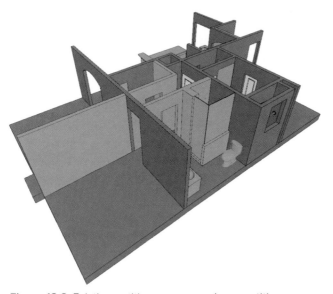

Figure 18.2 Existing entities are gray and new entities are green.

PROJECT TYPES

Every project requires different layers, different containers, and different organizational strategies. It is always best to think through your project's requirements before you start the model. When you approach and organize your models, keep the following tips in mind:

☑ Identify the layers your model will need based on what drawings you need. If you don't need a Finish Plan, you might not need to use the ARCH – Floor Finishes container and layer. If your model has only one floor, you won't need the CONC – Level 00 layers.

☑ A new construction project will not need the CONC – Existing or CONC – New layers because everything will be new.

- ☑ A rowhouse model might have several layers for the units, such as CONC – Unit A, CONC – Unit B, CONC – Unit C, etc.

- ☑ A campus model might have several layers for individual buildings, such as CONC – Building 1, CONC – Building 2, CONC – Building 3, etc.

- ☑ One of the simplest project types would be a one-level new-construction project.

- ☑ One of the most complex project types would be a multilevel, multiunit remodel.

- ☑ Think of each of the ARCH and SITE layers as nouns and the CONC layers as adjectives that describe the ARCH and SITE entities.

- ☑ Become comfortable with your location in the model. Pay attention to visual cues that identify the organizational levels of your model. Practice navigating the groups and components (use the Select tool, double-click, and the Esc key).

It is impossible to create one template that accommodates every project type. This means you'll be adding layers to almost all the new models on which you work. When you use the Layer dialog to add a layer, the newly added layer is visible by default in every scene. When you use the Add Hidden Layer ruby (see Chapter 8, "Ruby Scripts"), the new layer will be invisible in all existing scenes, which is more desirable.

Models have different needs. Visit **www.suexch.com/TSWFA** to see several models and model organization diagrams that represent different project scopes and types.

ACTIVITY

MODELING STRATEGY

At this point, it should be very clear that you can be very loose and sketchy in SketchUp, or you can be accurate and precise. Just as each project type has a unique organizational strategy, each project type has a unique modeling strategy. There are two schools of thought: model sketchy and then clean up, or model precisely from the beginning. There is no one right way to design in SketchUp, but some of the suggestions presented here can help you determine how SketchUp is best leveraged.

Sketchy Modeling

If you model without paying attention to precise dimensions, you are creating a *throw-away* model. When you create sketchy models, the amount of effort you'll need to edit the loose geometry back into precision is not worth the time it would take. Typically, it is easier to rebuild the design in a new file after you have poured your thoughts into the sketchy model. If you are going to model in this way, keep these tips in mind:

☑ Turn on length snapping to make the sketchy dimensions snap to a clean, round number. This will make it a little easier to transition if you are cutting and pasting into your precise model.

☑ Group everything! Once geometry is stuck together, it becomes much more difficult (but not impossible) to sort it all out.

☑ Assume that your sketchy model is going to be a throw-away model. Usually, it takes more effort to edit the geometry back into precise dimensions than it would to rebuild the model.

☑ During the Schematic Design phase, create a programming diagram, mass models, and quick plan sketches without being too hung up on precise modeling practices.

☑ A new construction project lends itself to brainstorming on a larger and freer scale, and sometimes without paying close attention to precise dimensions. Because you aren't limited by the constraints of an existing building, you are free to develop any style and space plan you desire.

Precise Modeling

Modeling with exact dimensions right from the beginning is the best method. Even though it is easy to push, pull, move, and scale without being precise, there is really no reason to do that. Keep your dimensions clean from the beginning by organizing your model and performing accurate operations. If you are going to model in this way, keep these tips in mind:

☑ If you have used a sketch model, or concept, then start a new file to create the SD/DD/CD model.

☑ Move groups, components, and entities between groups and components and even other files using the Paste in Place command. Copy or cut a selection, and once you are inside the desired model or container, click on the Edit drop-down menu and choose Paste in Place.

☑ From the beginning, a remodeling project lends itself to precise modeling because you need to work within the constraints of the existing construction.

Level of Detail

You need to determine the level of detail that should be included in your models. If you are creating a building model to be used for design, presentation, and construction documents, you should think in terms of 1/8″ plans. Typically, generic wall thicknesses provide plenty of detail, either to studs or including gypsum board. You don't need to model layers for drywall, studs, or plates in the main design model; you only need to include generic thicknesses and openings (Figure 18.3). Excessive detail is usually unnecessary, and it will slow you down. You can describe any detail beyond that in a detail drawing, detached from the main, proposed-conditions, design model.

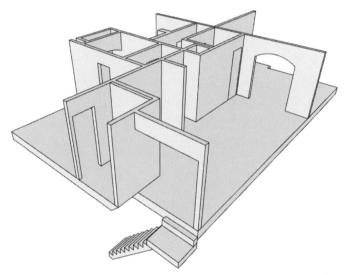

Figure 18.3 Wall, floor, and ceiling masses are typically enough detail to create the drawings needed to describe a design.

OBJECTS

Approaching and modeling objects is a challenging task. Typically, everyday objects that make a convincing scene are "organic" in shape. Many modelers approach these objects with the standard SketchUp modeling tools, which ultimately creates a hard-lined object that was obviously modeled in SketchUp (Figure 18.4). When you're modeling objects, keep the following tips in mind:

☑ Examine the object to determine the details that make it unique and recognizable.

☑ Think about your approach. What basic forms can be modified to create the desired object? Is an additive approach the best? Or would the subtractive approach be better?

☑ You will probably come to the conclusion that it is worth it to pay for professionally built models of objects at **www.formfonts.com**.

Many objects have a 3D form that produces the correct graphic when it is rendered in a plan— for example, couches, sinks, counters, and toilets (Figure 18.5).

Figure 18.4 A cartoonish chair (at right) conveys the form of a chair, but not necessarily a real style. The stylized chair (at left) is a more accurate representation of a real chair.

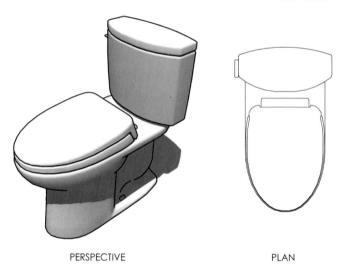

PERSPECTIVE   PLAN

Figure 18.5 The toilet component renders properly in 3D as well as in plan.

There are also many objects that have a 3D form that does not render correctly in plan. Some examples are doors, upper cabinets, and electrical outlets. To help you understand this concept, realize that a door shown in plan has a very graphical representation (Figure 18.6). Slicing through a three-dimensional door with a section plane will not produce the graphic you need for a plan. For any object like this, there will be a 3D object that will be visible in perspective and elevation views, and a 2D graphic that will be visible in plan views (Figure 18.7).

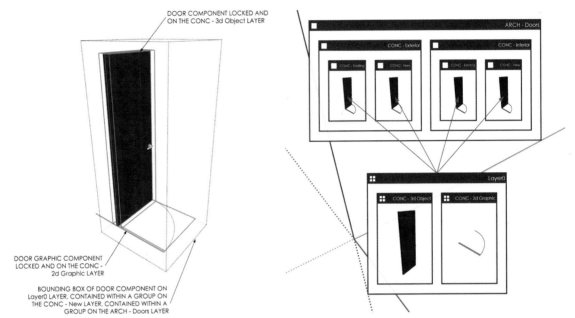

Figure 18.6 Utilizing a 2D graphic and a 3D object will allow the object to be represented properly in any drawing.

Figure 18.7 Model organization diagram of a door component

EXPORTING TO CAD

At some point you may want to move your SketchUp design into your favorite CAD program. The Model Organization tools in this book make it simple to export your design as a 2D or 3D model—and share your design with consultants so that engineering drawings can be completed. Typically, consultants do not work with SketchUp, so you will need to either export to a 3D format they can work with or to a 2D format that is easily adapted to their layering system.

Exporting 3D

Exporting your SketchUp model to another 3D model format is the easiest way to communicate with other programs. Depending on your needs, this method does not always provide the flexibility needed to utilize the model. If you do want to export to another 3D format, follow these steps:

1. Within SketchUp, click on the File drop-down menu and select Export > 3D Model (Figure 18.8).

2. Click on the Export Type drop-down menu and select the desired format. You can export to several formats, including .dae, .kmz, .3ds, .dwg, .dxf, .fbx, .obj, .wrl, and .xsi.

Figure 18.8 The AutoCAD Export Options dialog box

3. Click the Options button to adjust specific settings relating to the file type you are exporting. They will be different for each export file type.

4. Navigate to the TEMP folder (or the appropriate EXPORTS folder), add a YYMMDD folder, and then click the Export button to finish. A 3D model export maintains all layering and grouping; component instances are turned to blocks and maintain their connectivity.

TIP Exporting to Revit is the elusive holy grail of SketchUp workflow efficiency. The problem is that Revit is a completely different type of program than SketchUp. There is no clean, seamless import workflow that pulls all the intelligence from SketchUp and translates directly into the Revit format. Think about everything you have learned about the way that SketchUp works. There are *no* walls, floors, doors, or windows in SketchUp. You know what these entities are because you are putting them in containers and assigning layers. SketchUp can't communicate them to Revit because Revit actually has walls, doors, and windows. The best thing to do is import the 3D model as a mass and trace it in Revit. Another option is to import the 2D CAD drawings and trace those while applying the entity properties.

Exporting 2D

Typically, you export to 2D CAD to move into another CAD program, or you might just need to share 2D CAD backgrounds with other consultants. A major benefit of 2D CAD is that it is fairly fast and easy to use, and almost everyone in the design field knows how to use it. Sometimes you just need to get the job done. It is okay to think and design in SketchUp 3D, and then refine and document your design in a familiar 2D CAD program. *The SketchUp Workflow for Architecture* is extremely flexible, so don't hesitate to abandon ship at this point and use another program if that is what works for you.

Exporting to 2D CAD that everyone can use has different challenges. The main one is that the layers in most CAD programs are not set up the way they are in SketchUp. You can get around this by exporting 2D DWGs from SketchUp to CAD by layers or line weights. You will export once for the doors, windows, walls, fixtures, etc., and then export another set based on new and existing (Figure 18.9).

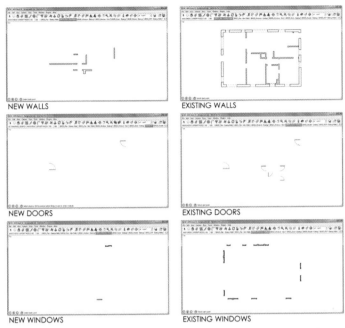

Figure 18.9 Exporting a separate .dwg file for each layer used in CAD gives consultants the flexibility to build any plan they need. Each scene will be its own .dwg export and its own external reference to the consultant's background drawings.

Creating the Export Model

If at all possible, you should always reference the proposed conditions model into another file in order to export the 2D backgrounds. Doing so limits the number of Scene tabs and clutter within the main design model. Follow these steps:

1. Start a new SketchUp model.

2. Within SketchUp, click on the File drop-down menu and choose Import.

3. Navigate to and select the BIC_3458 Steele St - Proposed Conditions.skp model. Click the Open button to finish the import.

4. Save the model as **BIC_3458 Steele St – Backgrounds** in the appropriate project folder.

Creating Scenes

Now it's time to set up the scenes that represent each piece of the **.dwg** backgrounds. You can visualize the scenes using a SOD (scene organization diagram) for the existing walls (Figure 18.10) and a SOD for the new walls (Figure 18.11). The 3D views shown in the figures are in perspective for effect; they will actually be top-down parallel projection views.

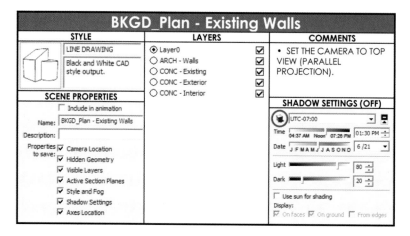

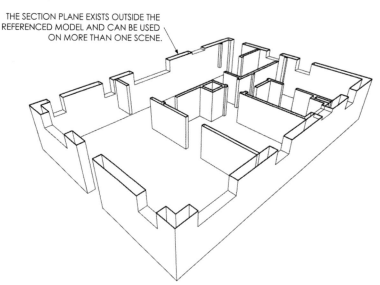

Figure 18.10 Swap the ARCH – Walls layer for other ARCH layers to create additional existing export scenes.

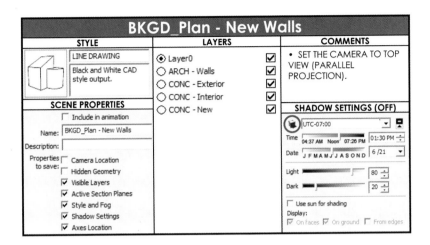

BKGD_Plan - New Walls		
STYLE	**LAYERS**	**COMMENTS**
LINE DRAWING Black and White CAD style output.	⦿ Layer0 ☑ ◯ ARCH - Walls ☑ ◯ CONC - Exterior ☑ ◯ CONC - Interior ☑ ◯ CONC - New ☑	• SET THE CAMERA TO TOP VIEW (PARALLEL PROJECTION).
SCENE PROPERTIES		**SHADOW SETTINGS (OFF)**
☐ Include in animation Name: BKGD_Plan - New Walls Description: Properties to save: ☐ Camera Location ☐ Hidden Geometry ☑ Visible Layers ☑ Active Section Planes ☑ Style and Fog ☑ Shadow Settings ☑ Axes Location		UTC-07:00 Time 04:37 AM Noon 07:26 PM 01:30 PM Date J F M A M J J A S O N D 6 /21 Light 80 Dark 20 ☐ Use sun for shading Display: ☑ On faces ☑ On ground ☐ From edges

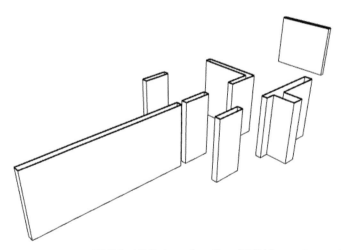

Figure 18.11 Swap the ARCH – Walls layer for other ARCH layers to create additional new export scenes.

1. Adjust the layer visibility, style, and shadow settings to reflect the desired background export.

2. In the Scenes dialog, click on the plus sign (+) to add a new scene.

3. Repeat this process for each desired background export.

TIP Every scene you create must have the same camera view. To ensure that they are all the same, set the camera view to top, select all of the BKGD scenes in the Scenes dialog, and then click the Scene Update button; update only the camera view and uncheck all other properties. Click Update. Now all the scenes have the same camera view.

Exporting 2D Graphic

Now that you have scenes created, export them to a **.dwg** for use in other CAD programs.

1. Click on the File drop-down menu and choose Export › 2D Graphic (Figure 18.12).

2. Click on the Export Type drop-down menu and choose **.dwg**.

3. Click on the Options button to open the Export Options dialog. Set the format to ACAD 2000. (The year 2000 is a pretty good year for compatibility between software packages and CAD versions. If you know exactly the version you need, choose it instead.)

4. Navigate to the appropriate EXPORTS folder, and add a folder with today's date in the YYMMDD format to keep things organized.

5. Click the Export button to finish.

Using the DWG Exports

Once all of the exports are completed, they can be compiled into a single CAD drawing to create any type of plan needed

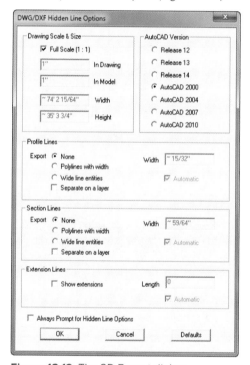

Figure 18.12 The 2D Export dialog

(Figure 18.13). Ideally, you will email all of these background **.dwg** files to consultants, or host them for download on a server. Then, the consultants can insert the drawings into their CAD program however they like. When you update the design, re-export the backgrounds and then just send a message to the consultants so they know to download and overwrite their files. This method is by far the most efficient way to keep everyone on the same page, but it requires all consultants to be proficient in 2D CAD.

For consultants who don't really know how to use CAD this way, you might find it easier to just do it for them. Simply reference the DWG exports into your favorite CAD program to create a series of drawings for them. Be sure to maintain the drawing origin for each reference, to insure that all drawings stack right into place. At this point, assign line weights to each of the external references as a whole.

TIP If you don't have a CAD program to compile the drawings, you can import all the drawings into SketchUp as .dwg files, and then export the entire file as a 3D .dwg.

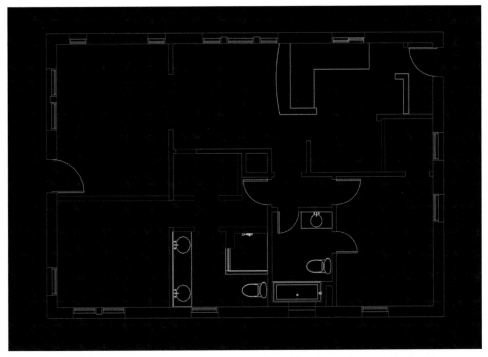

Figure 18.13 This proposed plan was created by referencing several .dwg exports from SketchUp into a 2D CAD program. Each .dwg reference is on a different colored layer, each different color represents the possibility for varying line weights.

You can also use the 2D export to abandon ship, and then finish the documentation in your favorite 2D CAD program. Reference the files in the same, and then you can explode, redraw, and modify your file at will. Keep in mind that when you export 2D CAD snapshots, there is no connectivity between the components—they do not become blocks. These DWGs are basically exploded, simple linework and might require some rebuilding and redrawing.

CHAPTER POINTS

☑ For an extensive collection of building model organization diagrams (MODs , scene organization diagrams (SODs), and their corresponding SketchUp models, visit **www.suexch.com**.

☑ While you're brainstorming in SketchUp, use the tools loosely and freely. Keep in mind that there are built-in ways to tighten up the dimensions and keep the geometry organized, even in a concept model.

☑ When moving a concept to a precise model, it is usually best to start a fresh model. Use Paste in Place to pull useful pieces of the concept model into the precise model.

☑ Typically, it is best to use precise dimensions and modeling techniques right from the beginning. Once you get the hang of the model organization and tool operations, it takes just as much effort to create a sketchy model as it does a precise model.

☑ A cloud file storage solution comes in really handy when you're distributing lots of large files to consultants.

Chapter 19

Design Development Rendering

During the Design Development phase, it is often necessary to present a refined design in 3D. By doing this, you will enable the client to fully understand the design and sign off so you can quickly move on to the Construction Documents phase. Throughout the architectural design process, you will still use the modeling and organization techniques from the previous chapters, but in this chapter you'll focus on presentation. You'll learn how to create beautiful SketchUp animations and renderings, prepare your model for photorealistic rendering, and explore your photorealistic rendering options.

POPULATING A SCENE

Any image you create will ultimately be used to sell an idea. Your design image should evoke excitement and the desire to be a participant in the image. You should put as much thought into populating your renderings as a realtor puts into staging a house for sale. Breathe life into the space by adding decorative objects, people, and action. Keep the following tips in mind when you're populating a scene.

☑ Address your audience. Who are you selling this design to, and what will get them excited about the space? Now is a good time to think back to your first meetings when the client expressed their main desires. If they expressed a strong desire for a fireplace, show the fireplace glowing with a family gathered around.

☑ Add decorative objects within the ARCH - Furniture container (Figure 19.1, Figure 19.2). Tables without food, magazines, or other details are boring. Such details are the objects that make a scene realistic; however, you don't want them to render in the furniture plan.

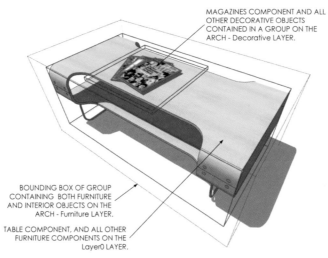

MAGAZINES COMPONENT AND ALL
OTHER DECORATIVE OBJECTS
CONTAINED IN A GROUP ON THE
ARCH - Decorative LAYER.

BOUNDING BOX OF GROUP
CONTAINING BOTH FURNITURE
AND INTERIOR OBJECTS ON THE
ARCH - Furniture LAYER.

TABLE COMPONENT, AND ALL OTHER
FURNITURE COMPONENTS ON THE
Layer0 LAYER.

Figure 19.1 Decorative objects such as magazines, plates, and pillows liven up a scene, but are not necessary to render in plan. Such entities belong on the ARCH – Decorative Objects layer.

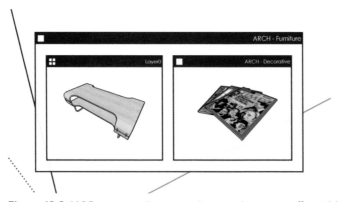

ARCH - Furniture

Layer0

ARCH - Decorative

Figure 19.2 MOD representing magazines resting on a coffee table

☑ Download professionally modeled and textured components at **www.FormFonts.com**.

☑ Use custom textures from Google image searches or from FormFonts. See Chapter 7, "SketchUp Collections."

☑ To sell the experience, populate models with people participating in appropriate activities. Add them to the SITE – Entourage container. For winter scenes, use people in jackets. At a restaurant, mix casually and professionally dressed people. For an office, add activity such as presentations and collaborative group discussions. Perform a Google search for **office** and investigate what a real office looks like. Take note of the clutter that can add realism to an image, then apply those subtle nuances when staging your scenes. (Figure 19.3, Figure 19.4).

Figure 19.3 This scene lacks decorative objects and people. The space is accurately represented, but the viewer has no idea how the space will be used.

Figure 19.4 This scene is full of life and activity. Decorative objects and people give the viewer an idea of how the space will be used.

RENDERING IN SKETCHUP

SketchUp renderings are traditionally "sketchy." Utilizing the loose lines and cartoonish materials available in SketchUp conveys design intent in a way that is much softer than a sharp photorealistic rendering.

Choosing an Appropriate Style

A style will drastically affect the way in which your audience receives your SketchUp rendering. If your design is still in a loose schematic state, present it with a sketchy style to remove some of the details you haven't thought out. If your design is fairly complete and advanced, use a hard-line style rather than a sketchy style to insure the details are clearly represented. See Figure 19.5, Figure 19.6, and Figure 19.7.

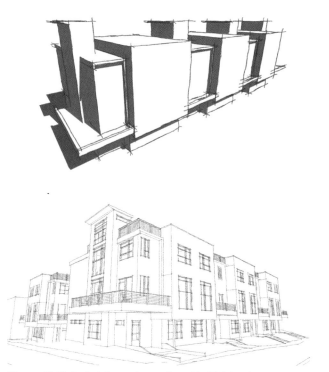

Figure 19.5 A sketchy style rendered in Hidden Line mode leaves much of the detail to the viewer's imagination or presenter's explanation, which is great for designs that are still in schematics. If you haven't addressed the materials, don't show them.

Figure 19.6 If a design is well developed, a sketchy style can sometimes come across as messy and cluttered.

Figure 19.7 A style with clean lines and textures is best for a design that has been well developed.

Creating Scenes

After you determine the style you want to use, you can create the scene.

1. Navigate to a desired view, and then select an appropriate style from the Style browser. You might want to click on the PRESENTATION utility scene tab and use the final PRESENTATION style that was created in Chapter 5, "The Professional's SketchUp Template."

TIP Use the Advanced Camera tools and Position Camera tools to place yourself in the model accurately, set the eye height, etc.

2. To add a new scene, click on the plus sign (+) at the top-right corner of the Scenes dialog.

3. Using the LO_ format, rename the scene **LO_Perspective 01**. Check on all of the Properties to Save.

4. Repeat to create additional scenes.

Exporting Images from SketchUp

The easiest way to produce an image is to use the Export 2D Graphic command in SketchUp. This creates a 2D snapshot of the screen in several formats, including raster and vector.

1. Click on the Scene tab that you would like to export.

2. Click on the File drop-down and select Export 2D Graphic.

3. Set the Export Type to .jpg if you plan to print or email the rendering as is. This is one of the most common raster-image formats. If you plan to perform a lot of post-processing, consider exporting the scene as a .tiff file.

4. Click on the Options button to set the image resolution as shown in Figure 19.8.

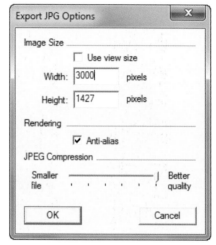

Figure 19.8 Image export options

Exporting Images from LayOut

Exporting images from LayOut is a very efficient way to export multiple views from SketchUp, and it allows you to leverage all of LayOut's professional export settings.

Adding Pages

Add a page within your LayOut presentation for each perspective rendering scene you created in SketchUp. Just follow these steps:

1. Within LayOut, start a new file using the BIC_8.5x11 – Landscape template. Save this file to your TEMP folder or an appropriate project folder and name the file BIC_Row House – Renderings.layout.

2. Click on the File drop-down and choose Insert. Navigate to the `BIC_Denver Row House.skp` model in the chapter files folder, select it, and click the Open button.

3. Click and drag on the edge of a viewport to loosely resize the viewport. Once you let go, immediately enter new viewport dimensions: **11", 8.5",** then press Enter (Figure 19.9).

Measurements   11",8.5"

Figure 19.9 Use the Select tool to scale a viewport with precise dimensions.

4. Center on the page horizontally and vertically. To do that, use the Custom Arrange toolbar, or right-click on the viewport and select Center > Horizontally on Page and repeat for Center > Vertically on Page.

5. Select the viewport, and then assign the LO_Perspective 01 scene, rendering type, and line weight in the SketchUp Model Inspector.

6. Duplicate the page and repeat the process for every desired scene.

Exporting Multiple Images

Although it is usually best to export a **.pdf** file, sometimes you'll want to export a series of images for post-processing in an image editor. Follow these steps to batch export raster images from LayOut.

1. Click on the File drop-down and choose Export > Images.

2. Navigate to the appropriate project folder, assign an appropriate name, choose a .jpg or .png export, and click on Save.

3. In the Image Export Options dialog, which is automatically launched, choose which LayOut presentation pages will be exported as well as the image resolution (Figure 19.10). Typically, 300 pixels/inch is an acceptable high-resolution export for print, and 72 pixels/inch is an acceptable resolution for screen presentations, such as a website.

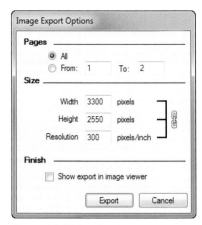

Figure 19.10 LayOut image export options

TIP It is okay to keep your large-format renderings in a separate LayOut presentation from your drawings. You can link one SketchUp model to as many LayOut presentations as you like.

Creating Animations

SketchUp animations are easy to create, and they provide an excellent way to explore a 3D space without having the model open and rendering in real time.

Creating an Animation Model

To create an animation file, follow these steps:

1. Within SketchUp, click on the File drop-down and select New to start a new model.

2. Click on the File drop-down and choose Import. Verify that the Files of Type drop-down menu is set to SketchUp Files (*.skp).

   Inserting one SketchUp model into another creates a link between the instance and the referenced model. This technique will limit the number of scenes and Scene tabs in the proposed conditions model. When you make changes to the original BIC_ Denver Row House.skp model, you can just right-click on the reference in the Animation file and select Reload to see the updated model.

3. Navigate to and select the `BIC_Denver Row House.skp file`. Click the Open button to import the model.

4. Save the file as **BIC_Denver Row House – Animation.skp**.

Adding Scenes

SketchUp animations are scene based. This means that SketchUp will link together all of the scenes in the animation into one movie. Be sure to check on all of the properties to save and choose which scenes should be included in the animation (Figure 19.11). Typically, every scene you create in the animation file will be included in the animation.

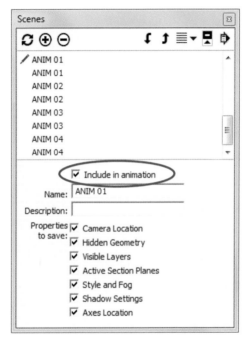

1. In the Scenes browser, click the Add New Scene button to create a new scene.

2. Name the scenes based on segments. For example, each scene in the first stream of animation should be titled **01**.

3. Click on the Window drop-down and choose Model Info. Click on the Animations tab.

4. Check on the Scene Transitions and adjust the amount of time between scenes based on personal preference. Typically, you should leave the Scene Delay set to 0 for a more fluid animation.

Figure 19.11 In SketchUp's Scenes dialog, the Include in Animation box is checked for each ANIM scene.

Exporting Animations

To export your animation, follow these steps:

1. Click on the File drop-down and choose Export › Animation.

2. Click the Options button at the bottom-left corner of the Export Animation dialog (Figure 19.12).

3. Navigate to your TEMP folder or an appropriate project folder, and select Export.

Animation Tips

Keep the following tips in mind when you're creating animations in SketchUp.

☑ Add a sky dome to the animation file to create a more realistic sky effect. Search the 3D warehouse for **sky dome** (Figure 19.13).

☑ Use ruby scripts to make your animations smoother. Visit **www.smustard.com** to purchase and experiment with Flight Path, Page Smoother, TimeEdit, and PageDelayEdit.

☑ The dimensions for high definition 1080p are 1920 pixels wide by 1080 pixels high. Thin out lines by exporting at a higher resolution, such as 3840 × 2160, and then crunching the file down in a video editor.

☑ Each instance of SketchUp utilizes one core. Therefore, if you have a quad-core system, you could maximize your machine by opening four instances of SketchUp and rendering the animation in four separate segments, and then compiling the segments in a video editor. To do this, you would need one animation file with all of the scenes set up. Every time you opened the animation file, you would need to uncheck different scenes to include in the animation.

☑ With more time between scene transitions, the camera will appear to fly slower.

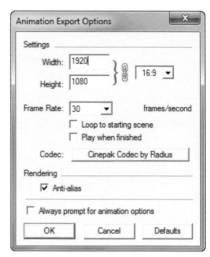

Figure 19.12 Animation export settings

Figure 19.13 A sky dome places a picture of a real sky behind an image, which will look better than a simple color sky.

- ☑ A higher frame rate will allow you to slow down an animation in a video editor without deteriorating the quality.

- ☑ By using simple video editing programs such as Windows Movie Maker or iMovie, you can add a lot to your animations. For example, you can add captions, fade effects, and chop out the "bouncing" effect often present in scene based animations.

- ☑ Sketchy styles do not typically render well in animations.

PHOTOREALISTIC RENDERING

Once a design has reached a level of detail that resembles a real space, it is best to render it as a photorealistic image. Photorealistic renderings make typical "cartoony" SketchUp renderings look real by adding soft shadows, reflections, light sources, and other natural properties of light.

TIP If a design is incomplete and isn't populated, your photorealistic rendering will look amateurish.

In the not-so-distant past, photorealistic rendering was a huge task involving exporting to expensive software packages that only Hollywood studios could afford and only Hollywood special effects wizards knew how to use. Today, photorealistic rendering can be accomplished in SketchUp. Most rendering plugins are extremely inexpensive, and they produce beautiful images that rival professional stand-alone rendering software (Figure 19.14, Figure 19.15).

Figure 19.14 Photorealistic rendering (rendered in Twilight Render)

Figure 19.15 Same view in SketchUp

Preparing a Model

Photorealistic rendering is a breeze with many of the available plugins for SketchUp, but you should first optimize the model for rendering using the Orient Faces utility scene (Figure 19.16). This utility scene displays the geometry in your model based on which side of the surface is facing you. The front is pink and the backs are green. Rendering the front of faces will produce more predictable results.

1. Click on the Orient Faces utility scene tab.

2. Double-click into Groups and Components, and then right-click on a green face and choose Reverse Faces to change it to pink. You can select multiple faces, right-click on the selection, and choose Reverse Faces to change more than one face at a time.

3. Click on the Design utility tab to verify that the correct material is applied to the surface. Usually, after reversing a face, you will need to apply a material to the front that was previously hidden.

4. Reverse the rest of the faces until all of them are pink.

GREEN REPRESENTS THE BACK OF A
FACE THAT IS FACING THE CAMERA.

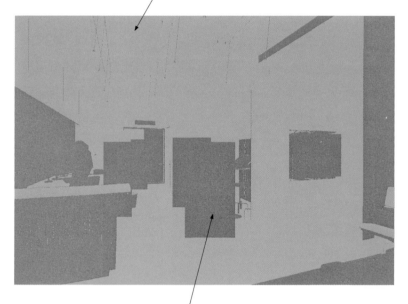

PINK REPRESENTS THE FRONT OF A
FACE THAT IS FACING THE CAMERA.

Figure 19.16 The Orient Faces utility scene makes it easy to identify the front and back of faces. Typically, your results will be more consistent when your render the fronts of surfaces.

Photorealistic Rendering Programs

Listed are several options for rendering inside SketchUp. Each program or plugin has its own unique features and benefits.

- ☑ Twilight Render: **http://twilightrender.com/**
- ☑ Shaderlight: **http://www.artvps.com/**
- ☑ Podium: **http://suplugins.com/**
- ☑ Render Plus: **http://www.renderplus.com/wp2/**
- ☑ Indigo Renderer: **http://www.indigorenderer.com/sketchup**
- ☑ Renditioner Pro: **http://www.imsidesign.com/Products/Renditioner/tabid/1756/Default.aspx**

- ☑ RenderPlus: **http://www.renderplus.com/wp2/wk/IRender_nXt.php**
- ☑ LumenRT: **http://www.lumenrt.com/**
- ☑ RenderIn: **http://www.renderin.com/**
- ☑ LightUp: **http://www.light-up.co.uk/**
- ☑ Vray: **http://www.chaosgroup.com/en/2/vrayforsketchup.html**
- ☑ Maxwell for SketchUp: **http://www.maxwellrender.com/index.php/maxwell_for_sketchup**
- ☑ Caravaggio: **http://www.caravaggio3D.com/**
- ☑ Lumion: **http://www.lumion3d.com/**

Post-Processing

It is always a good idea to run your final images through an image processor to fine-tune the brightness, contrast, color balance, etc. GIMP and Adobe Photoshop are powerful image editors that you install locally on your computer. There are also several image editors that can accomplish many of the same tasks for less money. Several cloud-based image editors are listed here:

- ☑ **http://www.photoshop.com/tools**
- ☑ **http://www.splashup.com/**
- ☑ **http://pixlr.com/**
- ☑ **http://www.picmonkey.com/**
- ☑ **http://www.sumopaint.com/app/**

CHAPTER POINTS

- ☑ Populate your scenes to sell your idea. Make the viewer want to participate in the image.
- ☑ To minimize cost and exports while maximizing efficiency and connectivity, pick a photorealistic renderer that works inside SketchUp.
- ☑ Use an image editor to fine-tune the final output.

Chapter 20

Construction Documents

During the CD phase, you (or the designer) will document all of the final design decisions and compile them into a set of construction documents. These documents are the culmination of *The SketchUp Workflow for Architecture*, and they are where all of your hard work and organization really pay off. In this section, you will see that you *can* create construction documents in LayOut and that the process is actually very efficient.

CRUCIAL CONCEPTS FOR DOCUMENTATION

Before you create the construction documents, you should understand some basic concepts that will help you create your drawings quickly and efficiently.

Section Planes

Section planes are the key to describing 3D spaces in 2D diagrams. Most people think section planes are just used for building sections; but really, any plan is also created using a section plane, placed horizontally (Figure 20.1).

Horizontal section planes can be placed at the main level of the model or in an ARCH container if needed. One reason for placing the section plane in an ARCH container is to cut different entities at different heights. Multiple section planes allow you to control which entities are being cut at what height (Figure 20.2). For instance, you might want the exterior walls to be cut at a different height than the interior walls. In such case, you could add several section planes within the ARCH containers to cut everything exactly as needed.

Section planes are separated by containers. In other words, a section plane within a group affects only the geometry in that group. This means that you can have multiple active section planes per scene , as long as each active section plane is in a separate container..

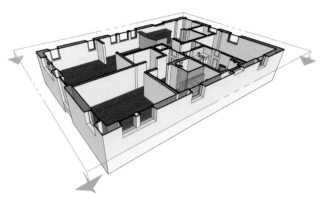

Figure 20.1 The horizontal section planes sit approximately 4' above the finished floor.

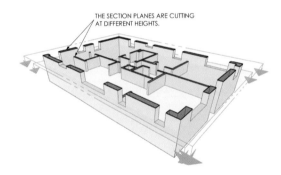

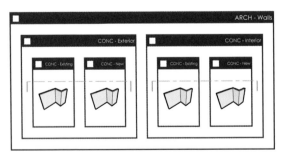

Figure 20.2 The section planes are placed in the CONC – Interior and CONC – Exterior containers of the ARCH – Walls container.

Vertical section planes are typically placed on the outside of the model, at the base level, because everything is cut at the same time for elevations and sections.

Stacking Viewports to Control Line Weights

The ability to completely control line weights in your drafting software is critical to any drafting workflow. To completely control line weights in LayOut, you will need to master the concept of stacking viewports.

Each plan drawing in your set of construction documents is composed of one or more viewports. Each viewport is linked to a plan scene within SketchUp. Each plan scene within SketchUp represents an array of line weights. This means that you will typically create one scene for "heavy" line weights (walls and floors) and one scene for "light" line weights (doors, windows, furniture, etc.).

To do this, you will need to actually stack the viewports in LayOut. Each viewport can have a line weight applied to it.

Each scene represented in LayOut has an array of line weights. (See the "Line Weight Theory" section in Chapter 10, "The LayOut Interface.") You apply a line weight to the viewport, and the style will translate that line weight into an array based on the profile and section cut settings. Figure 20.3 illustrates why it is best to assign line weights of .2 and .6. As you can see in the figure, these settings provide the largest array of line weights.

There is really no limit to the number of viewports you could stack; however, to keep your presentation and number of scenes manageable, two is usually enough, and three or more are necessary only if you need several different hatches.

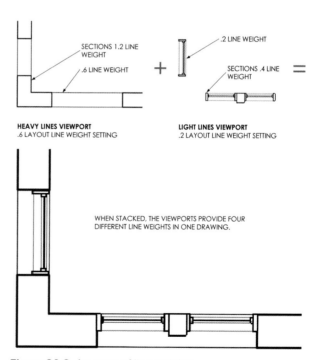

Figure 20.3 An array of line weights

All viewports that compose a drawing belong on the DRAWINGS layer in LayOut. You could use layers to control the stacking order, but then you would have a lot more layers to manage in LayOut. An easier way to manage the stacking order is to send the viewport backward and forward. Use either the Arrange toolbar, or right-click on a viewport and select Arrange › Send Backward/Forward to manage the stacking order, or sublevels of the layer.

The suggested stacking order and rendering settings of viewports is as follows:

☑ Light line weight on top, rendered as a hybrid (.2 line weight)

☑ Heavy line weight below, rendered as a vector (.6 line weight)

☑ Any hatching on the very bottom, rendered as a vector (line weight n/a)

TIP There is no need to insert the SketchUp model multiple times to create multiple stacked viewports. You can copy and paste the viewport right on top of the copied viewport. You can also use the Duplicate command available in the Edit drop-down menu to duplicate a selected viewport. Then hold down the Shift key and use the arrow keys to nudge the new viewport four times up and four times to the left so that it is once again aligned.

Hatching

Through the creative use of styles, or simply by drawing the hatch in LayOut, you can add hatching to your LayOut drawings. Each hatch method has its own limitations and requirements regarding efficiency and rendering settings. Before you incorporate hatching, explore all the options and then apply the best strategy for your particular design and set of drawings.

SketchUp Hatch

Using SketchUp to create the hatch provides a dynamically linked hatch in LayOut. This means that if you move a wall, the wall lines and hatch will update simultaneously in all the LayOut drawings. This method is ideal because it eliminates the need to redraw hatches as your design evolves.

A limitation to this method is that you can use only vector fills, and not the patterns or materials that most CAD users have come to expect. The good news is that if you are printing in color, you can use color fills.

If you are printing in black and white, you can create a nice array of fills with grays 10 to 25 percent apart. However, you will need to be selective with the amount of hatching you use in this way because each hatch requires its own viewport, which further complicates the stacking of viewports.

Create the Hatch – 50 (Figure 20.4) style now, and you can use it later when you create drawings composed of several stacked viewports. You can also create other hatch styles, such as HATCH – 25 and HATCH – 75 by adjusting the HLS lightness slider within the Style Edit tab.

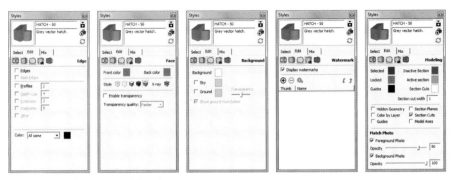

Figure 20.4 The Hatch 50 style

LayOut Hatch

Another hatching method is to use the Drafting tools in LayOut to create a solid vector fill (Figure 20.5). To do that, activate any of the Drawing tools, set the fill to the desired "hatch color," and turn off the stroke. Add LayOut shapes or lines with fill to define special hatched areas. Be sure to right-click on the fill and select Arrange › Send to Back so that the lines will be on top.

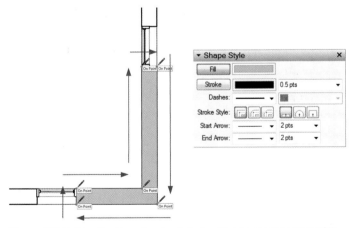

Figure 20.5 Use the Drawing tools in LayOut to create vector fills.

You could also use the fill you just created as a clipping mask for a hatch image or a .skp hatch file. To do that, create a repeating pattern in an image editor or in SketchUp and use the fill as a clipping mask (Figure 20.6).

The major downside to creating hatches in LayOut is that there is no dynamic link between the hatch and the drawing. If you update the plan, you will need to be aware of any conflicts created with the hatching. The benefit of this method is that you will be able to add as much hatching as you like with any pattern you need. Typically, this technique is best utilized for smaller areas of hatching.

TIP Right-click on any hatch and choose Send to Back. All hatches sit at the bottom of the stack on the DRAWINGS layer.

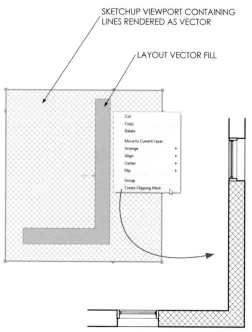

Figure 20.6 Draw repeating lines in SketchUp to create a hatch pattern fill to be used in LayOut.

Conceptual Layers

CONCEPTUAL layers are typically used as adjectives that explain the ARCH and SITE containers, but they can also help you achieve a desired look. As you saw in previous chapters, anything that does not render correctly in 3D can be corrected with a 2D graphic by using the CONC – 2D Graphic and CONC – 3D Object layers. In this section you will see how The CONC – Always Off and CONC – Details layers help you eliminate unneeded lines and excessive detail while maintaining model organization and efficiency.

CONC – Always Off

Because of the way SketchUp works as a surface modeler, there will be times when you don't want to see an edge but you won't be able delete it because it is needed to complete a surface. This often happens when containers meet—for example, at new and existing walls, between levels, and where exterior meets interior.

One option that will solve this problem is to hide the edge, but hiding is more of a modeling tool than a permanent fix. If you never want to see a specific entity, assign it to the CONC – Always Off layer, which is always turned off (Figure 20.7).

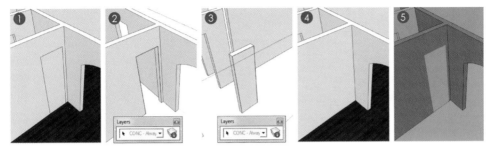

Figure 20.7 The CONC – Always Off layer allows you to show seamless transitions between containers.

Refer to the following images in Figure 20.7:

1. Notice that where the door was demolished and the new wall container meets the existing wall container, there are still lines. These lines need to remain in the model to make the surfaces, but they shouldn't be seen.

2. Double-click all the way into the existing wall's container and select the edges as shown. Assign them to the CONC – Always Off layer. The edges are not gone yet because they also exist in the new wall's container.

3. Double-click all the way into the new wall's container and select the edges as shown. Assign them to the CONC – Always Off layer.

4. The wall appears seamless now, as it should for perspective renderings and elevations.

5. Switch to the SCOPE utility scene, and note that both the new and existing functionality are maintained.

TIP Remember the "All edges and surfaces are drawn on Layer0" rule discussed in Chapter 4, "SketchUp Basics"? The CONC – Always Off layer is the one exception to that rule, although this layer is not limited to edges.

CONC – Detail

The CONC – Details layer helps you increase or decrease the level of detail shown for an object. There are often details associated with 3D objects that don't render properly in plan, so you need this layer "switch" to control the amount of detail shown. The entities placed on the CONC - Details layer are desirable in 3D views and elevations, but not in plan (Figure 20.8). Think of stair railings, door hardware, and window fenestrations (Figure 20.9).

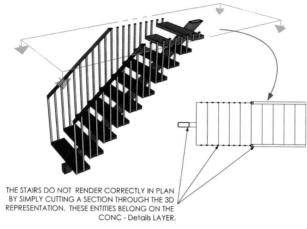

THE STAIRS DO NOT RENDER CORRECTLY IN PLAN
BY SIMPLY CUTTING A SECTION THROUGH THE 3D
REPRESENTATION. THESE ENTITIES BELONG ON THE
CONC - Details LAYER.

Figure 20.8 Some details of objects and architectural features do not render properly in plan, but are needed for a convincing elevation or 3D perspective view. Such entities belong on the CONC – Detail layer.

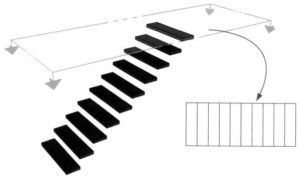

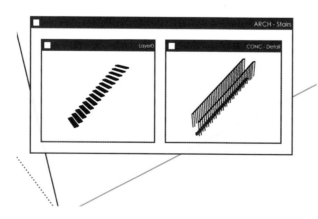

Figure 20.9 In this MOD, the stairs where the railings and main support are placed on the CONC – Detail layer. This will allow the stairs to render correctly when shown in plan.

DRAWINGS

Every drawing is composed of a scene, or combination of several scenes with varying styles, all combined and carefully stacked within LayOut. The following instructions explain how to make many common drawings that are needed to describe a building.

Plans

Each *plan drawing* is created by stacking two or more viewports on top of each other. Use the scene organization diagrams (SODs) to create the necessary scenes in SketchUp. Next, assign the scenes to viewports in LayOut and stack the plans as shown to create each plan drawing. While you're building these plans, keep in mind the following:

- ☑ All of the plans should share the same camera location, with the top-down view set to parallel projection.

- ☑ It is okay for several floorplan scenes to share the same section plane.

- ☑ Typically, the section plane for a plan should be approximately 4′ off the finished floor.

- ☑ Each viewport will be set to a scale appropriate for the plan. Assume that all plans, elevations, and sections for the model will be set to 1/8″ = 1′-0″, and enlarged plans will be set to 1/4″ = 1′-0″.

TIP This is a complicated process with a lot of steps represented by the Scene Organization Diagrams and Viewport Stacking Diagrams. Your first time through might be a little frustrating. Now would be a good time to visit **www.suexch.com** and watch the video tutorial on how to create these drawings, then use the book as a guide as you make the drawings yourself.

Existing Conditions Plan

The *existing conditions plan* represents the structure as it stands, before you make any changes (Figure 20.10). You will be using only the `BIC_3458 Steele St - Existing Conditions.skp` model for this drawing. This is the simplest plan drawing to create because it uses one model and only has two stacked viewports (Figure 20.11).

Demolition Plan

The *demolition plan* represents the pieces of the structure that will remain, as well as the pieces that will be removed (Figure 20.12). The demolition plan (Figure 20.13) utilizes the *existing conditions model* combined with the *proposed conditions model*.

EXISTING CONDITIONS PLAN					
	SKETCHUP SCENE	VISIBLE LAYERS	STYLE	RENDER SETTING	LINE WEIGHT
1	LO_Plan - Light	CONC - 2D Graphic CONC - Interior CONC - Exterior CONC - Existing ARCH - Doors ARCH - Equipment ARCH - Fixtures ARCH - Windows	LINE DRAWING	Hybrid	.2
2	LO_Plan - Heavy	CONC - Interior CONC - Exterior CONC - Existing ARCH - Floors ARCH - Stairs ARCH - Walls	LINE DRAWING	Vector	.6

[Top] VIEWPORT STACKING ORDER [Bottom]

Figure 20.10 The SOD for the existing conditions plan

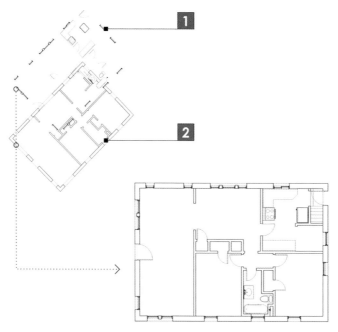

Figure 20.11 The stacked viewports of an existing conditions plan

Walls and entities to be removed are represented by dashed lines in this plan (Figure 20.14). To show the existing conditions dashed, you must first explode the existing conditions viewports. Although this removes the dynamic link between the SketchUp model and the viewport, it is okay because, technically, the existing conditions model is complete and will never change.

DEMOLITION PLAN				
SKETCHUP SCENE	**VISIBLE LAYERS**	**STYLE**	**RENDER SETTING**	**LINE WEIGHT**
1 LO_Demolition Plan - Light	CONC - Existing ARCH - Doors ARCH - Windows ARCH - Equipment ARCH - Fixtures	LINE DRAWING	Hybrid	.2
2 LO_Demolition Plan - Heavy	CONC - Existing ARCH - Walls ARCH - Stairs	LINE DRAWING	Vector	.6
3 LO_Existing Plan - Light	CONC - Existing ARCH - Doors ARCH - Windows ARCH - Equipment ARCH - Fixtures	LINE DRAWING	Vector, Exploded, Dashed	.15
4 LO_Existing Plan - Heavy	CONC - Existing ARCH - Walls ARCH - Stairs	LINE DRAWING	Vector, Exploded, Dashed	.5

(left side, vertical) [top] VIEWPORT STACKING ORDER [Bottom]

Figure 20.12 The SOD for the demolition plan

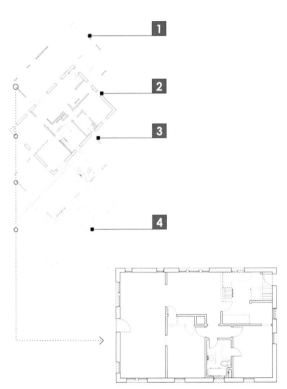

Figure 20.13 The stacked viewports of a demolition plan

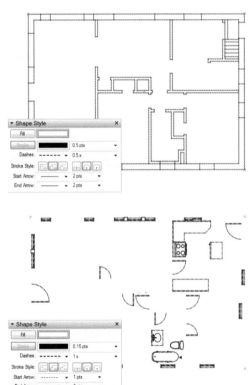

Figure 20.14 The Shape Style Inspector calling out the settings applied to the dashed drawings

Construction Plan

The *construction plan* describes what is to be built (Figure 20.15). New walls are delineated through the use of a hatch fill (Figure 20.16).

CONSTRUCTION PLAN					
	SKETCHUP SCENE	VISIBLE LAYERS	STYLE	RENDER SETTING	LINE WEIGHT
1	LO_Construction Plan - Light	ARCH - Doors ARCH - Equipment ARCH - Fixtures ARCH - Windows CONC - 2D Graphic CONC - Existing CONC - New CONC - Interior CONC - Exterior	LINE DRAWING	Vector	.2
2	LO_Construction Plan - Heavy	ARCH - Floors ARCH - Stairs ARCH - Walls CONC - Existing CONC - New CONC - Interior CONC - Exterior	LINE DRAWING	Hybrid	.6
3	LO_Construction Plan - Hatch	ARCH - Walls CONC - Exterior CONC - Interior CONC - New	HATCH	Vector	NA

(Top) VIEWPORT STACKING ORDER (Bottom)

Figure 20.15 The SOD for the construction plan

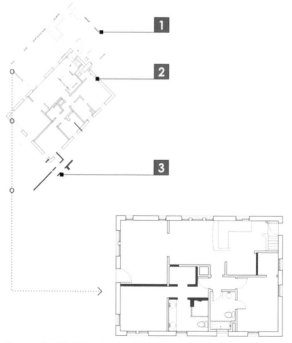

Figure 20.16 The stacked viewports for the construction plan

Finish Plan

The *finish plan* describes the materials that will be used to finish the space (Figure 20.17). You can use the standard LINE DRAWING style to create a black-and-white finish plan, or you can create a new LINE DRAWING style (Figure 20.18) that also shows colors and textures (Figure 20.19).

	FINISH PLAN				
	SKETCHUP SCENE	**VISIBLE LAYERS**	**STYLE**	**RENDER SETTING**	**LINE WEIGHT**
1	LO_Finish Plan - Light	ARCH - Doors ARCH - Equipment ARCH - Fixtures ARCH - Windows CONC - 2D Graphic CONC - Existing CONC - New CONC - Interior CONC - Exterior	LINE DRAWING w/Textures	Hybrid	.2
2	LO_Finish Plan - Heavy	ARCH - Floor Finishes ARCH - Floors ARCH - Stairs ARCH - Walls CONC - Existing CONC - New CONC - Interior CONC - Exterior	LINE DRAWING w/Textures	Vector	.6

[Top] VIEWPORT STACKING ORDER [Bottom]

Figure 20.17 The SOD for the finish plan

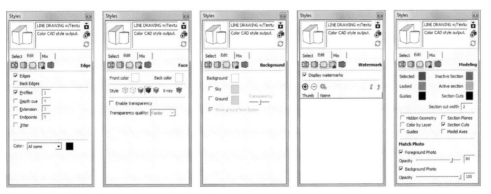

Figure 20.18 The line drawing with the Textures style

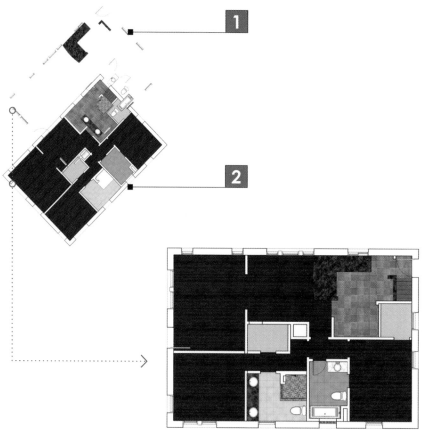

Figure 20.19 The stacked viewports for the finish plan

Reflected Ceiling Plan

A *reflected ceiling plan* describes what will be built on the ceiling of the space (Figure 20.20). Imagine looking down on a plan, through the ceiling, from above, and the floor is a mirror. What you would see is a reflected ceiling plan (Figure 20.21). This plan is very diagrammatic in nature, so creating it can be a little tricky.

Add the section plane above the window and door headers, but below the ceiling (Figure 20.22). Set the view from the bottom as a parallel projection, similar to a plan. Once you insert the drawing into LayOut, right-click on the viewport and choose Flip › Left to Right. This will make the reflected ceiling plan drawing read the same as the other plans.

REFLECTED CEILING PLAN					
	SKETCHUP SCENE	VISIBLE LAYERS	STYLE	RENDER SETTING	LINE WEIGHT
1	LO_Reflected Ceiling Plan - Light	ARCH - Ceiling Equipment CONC - 2D Graphic CONC - Existing CONC - New CONC - Exterior CONC - Interior	LINE DRAWING	Hybrid	.2
2	LO_Reflected Ceiling Plan - Heavy	ARCH - Ceilings ARCH - Walls CONC - Existing CONC - New CONC - Exterior CONC - Interior	LINE DRAWING	Vector	.6
3	LO_Reflected Ceiling Plan - Hatch 01	ARCH - Walls CONC - New CONC - Exterior CONC - Interior	HATCH - 25	Vector	NA
4	LO_Reflected Ceiling Plan - Hatch 02	ARCH - Ceilings CONC - New CONC - Exterior CONC - Interior	HATCH - 50	Vector	NA

(top) VIEWPORT STACKING ORDER (Bottom)

Figure 20.20 The SOD for the reflected ceiling plan

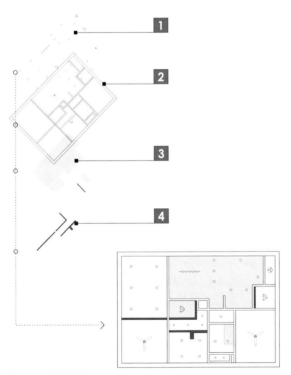

Figure 20.21 The stacked viewports for the reflected ceiling plan

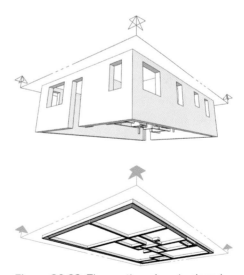

Figure 20.22 The section plane is placed.

Enlarged Plans

Sometimes you need a bigger plan to further explain a complex space and make room for cramped annotations and dimensions. To create a bigger plan, use the same methods you used for creating any plan—just use a larger scale (Figure 20.23).

Sections and Elevations

Creating section drawings and elevation drawings is much easier in that they only require one viewport. The downside is that you'll need to complete many of the graphics in LayOut. This will essentially break the dynamic link because you will need to update the LayOut geometry if you update the section drawing.

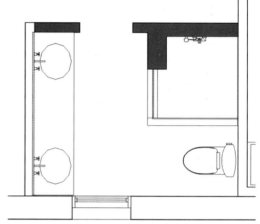

Figure 20.23 Using an enlarged plan makes dimensioning and annotating easier, and it still maintains the dynamic link.

To learn how to create sections and elevations, you will use a more complex and developed model, BIC_3458 Steele St - FINAL.skp, that includes multiple levels. Typically, a section or elevation section plane will exist at the base level of the model, outside of any container.

Building Sections

Building sections describe the relationship between the levels of a structure, and they provide interior elevation information. Keep these other tips in mind when you create section drawings:

☑ Place the building section plane at the base level of the model (Figure 20.24).

☑ Right-click on a section plane and choose Align View to set the camera view perpendicular to the section plane.

☑ Within SketchUp, right-click on a section plane and choose Create Group from Slice. Then, cut the group of linework and paste it into LayOut. Render it as a vector and explode. Now all of the linework for the section is readily available—but keep in mind, it is not dynamically linked to the section.

- ☑ Use the Line Drawing style to create a black-and-white drawing, or use the LINE DRAW-ING w/Textures style to create a color section.
- ☑ Use the Drawing tools in LayOut to create fills and accentuate the 2D SketchUp drawings to give them more visual pop (Figure 20.25).

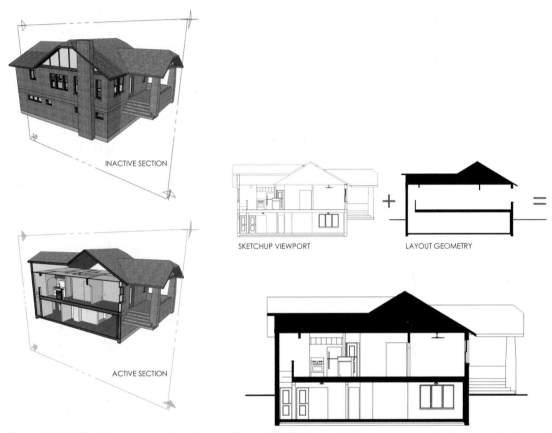

Figure 20.24 The Section plane location

Figure 20.25 The building section drawing is a combination of a SketchUp viewport complemented with LayOut geometry

Exterior Elevations

Exterior elevations convey materials and vertical heights. Elevations are possibly the simplest drawings to create because frequently they do not require any section planes and there is only one viewport. Keep the following tips in mind when you're creating exterior elevations.

- ☑ Right-click on a surface on the elevation that you are creating and choose Align View to set the camera perpendicular to the selected face. This technique is especially helpful when aligning the camera view with an angled wall.
- ☑ In SketchUp, use section planes to peel away unwanted portions of the site.
- ☑ In SketchUp, use fog to provide a sense of depth.
- ☑ In LayOut, use a clipping mask to remove unwanted portions of the site (Figure 20.26).
- ☑ You can get trees from 3D trees in SketchUp or from the pre-loaded 2D tree scrapbook collections in LayOut.
- ☑ Use the LINE DRAWING w/Textures style to make a color elevation, depending on the type of project and printing you are doing.

TIP Any LayOut entity that complements the drawing, such as a hatch or ground line, belongs on the **DRAWINGS** layer.

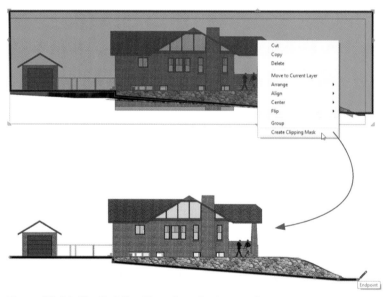

Figure 20.26 The Building Elevation clipping mask

Interior Elevations

Interior elevations are typically drawn at a larger scale than building sections, and they describe vertical dimensions and finishes. Keep the following tips in mind when you're creating interior elevations.

- ☑ Start by using a building section scene in SketchUp, or even using an existing building section scene.

- ☑ Turn off layers and hide as much geometry as possible in SketchUp. LayOut will process all the geometry that is turned on, even if it is not shown in your viewport.

- ☑ Apply a clipping mask in LayOut to isolate the desired portion of the drawing (Figure 20.27).

- ☑ Use the Line Drawing style to create a black-and-white drawing, or use the LINE DRAWING w/Textures style to create a color interior elevation.

- ☑ Use the Drawing tools in LayOut to create fills. This will give your drawing more pop.

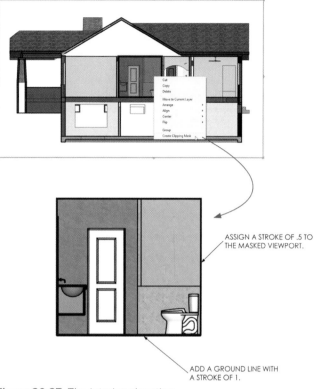

ASSIGN A STROKE OF .5 TO THE MASKED VIEWPORT.

ADD A GROUND LINE WITH A STROKE OF 1.

Figure 20.27 The interior elevation

Schedules

Schedules are used to convey the quantities you'll need of products, such as doors, windows, and finishes (Figure 20.28). A *schedule* in LayOut is actually very simple, created mostly of text boxes with different fills, strokes, fonts, and text sizes (Figure 20.29). Keep the following tips in mind when you're creating schedules in LayOut.

- ☑ There is no dynamic link to the entities you are scheduling, so make sure you count carefully. It is usually easier to catch schedule mistakes when the schedule and drawings are printed.

- ☑ Once you build a schedule, add it to a scrapbook collection for use on other projects.

- ☑ Use the Drawing tools in LayOut to complement complex schedules.

RE-USE EXISTING	#	DOOR SIZE	TYPE	FRAME	FINISH DOOR	FINISH FRAME	HDWR. GROUP	GENERAL NOTES	FIRE RATING
-	1	3'-0" X 7'-10"	1	HM	STAIN	PAINT	1	TYPICAL DOOR	1 HOUR
-	2	3'-0" X 7'-10"	1	HM	STAIN	PAINT	1	TYPICAL DOOR	1 HOUR
-	3	3'-0" X 7'-10"	1	HM	STAIN	PAINT	1	TYPICAL DOOR	1 HOUR
-	4	3'-0" X 7'-10"	1	HM	STAIN	PAINT	1	TYPICAL DOOR	1 HOUR
-	5	3'-0" X 7'-10"	1	HM	STAIN	PAINT	1	TYPICAL DOOR	1 HOUR
-	6	3'-0" X 7'-10"	1	HM	STAIN	PAINT	1	TYPICAL DOOR	1 HOUR
-	7	3'-0" X 7'-10"	1	HM	STAIN	PAINT	1	TYPICAL DOOR	1 HOUR
-	8	3'-0" X 7'-10"	1	HM	STAIN	PAINT	1	TYPICAL DOOR	1 HOUR
-	9	3'-0" X 7'-10"	1	HM	STAIN	PAINT	1	TYPICAL DOOR	1 HOUR
-	10	3'-0" X 7'-10"	1	HM	STAIN	PAINT	1	TYPICAL DOOR	1 HOUR
-	11	3'-0" X 7'-10"	1	HM	STAIN	PAINT	1	TYPICAL DOOR	1 HOUR
-	12	3'-0" X 7'-10"	1	HM	STAIN	PAINT	1	TYPICAL DOOR	1 HOUR

Figure 20.28 Schedules are composed of text boxes and shapes of varying sizes, fills, and strokes.

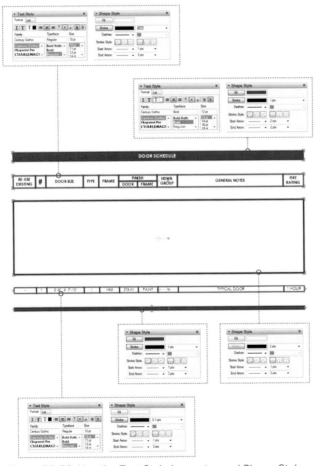

Figure 20.29 Use the Text Style Inspector and Shape Style Inspector to create numerous schedule options.

Details

A *detail* explains the finite construction of a specific building condition. When you're creating details in any drafting program, there is a disconnect between the dynamically linked design model and the detail drawings. It would be nearly impossible to build a model with the level of detail and organization necessary to show all levels of detail at any architectural scale. Because of this, it is okay to "detach" your details from the design model.

Draft the details in 3D SketchUp just as you would in 2D CAD (Figure 20.30). Use SketchUp's ground plane as your digital drafting table. Consider using a separate SketchUp model, or even a "throwaway model," when you're creating details.

Once you have finished drafting the detail, select all of the lines, and then cut the lines out of SketchUp. Paste the lines into LayOut to insert them as a linked SketchUp model (Figure 20.31).

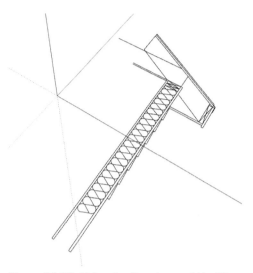

Figure 20.30 Using the Drawing and Modification tools, draft the details in SketchUp.

With the viewport still selected, use the SketchUp Model Inspector to set the viewport to Top View, Ortho, Vector Rendering, and choose an appropriate scale for a detail drawing, such as 1″ = 1′-0″ (Figure 20.32).

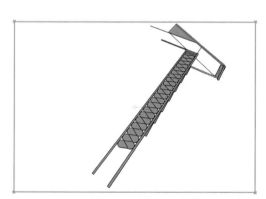

Figure 20.31 The pasted SketchUp lines are actually a .skp file linked to the LayOut presentation.

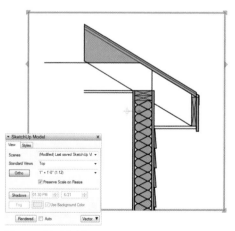

Figure 20.32 The detail drawing is shown optimized in LayOut.

Explode the viewport so that you can control the line weights. Once it's exploded, you will probably need to ungroup several LayOut groups. To do that, right-click on the group and select Ungroup. Then, use LayOut's Drawing and Modification tools in conjunction with the Shape Style Inspector to complete the detail drawing (Figure 20.33).

SketchUp is a 3D program, so there is no reason you shouldn't branch out and create 3D details. Often 3D details can do a better job explaining conditions than 2D can. As a starting point, try searching the 3D Warehouse for **Construction Details** (Figure 20.34).

TIP Save all of your details in the Scrapbooks library so you can use them on other projects. Frequently, a typical project type uses standardized details, and you can save a significant amount of time by building a collection of details.

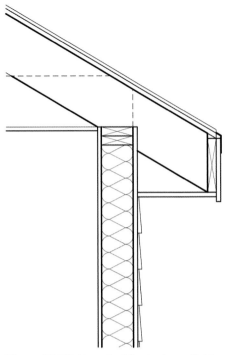

Figure 20.33 Use all of the tools available in LayOut to complete the detail drawing.

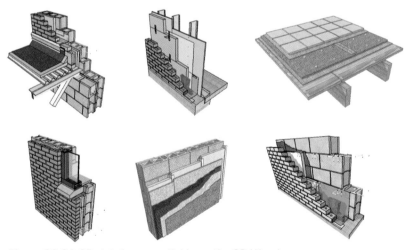

Figure 20.34 3D details are available on the 3D Warehouse.

ANNOTATIONS

Annotations are the extra layer of information that further describe the drawings. Annotations complement the graphic with accurate dimensions and precise descriptions. Keep these tips in mind when you annotate your drawings:

☑ Because it is difficult to draw accurate column lines in LayOut, draw them in SketchUp. Treat column lines as 2D Graphics that compliment a 3D object of a beam.

☑ Door and window center lines are drawn in LayOut

☑ Be sure to switch to the ANNOTATIONS layer, which should be active most of the time.

☑ It is okay to link your model to several different layout files to break up the set. This will reduce rendering time and allow you to distribute work among the team.

☑ When you're dimensioning, typically it is best to turn off Auto Scale and set the Dimension Scale manually in the drop-down menu. This will eliminate potential errors from snapping to a point outside of a viewport.

☑ If you find yourself using the same annotation, take the time to add it to your scrapbooks.

CHAPTER POINTS

☑ Leverage conceptual layers to achieve a desired look and level of detail within your drawings.

☑ You can download professionally built title blocks and scrapbooks at **www.suexch.com**, as well as review extended content regarding the creation of construction documents with SketchUp Pro and LayOut.

☑ Any drawing can be exploded to provide you with complete line-weight control in LayOut.

Index